THE MICROPUB
GUIDE

THE MICROPUB GUIDE

Mat Hardy and Dan Murray

Duncan Petersen

1st edition

123456789

Conceived, designed and produced by
Duncan Petersen Publishing Ltd,
Studio 6, 82 Silverthorne Road, Battersea, SW8 3HE

Copyright © Duncan Petersen Publishing Ltd 2017

Editor Natasha Lodge
Contributors Helen Fanthorpe, Richard Reeve, Alexander Duncan,
Giulia Sgarbi
Cover and layout design Carl Hodson
Maps Map Creation Ltd
Layout Natasha Lodge
Photo credits Many of the photos were supplied by the micropubs and have
been reproduced with their permission. Other photos were taken by: Richard
Reeve, Alexander Duncan, Natasha Lodge, Giulia Sgarbi, Lulu Lodge,
Mark Newton
Special thanks to Thiha Soe, Owen Voge and Lulu Lodge
Editorial director Andrew Duncan

A CIP catalogue record for this book is available from the British Library

ISBN 978-0-9930946-9-9

DTP by Duncan Petersen Publishing Ltd
Printed in Britain by Latimer Trend, Plymouth

Martyn Hillier's opinions as expressed on pages 6-10 are his personal views. He
is not responsible for any views expressed elsewhere in the guide.

Opening times were correct when we went to press but we recommend
checking the website or facebook page before visiting.

**Some microbreweries - not the micropubs - have paid to advertise in this guide.
Their advertisements appear under the heading 'Who brews the beer?' We are
very grateful for their support. The micropub reviews are entirely
independent.**

Contents

Martyn Hillier, above left, founder of the micropub movement, landlord of The Butcher's Arms, Herne, above right, and co-founder of The Micropub and Microbrewery Association.

This excellent guide – the first and only one to micropubs in Britain – tells the story of the first decade of the micropub revolution. I like to call it a revolution, but perhaps it's more accurate to call it a movement because nothing was overturned. The micropub concept has exploded with the fastest growth rate in the industry. There are now well over 200 across the country. Not bad from a standing start!

For decades the pub industry was controlled by the large brewers. Anyone wanting to get an 'on licence' independently had to fight the big guns in court, which was beyond most people's finances – huge legal costs without any guarantee of winning.

But in the last 20-30 years, power began shifting away from the big brewers, and it is now the big four supermarkets that control the retail drinks industry. They put pressure on the government of the day to change the outdated licensing laws, bringing in the 2003 Licensing Act which made it no longer essential to prove the need for a licence to sell alcohol. As a result, on Thursday 24 November 2005, the very first day allowed under the radical new Licensing Act, I opened The Butchers Arms. It was the first micropub in

Britain, and after only three years it was on the map – voted Kent Pub of the Year by the county's CAMRA members.

I don't want to beef too much about CAMRA, but it does strike me as odd that an organization set up to promote cask ale and the pubs that serve it has failed to get behind micropubs. They asked me to give a presentation to their AGM in 2009 about the micropub concept. I had my doubts about giving away the secrets of what was then a unique new concept, but I did it anyway. The following month, they printed a letter in their journal *What's Brewing* describing micropubs as a frivolous idea and totally rubbishing my presentation. That really started the debate! In hindsight, it did the movement a big favour. You couldn't move for people wanting to know about micropubs. Given the enthusiasm with which the 400 CAMRA members at the AGM greeted my presentation, I thought that the CAMRA powers-that-be might spread the word to the rest of their then 145,000 members, say with a piece in *What's Brewing*, but for some reason that just didn't happen.

Why micropubs work

People are turning away from mainstream pubs because they try to please everybody and, in doing so, please nobody.

Traditionally, large mainstream pubs have had as many as three bars, a public bar, saloon bar and a snug – in other words three micropubs under one roof. Nowadays, purely to reduce staffing and increase profits, they have been converted into one large bar. The largest still try to meet all needs, however conflicting: sports TV, gaming machines, pool, juke boxes... And as for conversation or a quiet pint – forget it! A micropub does just one thing in one small room simply and well – selling cask-conditioned ale. That's why it's unique: any other type of beer can be bought at a supermarket for a third of the price.

When I started planning The Butchers Arms I spent time thinking about what I liked and disliked about the pubs I went to. I didn't like smoking. I didn't like TV or background music. Worst of all, I detested tasteless, gassy draft lager. And I wasn't going to have a bar. As a pub-goer I was infuriated by bars. I hate queuing. I was also fed up with having to fight my way to the beer through a stockade of backs and shoulders, both standing and blocking

Needle and Pin, Loughborough: Kentish-style high seating at the edge of the room.

the way with bar stools, together with the attitude of resentment (even menace) and entitlement by the bar-hoggers – to say nothing of the difficulty of lifting full pints over their arms and clothing without spilling. (To be fair, that wasn't too difficult because the sort of pub that attracted bar-hoggers usually didn't fill a rim glass full enough for slopping to be a problem.) No, I was going to have a pub where people could get their ale with minimal hassle. Without a bar as a focal point, people would spread out and look inwards into the room. They would face each other – and talk! That's what happens in micropubs. It's the norm to talk with strangers. You can't say that of the aircraft-hangar pubs that litter our town centres.

It wouldn't help my concept to sell hot food. Groups eating meals all sit round a table and face inwards. They don't join the general conversation which is what my pub would be about. So The Butcher's Arms excluded all those things that I didn't like and concentrated on what I did like: good beer and good conversation.

The rise of the supermarkets has, I must admit, helped the micropub movement. Everywhere, high street shop units were becoming empty, and rents went down accordingly. So start-up costs for micropubs in one of these units were and still are reasonable, especially as there's no need to buy in standard pub furniture. Tables, chairs and decoration could be got in from anywhere, including the junk yard or skip. The more homely and less like a mainstream pub you can make it, the better. Kentish-style seating – tall chairs and tables around the edge of the room – is important because it encourages conversation and evens up people's eye levels, however tall or short they are. It's also important to have some clutter around, to absorb sound.

Keep it local, keep it real

I named my micropub The Butchers Arms because it had been a butcher's shop since the late 1800s. I was tapping into the history of the village and everyone knew where it was.

The term micropub came about because small, craft breweries are called 'microbreweries', so I followed suit. It also makes the connection between microbrewers and the places that sell their ale.

Cask ale is like a proper loaf of bread made at a small local bakery. By contrast, the large brewers make a standard, sliced white loaf, in something more like a factory than a brewery. If you've never drunk cask ale before, you have a treat in store, it's a different, wonderfully varied world.

Real ale develops in the cask. That's what gives it its extra character. But it brings challenges for the publican. Looking after it is not rocket science and if you want some tips, get in touch with me. I'll tell anyone.

Community hubs

Over the ten years that they have been in existence, micropubs have gained the reputation of being well-run, civilised establishments, good neighbours and community hubs. Councils are learning this and, as a result, are looking increasingly favourably on granting planning permission. Even the Archbishop of Canterbury went into a micropub in 2016 and local estate agents now use the presence of a nearby micropub as a selling point for private properties.

By contrast, especially in city centres, bars and pubs are often characterized by absent managers and bored or rude staff. They're noisy and impersonal. And when you leave at closing time you're surrounded by kids throwing up on the pavement.

Micropubs take drinkers back

The Butchers Arms, Herne: community hub.

The Thomas Tallis, Canterbury: a place to meet new people.

to the days of the old ale houses, where ale was served from a firkin in someone's front room. A landlord who enjoys his work, loves cask ale and is grateful to have found an independent living will make it his business to create a friendly and inclusive atmosphere in his micropub. More to the point, the small size of his premises means that this comes naturally, especially when there's no bar and he and his helpers have to take the ale from the cold room to each customer as they order, mixing with people and making introductions as they go.

All kinds of micropubs

The micropub concept is clear. But it is not prescriptive. If you travel around the excellent micropubs featured in this guide, the first thing you will spot is that they are variations on a theme. Micropub is not a straitjacket. So micropubs are diverse, and each is as original as the independently-minded person who opened it. Is a small pub which sells nothing but 'craft keg' a micropub? Or merely a fashionable, small pub? Is a large pub that sells nothing but cask ale a big micropub?

The hallmarks of a micropub are:

- Conversation — you are joining a welcoming community with whom you already know you share at least one interest.
- Real Cask Ale — excellently kept and served.
- No distractions.

Spread the word!

We've divided the guide into two sections – Mainstream micropubs (starting page 24) and Other micropubs (starting page 306). The criteria for putting a place in one section or the other aren't rigid – and we like all the micropubs in this guide.

However, we believe that there's an interesting distinction between micropubs that stick closely to the core principles, and those that don't – and that enthusiasts will want to see the difference highlighted.

MAINSTREAM MICROPUBS:
- Focus on cask-conditioned real ale. Wine, spirits and cider are often available too, but the landlord is dedicated to real ale and keeping it in great condition, typically in a cold room. Gravity poured ale from the cask maintains its natural condition.
- Encourage conversation. Talking to strangers is the norm. Friendly, welcoming owner and helpers.
- Usually just one room, which looks personal and inviting. Often, but not always, the landlord has created a home-from-home ambience using ordinary furniture rather than pub furniture.
- Bar snacks only.
- Often, but not always, there's high Kentish-style seating around the edge of the room to promote conversation and discourage people forming inward- facing huddles.
- Many have no bar, offering table service to avoid queuing and prevent a barrier between owner, his helpers and the drinkers.
- Usually one off, owner managed and not part of a chain.
- Locally oriented - a community hub.
- Put new life into old retail units on declining high streets.

OTHER MICROPUBS
- Often have more than one room.
- Serve roughly as much key keg and lager as real ale.
- Often music and sports TV play a major part.
- Food – not just snacks – is an important feature.

Name of micropub. ————

City, town or village and county, in which the micropub is located. ————

Postal address and other key information. ————

Opening hours as we went to press - check online. ————

Independent review. ————

Places of interest near the micropub. ————

THE JUST REPROACH

Deal, Kent

ESSENTIAL INFORMATION
14 King St, Deal CT14, 6HX
Email: mark.robson@btinternet.com
Facebook: www.facebook.com/
  The-Just-Reproach-Deals-
  Micropub-214290775307658

Opening hours:
Monday 1200-1500 then 1700-2000
Tuesday-Thursday 1200-1400
then 1700-2100
Friday 1200-1400 then 1700-2300
Saturday 1200-2300
Sunday 1200-1600

Other reasons to go: Deal Castle
www.english-heritage.org.uk;
Walmer Castle
www.english-heritage.org.uk;
Royal Cinque Ports Golf Club
www.royalcinqueports.com

One hundred per cent in its skin: everything feels just right. It's solidly built, in a pleasant corner site with bus stop, train station and car parking two to three minutes away; the beach is 100 yards off; inside it's just the right size and decorated – but not cluttered - with interesting memorabilia hung on cream painted tongue and groove; the layout is classic Kent micropub - chunky high wooden tables round the edge of the room with high seating. Deal is a more attractive seaside town than its neighbour Dover.

The name is properly local – see the poem mounted on the wall. "Defoe alleges that the local inhabitants were reluctant to put to sea to rescue sailors in trouble from the hurricane, though were not averse to plundering boats when the opportunity arose. Locals still resent this assertion!"

Affable owner Mark Robson (below middle) who runs the place with his daughter Bronwen is a fan of Defoe, admiring his nonconformism. He was a head teacher in a Kent special school for children with autism. When our reporter said he guessed that running a micropub must be easy compared with that, he replied "On the whole, but with a few of the customers it's a close-run thing."

Like many another micropub, The Just Reproach was inspired by visits to The Butcher's Arms, page 140, but opening wasn't a snap decision. It took Mark five years to take the plunge – "I waited til the children had grown up and the mortgage was paid off."

Everyone really does talk to each other in this place – the buzz of conversation can be heard down the street. Many micropubs believe they've created a community, but

This information is only an indication for wheelchair users. Always check on suitability with the micropub.

Quotes and opinions from regular customers.

here it's no idle claim, and is supported by the micropub's success in fundraising. Mark operates a zero tolerance mobile policy – witness the phones nailed to the wall.

Four real ales (five at weekends) are served by hand from the cold room, plus local wine, a house wine and four ciders. On our visit we enjoyed Wantsum Brewery's 4.2% Challenger Green Hop – fruity with a depth of flavour combined with freshness.

We rate this place one of the best in the guide. Mark also owns The Thomas Tallis in Canterbury, page 134.

Disabled access √ not to WC and small step at entrance
Child friendly √
Dog friendly √

WHAT THE REGULARS SAY
'I just love this micropub. Superbly friendly staff and such a relaxed and friendly environment.'

'There is no bar, take a seat and check out the list of beers available. The beer is well kept and local and is very reasonably priced. So onto a winner there.'

99

Paid advertising of micro-breweries. We are very grateful for their support.

13

Time ran out on the first edition of the guide in late 2016, leaving us unable to include several micropubs that deserve an entry in the main section. As new micropubs open most months, there will be some that didn't even make this list. Sorry... Let us know if you've been left out and we'll catch up with you in the next edition.

Crossways Micropub, Blythe
Uttoxeter Road, Blythe Bridge, Stoke-on-Trent , ST11 9LY; 07527 669965.
Four handpumps serve three real ales and one cider. Friendly, simple place owned by the Peakstones Rock Brewery. At least two of the ales will be from this microbrewer.

Black Rat, Bradford
530 Leeds Road, Thackley, Bradford, BD10 8JH; 07930 158856.
Three real ales, two real ciders and a selection of small batch gins. The ales are mainly from Yorkshire brewers. No frills, genuine place.

Queen's Head, Chepstow
Moor Street, Chepstow, NP16 5DD; 07793 889613.
The first micropub in the Chepstow area. In a small room once part of a mainstream pub, eight handpumps on the bar serve mainly real ales, with an emphasis on Welsh microbrewers.

The Bitter and Twisted, Coalville
16 High Street, Coalville, LE67 3ED; 07773 341531.
In a former pet shop and butcher's shop, this is a genuine place offering a well chosen variety of real ales and real ciders.

The Jolly Porter, Diss
Station Road, Diss, IP22 4HN; 01379 308320.
Occupies the same premises as the mainstream pub with the same name in what used to be the taxi office at Diss railway station. Three regular real ales, one always from Hoxne Brewery.

Doncaster Brewery Tap, Doncaster
7 Young Street, Doncaster, DN1 3EL.

Attached to Doncaster Brewery, this is an outlet for their beers with two of six ales being from guest breweries. There is a window from the pub into the brewery to allow customers to watch the process.

The Saxon Tavern, Earls Barton
26 The Square, Earls Barton, NN6 ONA; 07956 462352.
Serving six changing cask conditioned real ales racked behind the bar, some ciders and wine, this is a super-homely place in a single room decorated "like your front room" says the owner - with one of the very few real log fires you'll find in a micropub.

The Open Arms, East Grinstead
51 Railway Approach, East Grinstead, RH19 1BT; 01342 327727.
On a corner site, with a smart exterior. Serves five regular beers straight from the cask.

Beer in Hand, Hereford
136, Eign Street, Hereford, HR4 0AF; www.beerinhand.co.uk.
The taphouse of Odyssey Brew Co, known for its US-inspired full flavoured beers. Serves a mix of cask conditioned real ale and craft keg.

Ales of the Unexpected, Margate, Kent
105 Canterbury Road, Margate, CT9 5AX; 07958 647753.
Shame owner Carl didn't give us full information otherwise it would be in the main part of the guide. It's a genuine micropub which our reporter Richard Reeve sums up as an 'all-round good micropub' which is borne out by Carl's view of his job: "It's my social life – I love to talk to people and I love real ale."

The Gas Tap, Melton Mowbray
11a Burton Street, Melton Mowbray, LE13 1AE.
Hundred per cent pure micropub in a former sandwich bar, accommodating 25 people in one room. Serves only cask conditioned real ales, some cider and wine. Also known as Gas Tap Real Ale & Cider House.

Continued on next page

Biergarten, Milton Keynes
Unit 3, The Triangle, Wolverton Park Road, Wolverton, Milton Keynes MK12 5FJ; www.mkbiergarten.co.uk.
Friendly place modelled on a German beer garden, but it serves one cask-conditioned real ale beside two keg lines. The main feature, though, is the interesting range of craft bottled beers from Germany, Belgium, America, the UK and Scandinavia.

Early Doors, Skipton
14 Newmarket Street, Skipton, BD23 2HX; www.earlydoorspub.co.uk.
The name comes from a sitcom about a pub in Manchester – there's nothing unusual about the opening times. A genuine no-frills micropub serving five changing real ales from handpumps.

The Pup and Duckling, Solihull
1 Hatchford Brook Road, Olton, Solihull, B92 9EU.
Six real ales and six real ciders. There are two drinking spaces, a large room at the front with a bar and a small cosy room at the back.

The Floodgate Alehouse, Stafford
147 Newport Road, Stafford, ST16 2EZ; 07917 885821.
Called The Floodgate because the council insisted on flood defences - although no one can recall flooding in the area. Stays close to core micropub criteria except for a large range (27) of single-malt whiskies – which doesn't cause problems.

Upminster TapRoom, Upminster
1b Sunnyside Gardens, Upminster, RM14 3DT.
Real ales served straight from the cask in a cool room seen through a window in the bar. Table service. Parking is difficult, so use public transport – Upminster station is about ten minutes' walk.

The Gas Tap, Melton Mowbray.

Please write and tell us about your experience of micropubs whether good or bad, whether listed in this edition or not.

The address to write to us is:
Print editor, Duncan Petersen Publishing Ltd
Studio 6, 82 Silverthorne Road,
London,
SW8 3HE

Checklist
Please use a separate sheet of paper for each report; include your name, address and telephone number on each report.

Your reports will be received with particular pleasure if they are typed, and if they are organized under the following headings:

Name of establishment
Town or village it is in, or nearest
Full address, including postcode
The building and setting
Atmosphere, welcome and service
Value for money

We assume that in writing you have no objection to your views being published unpaid, either verbatim or in an edited version. Names of major outside contributors are acknowledged, at the editor's discretion, in the guide.

LOCATION MAPS

SOUTH-WEST
ENGLAND,
WALES,
WEST MIDLANDS.

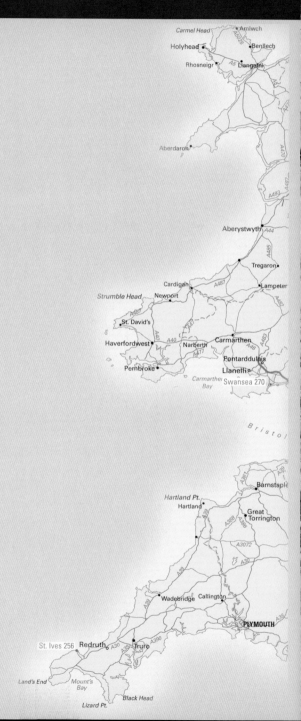

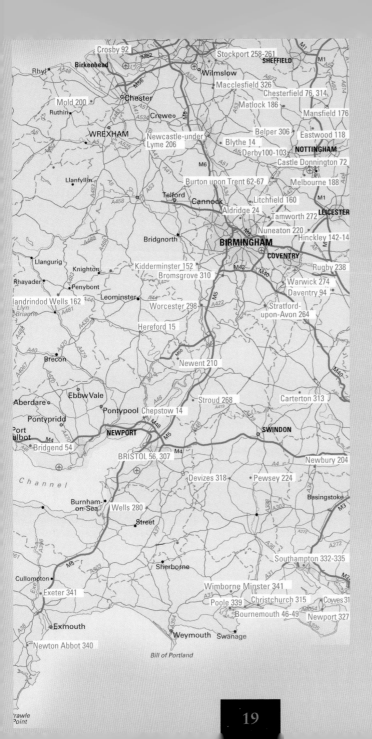

Crosby 92
Birkenhead
Rhyl
Stockport 258-261
SHEFFIELD
Wilmslow
Macclesfield 326
Mold 200
Chester
Chesterfield 76, 314,
Ruthin
Matlock 186
Crewe
Mansfield 176
WREXHAM
Newcastle-under-
Belper 306
Eastwood 118
Lyme 206
Blythe 14
Derby 100-103
NOTTINGHAM
Llanfyllin
Castle Donnington 72
Telford
Burton upon Trent 62-67
Melbourne 188
Cannock
Litchfield 160
Bridgnorth
Aldridge 24
Tamworth 272
LEICESTER
Knighton
BIRMINGHAM
Nuneaton 220
Hinckley 142-14
Llangurig
COVENTRY
Rhayader
Kidderminster 152
Rugby 238
Penybont
Bromsgrove 310
Warwick 274
landrindod Wells 162
Leominster
Daventry 94
Llyn
Worcester 298
Brianne
Stratford-
upon-Avon 264
Hereford 15
Brecon
Newent 210
Ebbw Vale
Aberdare
Carterton 313
Pontypridd
Pontypool
Chepstow 14
Stroud 268
Port
NEWPORT
albot
SWINDON
Bridgend 54
BRISTOL 56, 307
Newbury 204
Channel
Devizes 318
Pewsey 224
Burnham-
on-Sea
Wells 280
Basingstoke
Street
Southampton 332-335
Cullompton
Sherborne
Exeter 341
Wimborne Minster 341
Poole 339
Christchurch 315
Cowes 31
Exmouth
Bournemouth 46-49
Newport 327
Newton Abbot 340
Weymouth
Swanage
Bill of Portland

rawle
Point

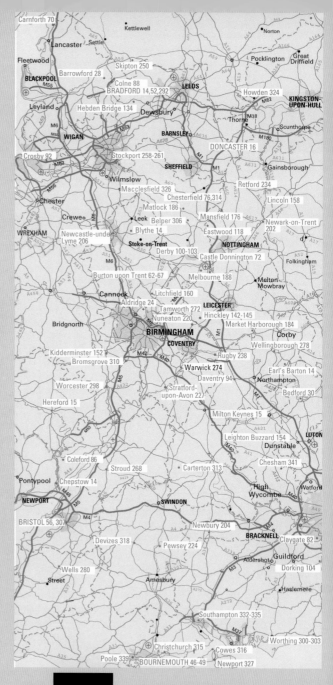

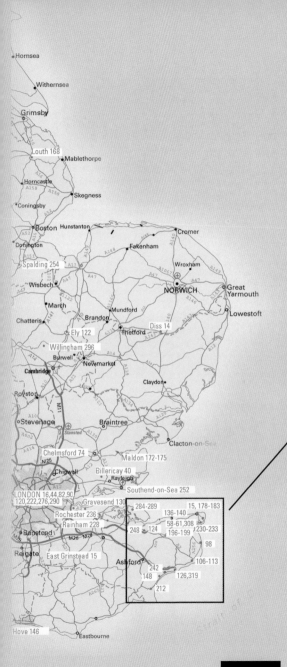

Whitstable 284-289
Sittingbourne 248
Faversham 124
Herne 136-140
Broadstairs 58-61, 308
Minster 196-199
Ramsgate 230-233
Deal 98
Dover 106-113
Folkestone 126, 319
Sandgate 242
Hythe 148
New Romney 212

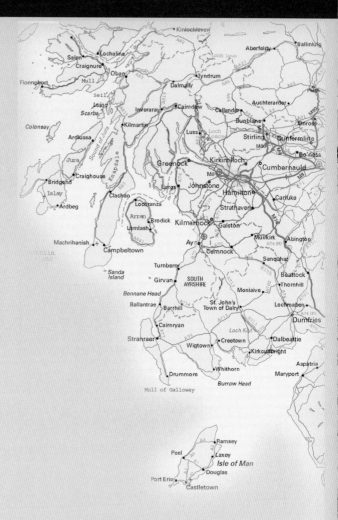

Montrose
Forfar
Lunan Bay
Arbroath
Carnoustie
DUNDEE
St. Andrews Bay
Fife Ness
Leven
Isle of May
Kirkcaldy
Firth of Forth
Grantshouse
Ayton
Penicuik
Berwick-upon-Tweed 36
Lauder
Greenlaw
Galashiels
Kelso 150
Wooler
Hawick
Alnwick
Amble
Otterburn
Kielder Water
Langholm
Morpeth 342
Whitley Bay
Longtown
Haltwhistle
Newcastle-upon-Tyne 208
Gretna
Prudhoe 226
GATESHEAD
SUNDERLAND
Consett
Alston
Stanhope
Durham 341
Hartlepool 132
Stockton-on-Tees 262
Redcar 331
MIDDLESBROUGH 190-195
Brough
Whitby
Stokesley
Robin Hood's Bay
Northallerton
Scarborough 244
Filey 341
Kettlewell
Bridlington
Carnforth 70
Driffield 114
Lancaster
Fleetwood
Skipton 250
Daventry 94
Cross Hills 327
Beverley 38
BLACKPOOL
Saltaire 52
Hedon 324
BRADFORD 14
KINGSTON UPON HULL
Leyland 156
Wibsey 232
Howden 326
Chorley 78
Huddersfield
Scunthorpe
Ormskirk
Standish 294
Pontefract 342
WIGAN
Barnsley 340
Doncaster 14
Brigg
LIVERPOOL
MANCHESTER
Market Rasen
SHEFFIELD
Knutsford
Wilmslow
Worksop
Gainsborough
Retford 234
Macclesfield 326
Lincoln 158
Matlock 186
Chesterfield 76
Mansfield 176
Crewe 319
Newcastle-under-Lyme 206
Newark-on-Trent 202
Hucknall
Sleaford

Aldridge, Walsall, West Midlands

ESSENTIAL INFORMATION
14 Croft Parade, Aldridge, Walsall, WS9 8LY
Telephone: 07513 320525
Website: www.theturtleshead.co.uk
Facebook: www.facebook.com/pg/
TheTurtlesHeadAldridge

Opening hours:
Monday Closed
Tuesday-Thursday 1200-2200
Friday-Saturday 1200-2230
Sunday 1200-2100

Other reasons to go: Woodlands Adventure
woodlandsadventure.co.uk;
Park Lime Pits Local Nature Reserve
www.facebook.com/pg/
FriendsOfParkLimePits;
Aldridge Transport Museum
www.amrtm.org

A fairly recent addition to the micropub scene but by no means the newest, this place opened in a former hairdressers in 2015. It's a family run business which actively welcomes children and dogs (there are dog treats available at the bar).

The outside appearance within a 1960s shopping centre doesn't do it justice and it's easy to bypass, but once inside you're in a haven of real ale and enthusiastic chatter. It's perhaps not your average micropub. There's a red chesterfield sofa and tub chairs with low wooden tables, the walls are lined with bookshelves filled with knick-knacks along with film posters. There's a statement red wall bringing a bit of life to the otherwise cream and neutral colour scheme. The feel is cosy and relaxed, you can easily spend your whole evening here, and indeed many people do.

Landlord Adrian Morrell lost his job and was deemed unemployable by the local job centre. This spurred him on to start his own business and The Turtles Head was born. It was quite a jump from his previous career in the funeral industry but he has taken to his more cheerful new calling.

There are four constantly changing ales served via handpump from the bar. You can taste before you buy and Adrian is more than happy to help if you are unsure. They also offer eight real ciders, wine and a craft lager from Wye Valley.

The name is quite amusing, a play on the endless use of The King's Head in pub names. It was dreamt up over a few pints and, as Adrian puts it, reflects his jokey side. The artwork is great and should be admired before entering.

On our visit we enjoyed: Church End Brewery's Screw EU, a 3.8% malty and

toffee flavoured beer, made specially for Brexit; Wellingtonian from Froth Blowers Brewery, a 4.3% blonde coloured beer made with three types of New Zealand hops; and Fownes Brewery's Gunhild, a 4% honey ale with Czech Saaz hops. The honey comes from Paynes Bee Farm in Sussex and the hops used bring out the honey flavour.

Disabled access ✓ **Child friendly** ✓
Dog friendly ✓

WHAT THE REGULARS SAY

'Fantastic establishment! Wonderful beers and ciders. Lovely staff!'

'Ade and his family make it a very warm friendly relaxing place with superb real ales.'

'A very warm welcome, good real ales, and a complementary cheese board. You can taste the ales before you choose which one you want. Dog friendly and a great place to relax.'

Barfrestone, Kent

ESSENTIAL INFORMATION
Pie Factory Road, Barfrestone, Dover,
CT15 7JG
Telephone: 07522 554118
Email: thewrongturn@outlook.com
Facebook: www.facebook.com/
   thewrongturnmicropub

Opening hours:
Monday-Tuesday Closed
Wednesday 1500-2100
Thursday 1500-2000
Friday 1500-2100
Saturday 0000-2100
Sunday 0000-2000

Other reasons to go: Dover Castle
www.english-heritage.org.uk;
White Cliffs of Dover;
Deal Castle www.english-heritage.org.uk

Turn right off Barfreston village's main road down a short lane, left into a wooded private drive and at the end, in the grounds of a house, is what looks like a large timber summer house. You think you have taken a wrong turn, but you haven't because here is the most unexpected micropub we've seen on our travels. It was probably the first in a non-commercial countryside location, opening in 2014.

The setting is leafy and peaceful, and the countrified ambience continues as you step inside off the front deck. With a bar to one side and pine kitchen tables and chairs plus other furniture providing conventional-height seating for perhaps 24 in comfort (plus standing room for ten) it's homely and relaxed. There are feminine touches such as a sofa in the corner with a throw and floral pattern cushions; an upright piano stands on the back wall and a collection of wicker baskets hangs from the A-frame beam. As we went to press owner Ginny Timms had plans to extend and improve the garden seating area (opposite, centre).

Ginny is an artist who has lived in the neighbourhood for around 20 years and this was once her studio, before that a garage. She got help in setting it up from Carl at Ales of the Unexpected (page 15) – and from the closure of the local mainstream pub.

All ages and types can feel comfortable here: you will often find oldies installed as if in their local, near the log burner, but also people visiting Barfrestone's Norman church, people from the nearby campsite and walkers on the North Downs Way. Heads don't turn when you walk in – there's no cliquey band of regulars and no one rough. Swearing is frowned on. It's a

community hang out for Barfrestone, but people also come from nearby villages, even from Dover. Events include a Halloween fancy dress party, a carol service and occasional musical or jamming sessions.

Ginny serves three ales at a time (IPA, bitter and mild) balancing local brewers with guest ales from further afield, plus cider, wine, Prosecco and bottled craft lager. Food is minimal, but there is quite a substantial cheese, ham and onion quiche and a popular cheese board.

On our visit we drank Gadds' No 5 traditional bitter - dark in colour with a flowery, malty taste – hops take a back seat.

Disabled access ✓
Child friendly ✓ in the garden
Dog friendly ✓

WHAT THE REGULARS SAY

'I like the cosy log burner and garden.'

'A little gem in the middle of nowhere.'

Barrowford, Lancashire

ESSENTIAL INFORMATION
The Old Bank, Gisburn Road, Barrowford,
    Lancashire, BB9 6HQ
Telephone: 07739 870880
Email: TheBankersDraft@aol.co.uk
Facebook: www.facebook.com/
    thebankersdraft

Opening hours:
Monday-Tuesday Closed
Wednesday-Thursday 1600-2100
Friday 1600-2230
Saturday 1400-2230
Sunday1400-2100

Other reasons to go: Pendle Cycle Tours
www.visitpendle.com;
Higherford Mill Artists
higherfordmillartists.wordpress.com;
Pendle Heritage Centre
www.pendleheritage.co.uk; The Harris
Museum www.harrismuseum.org.uk

Both the premises and the owner of this place began life in financial services. The imposing building was once a bank, and owner Tracey worked in a financial services business. When it was sold she used her share of the proceeds to open The Banker's Draft on Halloween 2014 – an auspicious day because nearby Pendle is famous for witches, and for its witch trials in 1612.

She'd always planned to open a tea-room or shop, but with two children she couldn't find the time. Then, partner David got her into real ale and they visited some beer festivals and micropubs, including The Market Alehouse (page 156) in Leyland.

Tracey knew that this characterful building in a small village opposite a park was right the moment she walked in. It's not big, but has a more spacious feel than most micropubs. The ceilings are high and ornate, and there are plenty of characterful features, which Tracey has preserved as far as possible. The old manager's office has been turned into the cold room. It's sparsely decorated with a few pictures and old pump clips above the picture rail.

The bar offers five rotating ales, wines and ciders. We tried Dancing Duck

Brewery's Dark Drake, a 4.5% malty, caramel and liquorice flavoured ale with a coffee and toffee finish; and Rudgate Brewery's Chocolate Stout, a 5% rich ale with a subtle chocolate finish.

The Banker's Draft is between two mainstream pubs and doesn't seem to suffer because the others are food and TV orientated. It's almost always busy, in fact it can claim to have become the village hub.

Disabled access ⊗ **Child friendly** ✓
Dog friendly ✓

WHAT THE REGULARS SAY

'Love this place, Tracey always has a warm welcome and a recommendation of what to try.'

'Nice to go to a proper drinking establishment where they serve a good hand pulled pint.'

'If you want no telly, no juke box and somewhere you can take the dog this is it.'

SAINT PETER'S ALE HOUSE

Bedford, Bedfordshire

ESSENTIAL INFORMATION
38 St Peter's Street, Bedford, MK40 2NN
Telephone: 07511 649795
Email: rob.taylor@redbrewery.com
Facebook: www.facebook.com/
    StPetersAleHouse
Twitter: @stpetersale

Opening hours:
Monday-Thursday 1500-2300
Friday 1300-2300
Saturday 1200-2300
Sunday Closed

Other reasons to go: The Higgins Bedford
www.thehigginsbedford.org.uk;
The Panacea Museum panaceatrust.org.uk;
The Quarry Theatre www.quarrytheatre.org.uk

Saint Peter's Ale House opened in November 2015 as Bedford's first micropub. It is a smart and modern former hair salon owned by John Kearney's Red Brewery. John's son Joseph runs the Ale House as a separate venture with his childhood friend Rob Taylor. Although the Red Brewery sell their own beers and ales here, Saint Peter's also stocks a selection of beers from other breweries in Bedfordshire, Cambridgeshire, the home counties, and London. Joseph and Rob are slowly but surely drawing in a loyal customer base. They are noticing the benefits of selling Red Brewery beers directly through their micropub: with lower overheads and negotiable prices, the pints can be sold for less – meaning happy customers. In addition, they hope to create links with other micropubs and get them selling Red Brewery products too.

The alehouse is in a pleasant spot in town, near shops and restaurants. Its front is almost entirely glass, giving plenty of natural light. The rest is painted white with post-box red around the door: they are going for simple and bold. The inside follows suit, with cream and stone tones, and red lamp shades. The decoration is minimalist compared to other micropubs I've visited, although there is a simple clock face, a curious metallic artwork and a 'periodic table of beer' poster. There is space for 36 to sit (around five small tables and two larger ones) on uniform metal-framed chairs. It feels spacious and there's plenty of room to stand.

The stillage array can be seen behind the attractive wooden bar counter. It can fit 11 casks, but when we visited the pub had been open for just a month and

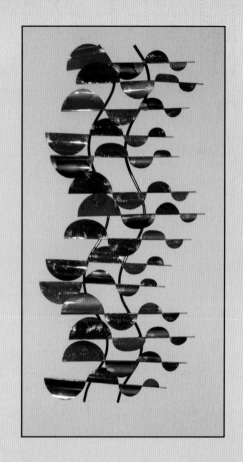

there was a choice of five beers. I enjoyed Milton Brewery's Minerva, a 4.6% ABV, pleasantly bittered Golden Ale and Gundog Ales Ltd Lord Barker, a 4.2% smooth and chocolatey stout.

We learnt as the book went to press that this place closed in early 2017.

Disabled access √
Child friendly √ until 1900
Dog friendly √

WHAT THE REGULARS SAY
'A warm and friendly welcome with knowledgeable staff.'

'We come for the beer but also like the fact there is a choice of wines.'

'There is now a resurgence and interest in great beer where there was previously a dearth. There is now more choice in beers with great flavour.'

POTTLE OF BLUES

Beeston, Nottinghamshire

ESSENTIAL INFORMATION
1 Stoney Street, Beeston, Nottinghamshire,
NG9 2LA
Telephone: 07923 517331
Email: apottleofblues@hotmail.com
Facebook: www.facebook.com/
   APoBlues/?fref=nf
Twitter: @APottleOfBlues

Opening hours:
Monday 1200-2200
Tuesday Closed
Wednesday-Thursday 1500-2300
Friday-Saturday 1200-2300
Sunday 1200-2200

Other reasons to go: Attenborough Nature
Centre and Reserve
www.attenboroughnaturecentre.co.uk;
Holme Pierrepont Country Park
www.nwscnotts.com;
Wollaton Hall
www.wollatonhall.org.uk

Jen and Ralph Glover opened this place in April 2016, giving it a highly appropriate name. Jen is the daughter of Gary Pottle, co-owner of the Copper Pottle in Herne Bay (page 34). Seeing how much her father enjoyed his micropub, she gave up teaching to open her own. With her husband Ralph, a blues enthusiast, they took careful note of how Gary organised his venture in Kent and have reproduced its success in Nottingham. It's a lively and engaging place; come here for great company and sometimes even some blues playing from Ralph, if he's not too busy serving drinks.

Their site was previously a candle shop, but now the walls are decorated with musical instruments, vinyl records and blues posters. There is even a violin case fashioned as a drinks cabinet. A guitar has been transformed into a plant pot and two others serve as lighting features. There is also a piano, slightly out of tune, advertising future beers and is there for anyone to play. The music theme continues into the lavatory where guitar backs have been painted with appropriate stick figures.

The furniture consists of two wall-mounted benches and several bar-high chairs. When we visited there were plans for outdoor seating. Jen and Ralph are also hoping to exhibit local artwork and hold regular live music events.

Between four and five beers are on offer at a time in addition to four regularly changing ciders. They also stock wines and soft drinks, crisps and pork scratchings.

I drank Springhead Brewery's Drop O' The Black Stuff 4% ABV, an aromatic roasted barley porter, smooth and slightly smoky; and Black Iris Brewery's Bleeding Heart 4.5% ABV.

There is currently no disabled access but there are plans to install a ramp which will give access to the bar.

Disabled access ⊗ **Child friendly** ✓
Dog friendly ✓

WHAT THE REGULARS SAY

'Cracking night - everyone was very tolerant of my guitar playing.'

'Enjoyed it so much, one pint became four.'

Beltinge, Herne Bay, Kent

ESSENTIAL INFORMATION
84 Reculver Road, Herne Bay, CT6 6ND
Telephone: 07873 436122/ 07710001261
Email: info@copperpottle.co.uk
Website: www.copperpottle.co.uk
Facebook: www.facebook.com/
  copperpottle
Twitter: @copperpottle

Opening hours:
Monday Closed
Tuesday-Saturday 1200-1400
then 1800-2100
Sunday 1200-1500

Other reasons to go: Monkton Nature
Reserve www.monkton-reserve.org;
The Seaside Museum
www.theseasidemuseumhernebay.org;
Wildwood www.wildwoodtrust.org

A pottle is a half-gallon measure for liquids, or a type of small pot. It also happens to be the surname of Gary Pottle, who runs this rather eccentric micropub with his collaborator Gavin Elgar. And Gavin has copper-coloured hair.

Gary was originally employed in the sport and leisure industry while Gavin worked for Martyn Hillier in The Butchers Arms (page 140), the first micropub to open in Britain. Trading on these transferable skills, they opened The Copper Pottle in June 2015 in a small shop formerly occupied by Smackerjack's Pet Foods.

The exterior resembles a fish and chip shop, with cobalt blue tiling and an almost entirely glass front. Inside, it's more akin to a scout hut with garlands hung from the walls. Quirky, maybe, but successful. Gadgets are banned – defy this and you will be fined – proceeds to the Strode Park Foundation.

Gary and Gavin have certainly earned their DIY badges, having refurbished the place entirely by themselves. The furniture consists of simple wooden chairs and benches with a couple of long tables. Two of the most interesting features are the bar, made of Herne Bay driftwood and old scaffolding board; and a table decorated with a butterfly pattern that Gary's uncle picked up somewhere during his time in the Merchant Navy. The soundproofing consists of golfing umbrellas hung from the ceiling – something like The Royal Albert Hall. Whether or not they're effective is unclear.

Real ales and ciders are served from a temperature-controlled cellar room and outside there is a designated smoking area in which they plan to provide some seating.

Aside from beers and ciders, wine and soft drinks are available along with a selection of crisps, cheese thins, pork scratchings and nuts. During our visit, we enjoyed a pint of Adnams Ghost Ship, a 4.5% nicely bittered Pale Ale; and Old Dairy Copper Top, a 4.1% spicy caramel Premium Bitter.

Disabled access ⊗ **Child friendly** ✓
Dog friendly ✓

WHAT THE REGULARS SAY
'Amazing place, great company. Thoroughly recommend the fruity cider! Well worth a visit.'

'Absolutely brilliant, perfect micro pub.'

CURFEW

Berwick-upon-Tweed, Northumberland

ESSENTIAL INFORMATION
46A Bridge St, Berwick-upon-Tweed,
TD15 1AQ
Telephone: 07842 912268
Facebook: www.facebook.com/
    curfewmicropub
Twitter: @CurfewMicropub

Opening hours:
Monday-Thursday 1200-2100
Friday-Sunday 1200-2200

Other reasons to go: Berwick Castle
www.english-heritage.org.uk;
Paxton House paxtonhouse.co.uk;
Royal Border Bridge;
The Maltings Theatre and Cinema
www.maltingsberwick.co.uk

Berwick is England's most northerly town, some two miles south of the Scottish border, where the Tweed runs into the North Sea. Some of the folk on the streets look distinctly rough and while the centre isn't exactly run down, you don't see smart little boutiques on the main drag – rather, cut price stores.

The Curfew, located in Bridge Street, less than five minutes downhill from the main street, comes as a pleasant surprise. It's up an alley, clearly signposted from the street, which opens out into a fair-sized, nicely sheltered outdoor seating area in front of the micropub itself, which was once a bedsit and before that a cow shed.

The name of the game here, as you might expect, is no frills – instead, honest simplicity and getting the basics right. Gemma (pictured opposite, top right behind the bar), and David Cook, who were inspired to open by a day trip to Rat Race Ale House in Hartlepool (page 132), had hospitality trade experience when running a local B & B. The outdoor area, with simple garden seating, is a sun trap backed by the old city walls, and includes the 'cellar' - a hut where the firkins are housed. Inside, it's narrow, long and light with low seating and round tables. Dominating the walls are black boards carrying neatly chalked names of the four regularly changed cask-conditioned real ales, a respectable range of bottled beers and the bar snacks, which are more imaginative than many you'll find in a micropub, including haggis eggs.

This is Berwick's first and only micropub, and a novelty to many of the locals, some of whom think it might be a microbrewery, not a drinking place. (The Barrels, by the way, just along Bridge Street, may look a little

like a micropub but isn't.) The Curfew won the Overall Northumberland Pub of the Year award in 2016.

On our visit we drank Pollards from Thornbridge Brewery - a notable experience. It's a 'coffee milk stout', made not just with coffee but with oats, providing an espresso-style shot in the arm – skip porridge and coffee for breakfast and drink Pollards instead – you'll be up for most things.

During the Anglo-Scottish Wars of the Middle Ages Berwick changed hands again and again, seeing more than its share of raids, sackings and massacre. It isn't clear whether this is why the 8 o'clock curfew bell carried on being rung (and still is) when elsewhere the practise stopped long ago. But it's in keeping with the town's slightly forbidding atmosphere, and although these days the bell is rung symbolically, rather than to get everyone indoors, Gemma and David close early during weekdays, at 9 pm. Things can get wild after 10.

Disabled access ⊗ **Child friendly** ✓
Dog friendly ✓

WHAT THE REGULARS SAY

'Mainstream pubs are now too generic. Here is more personal, individual and intimate.'

'Much friendlier, a more cosy attitude and no pretentiousness.'

'There is a sense of community and they listen to what the public wants.'

CHEQUERS MICROPUB

Beverley, East Yorkshire

ESSENTIAL INFORMATION
15 Swabys Yard, Beverley, HU17 9BZ
Telephone: 07964 227906
Email: mildorbitter@gmail.com
Facebook:www.facebook.com/
   ChequersMicropub
Twitter: @chequersmicro

Opening hours:
Monday Closed
Tuesday-Wednesday 1200-2200 ish
Thursday-Saturday 1200-2300 ish
Sunday 1200-2200

Other reasons to go:
Beverley Minster
www.beverleyminster.org.uk;
Beverley Racecourse
www.beverley-racecourse.co.uk;
Beverley Westwood

Ian Allott opened the first micropub in Yorkshire after getting fed up with driving 50,000 miles a year as a regional manager for a fuel distribution company. He wanted to spend more time at home, and gives a slightly hollow laugh when explaining that the new venture gives him that "in theory".

One day in 2012 he heard a short interview with Martyn Hillier of The Butcher's Arms, page 000, on Radio Four's lunchtime programme. Heading south a few days later he detoured to Herne Bay and within ten minutes of entering The Butcher's Arms reckoned that Yorkshire needed a similar place. He did his homework, looking at a few others, and opened in 2013 in a former patisserie, coffee and sandwich shop.

Chequers stands out in several ways. The black- and-white tiled floor is distinctive, and of course appropriate, but what we haven't seen elsewhere are stairs behind the bar leading to an upper floor. They are the way up to the toilets, the cold room and store room and give the set-up a quirky feel.

Above the panelled bar hangs a sign saying 'Patent, medicines, pure drugs and chemicals and surgical appliances' which Ian salvaged from an 'emporium' in Hull. To furnish the place he bought furniture that everyone else was chucking out, for example old settles and round bar stools. The aim was a mid 20th-century ambience.

The drinking area is on two levels, separated by a couple of steps but the focus is usually around the bar where often everyone knows each other and the conversation is shared by all.

Ian describes his place as a local's local, but because of its location in a shopping precinct off Beverley's Saturday market area, the clientele, although 80 per cent local, is

diluted at weekends by passing trade of all sorts including tourists. Everyone integrates happily. Ian keeps closely to micropub values – just five continuously changing real ales served by handpump from the cold room above – and no spirits. The formula works: on our visit the place was packed at 6 pm and same again when we went back at 9. They've also won five CAMRA beer and cider awards.

We started with North Riding Brewery's 4.5% Dandelion and Burdock Porter, jet black and tasting genuinely of dandelion and burdock – amazing. Later we tried Cat's Whiskers 4.8% Cream Stout from Colchester Brewery, very smooth and slightly sweet.

Disabled access ⊗
Child friendly ✓ until 2000
Dog friendly ✓

WHAT THE REGULARS SAY

'The best place to go, if you haven't gone before go, it's great. Customers and the bar staff are the best.'

'Tremendous, tiny tavern. Amazing selection of ales served by friendly and knowledgeable staff. Highly recommended.'

'Delightful beer. No messing just beer.'

Billericay, Essex

ESSENTIAL INFORMATION
54c Chapel Street, Billericay, CM12 9LS
Telephone: 01277 500121
Email: info@billericaybrewing.co.uk
Website: www.billericaybrewing.co.uk
Facebook: ww.facebook.com/
   BillericayBrew
Twitter: @BillericayBrew

Opening hours:
Monday-Wednesday 1000-1800
Thursday-Saturday 0900-2100
Sunday 1100-1700

Other reasons to go:
Billericay Community Cinema
www.billericaycine.com;
Cater Muesuem www.catermuseum.co.uk;
Lake Meadows www.lakemeadows.org.uk

The Billericay Brewing Company Shop and Micropub (to use its full name) was opened by Trevor Jeffrey in 2013. Trevor is a former industrial chemist who was drawn into the micropub world after spending a day brewing his own beer at the Brentwood Brewing Company – an experience also on offer at the Billericay Brewing Company. The microbrewery, pub and shop are the culmination of five years hard work, and are now fully established and thriving.

The site looks like a typical small garage, but, the sign outside makes it clear what the place really is. Go inside, and you immediately see the changes that have taken place - there's no sign of any oily rags. Four richly stained high tables and several wooden high chairs and stools give it the typical micropub appearance. The casks of ale and the bottle stock are clearly displayed and the decorations are sparse. The most attractive features are the exposed wooden rafters and the appropriate choice of lighting – beer bottle lampshades.

Typically of a weekday there are around five beers on offer with at least six and sometimes more at the weekend. The range aims to include two golden ales, two amber ales and two bitters. Soft drinks are sold by the can, cider and Perry is sold in draught and bottled form, and there is a small selection of wines supplied by Dedham Hale and New Hall. The only snacks available are crisps. In addition to stocking their full range in bottles, they also have more than one hundred beers mostly from Essex breweries but some from London. In addition they have a frequently changing programme of guest ales, both regional and national.

During my visit I sampled Billericay Zeppelin 3.8%, a pale amber session bitter,

which was there to commemorate the centenary of the L32 Zeppelin crash near Snails Farm, Great Burstead in 1916. It had a pleasant light, bitter and slightly smoky flavour; I also enjoyed the guest ale, Hope SX Demon 4.4%, a dark ale, rich and malty with a slightly bitter finish.

Disabled access ✓ not to WC
Child friendly ✓ **Dog friendly** ✓

WHAT THE REGULARS SAY

'I come here because there is frequently a great selection of great bitters.'

'Great tour and tasting. Excellent beers!'

'Top place to visit if you like a pint of real ale and would like to see the brewery that made it.'

THE WHEEL ALEHOUSE

Birchington-on-Sea, Kent

ESSENTIAL INFORMATION
60 Station Road, Birchington-on-Sea,
Isle-of-Thanet, Kent, CT7 9RA
Telephone: 07826 130927
Email: alan@thewheelalehouse.co.uk
Website: www.thewheelalehouse.co.uk

Opening hours:
Monday-Saturday 1200-1400
then 1700-2100 ish
Sunday 1200-1400

Other reasons to go:
Quex Park and Powell Cotton Museum
www.quexpark.co.uk;
Minnis Bay ww.visitthanet.co.uk;
Shell Grotto www.shellgrotto.co.uk

The Wheel Alehouse is on the main, busy high street of Birchington-on-Sea. It's a supporter of the Royal National Lifeboat Institute – all quiz entry fees are donated and a collection boat is contributed to by customers, so much so that the place was awarded a plaque for the highest donations in the area. This shows you what kind of a place The Wheel Alehouse is - welcoming and friendly.

Alan Ross (opposite, bottom left) ran a fish and chip shop in Garlinge before deciding to open this place in 2013. He's also an ex navy man and is chatty and greatly knowledgeable about his ever changing ales if you're unsure what to try.

The size of the place is slightly larger than most micropubs but they adhere to all the criteria and their size only serves to provide more room for their keen customers. It's on two levels with the upstairs level used for quizzes (every second and last Wednesday of the month) and live music events, for those who just want a drink the micropub atmosphere is maintained on the ground floor.

The nautical theme unsurprisingly comes from their location on the Isle of Thanet, being surrounded by sea on three sides. The micropub itself is only half a mile from the sea. The name however comes from a joke in Stage Fright - Only Fools and Horses (1981-2003) where a singer can't pronounce the letter r – so real ales became wheel ales.

The walls and ceilings are adorned with nautical memorabilia as well as the customary pump clips. Several large barrels serve as tables with bar-stools, and there are also some regular height tables and chairs.

This place is dog-friendly. Alan often has his own dog behind the bar with him and on our visit, Dougal, who also works behind the bar, had brought along his dogs, Ted and Bubbles.

A few beers they have had on offer are Mighty Oak's Yellow Jersey, a one off 4% golden ale created using the rare US hop Comet as well as Caramalt, and Marris Otter which give this ale a biscuity flavour; Black Paw Brewery's Archbishop's Ale, a 4.1% ruby bitter; and Pheasantry Brewery's Lincoln Tank Ale 4.2%, created to raise money for the Lincoln Tank Memorial (a 2D model of a Mark 1 tank, the first ever tank to be created. The model sits on Lincoln's Tritton Road).

Being so close to the sea Alan says he had to offer rum, so besides real ale, rum, vodka, brandy, port and G&Ts are also available. There's also wine, cider and soft drinks.

Disabled access ⊗ **Child friendly** ✓
Dog friendly ✓

WHAT THE REGULARS SAY
'Very friendly atmosphere with good beer at a reasonable price.'

'Great beers and great company.'

'This is a micropub that sells fabulous beer in a very friendly environment. Very welcoming and sociable.'

THE BROKEN DRUM

Blackfen, Greater London

ESSENTIAL INFORMATION
308 Westwood Lane, Blackfen, DA15 9PT
Telephone: 07803 131678
Email: thebrokendrum42@gmail.com
Website: www.thebrokendrum.co.uk
Facebook: www.facebook.com/
   thebrokendrum42
Twitter: @TheBrokenDrum42

Opening hours:
Monday-Thursday 1500-2200
Friday-Saturday 1200-2200
Sunday 1300-1600

Other reasons to go: Hall Palace &
Gardens www.bexleyheritagetrust.org.uk;
Danson House
www.bexleyheritagetrust.org.uk;
**Butterfly Jungles Experience & Plant
Centre** www.butterflyjungles.com

Fans of the late Terry Pratchett's *Discworld* book series will know that The Broken Drum was a dimly-lit and disreputable tavern, visited by trolls and axe-wielding ne'er-do-wells, notorious for its nightly brawls and beer that tasted like battery acid. Happily, for those looking for cask ale variety in Blackfen, the similarities between the fictitious Broken Drum and its 'roundworld' namesake end at the sign above the door.

This tidy little establishment is the realisation of a dream for owner and former computer programmer, Andy Wheeler (opposite, encircled). Post redundancy, Andy transformed a disused nail bar into a profitable reality, opening Bexley Borough's third micropub in April 2015.

The pub enjoys a light, bright, open-plan layout with minimal decoration, save for an arrangement of historic photos of the local area and some Terry Pratchett references. Andy has thought a great deal about the furnishings, and took advice from his friend and fellow micropub

owner, Ray Hurley of The Door Hinge in nearby Welling (page 276), who helped build and install the two benches. From the false ceiling with cavity, the sound dampening carpet and soft-cushioned chairs, this is one sound-proofed pub — staying true to the micropub ethos of minimising disturbance to the neighbourhood peace. The resident living upstairs has no complaints.

It seats around 26, but if all are taken, there's still room to stand and chat. The small bar and kitchenette leads to the chilled tap room where a modest but well-kept range of ales are dispensed straight from the cask. There is a small unisex WC just off the serving area.

At the time of our visit Andy had no house beer – ales are changed regularly and so far nothing had been repeated. He knows most of the Kentish breweries and tends to concentrate on sourcing from these, relying on a friend for advice on ales procured outside the county. While there we savoured a 3.7% amber ale Guinea Guzzler produced by the local Millis Brewery Company, and a 4.6% dark ruby bitter, The Knights Ale from The Canterbury Ales, both of which were excellent. Standard pub fare is available: crisps, scotch eggs, nuts, pork pies and soft drinks.

Discworld enthusiasts may recall that The Broken Drum eventually changed its name in an attempt to reinvent itself and leave behind its contemptible reputation. It became The Mended Drum – an

apt metaphor, perhaps, for what those micropub entrepreneurs – like Andy – are doing in 'mending' the declining pub industry. They are providing an ever-increasing number of dissatisfied folk with what they've been seeking – namely a simple, congenial environment where they can enjoy lively conversation and a range of affordable, quality ales, ciders and wines.

Andy has definitely succeeded in changing his tune and marching to a different beat. We dare say it won't be long before there'll be a CAMRA fanfare coming his way, especially given that other fledgling micropubs in the region have already been rewarded with accolades for similar efforts.

Disabled access ✓ not to WC
Child friendly ✓ until 2000
Dog friendly ✓

WHAT THE REGULARS SAY
'Conveniently located for me and welcoming, with top quality interesting ales, it's always a pleasure to enjoy a pint or two at the Broken Drum.'

THE FIRKIN SHED

Bournemouth, Dorset

ESSENTIAL INFORMATION
279 Holdenhurst Road, Bournemouth,
BH8 8BZ
Telephone: 07719491971
Email: thefirkinshed@yahoo.co.uk
Website: thefirkinshed.wordpress.com
Facebook: www.facebook.com/
    thefirkinshed
Twitter: @thefirkinshed

Opening hours:
Monday 1600-2100
Tuesday-Thursday 1600-2230
Friday-Saturday 1200-0000
Sunday 1200-2100

Other reasons to go:
Bournemouth's East Cliff Beach BH1 2EW;
Boscombe's one-off shops and restaurant
choices; Bournemouth city centre museum:
www.galleriesofjustice.org.uk

A pirate micropub. The owner, Paul Gray, comes complete with a beard dyed blue, anarchist tendencies and says of his micropub's decoration: "the walls are smeared with the insides of my head." To get an idea of what this means, look at the pictures on these pages. We especially liked the one of the decapitated head (opposite, top left) with a mobile stuffed between its teeth. Paul really hates mobiles: if yours rings, the fine is £1 for the air ambulance collection box.

If it sounds a little alarming, it's not. This is a slightly off-the-wall but friendly place and Paul is probably more of a Robin Hood than a Bluebeard. He does a terrific double act with his daughter Ruby (opposite, top right), who provides the softening touch with a great smile. A natural behind the bar, she radiates good humour, but, we suspect, is more than capable of dealing with most situations. She has been much involved in the venture from the start and Paul regards it as her business as much as his.

This was Dorset's first micropub, and like its neighbour The Wight Bear, (page 50), fiercely loyal to the micropub core principles. Unlike its neighbour, it has a bar, but with Ruby behind the counter it doesn't feel like a barrier. Paul claims that she knows more about beer than any barman in Bournemouth, and he prides himself on having ended Bournemouth's reputation as a place where you couldn't get a decent pint. Of the six beers always on the go, there will usually be one that you've never come across. He is shopping further and further afield to come up with ales that the local competition aren't offering.

The overall effect of the decoration is woody – and cluttered. You could spend all

'Friendly, quirky.'

'Awesome place, great staff.'

'The best pub in Bournemouth'

evening taking it in, from the macabre corpse statue (centre above) - "he's head of security" - to the huge blue letters spelling out BLUES ROCK – once part of the Blockbuster Video sign that hung outside the premises in its previous incarnation. Paul is an addictive junk collector and Ruby has been heard to remark that most of the interior came off skips. There are clever practical touches too, such as the decorative rectangular panels on the walls containing sound absorbing material.

They have occasional live musicians, from all over the globe playing their own eclectic mix of folk, blues/ bluegrass and country. There are also Vinyl Revival nights which are on Thursday nights unless there's have a band in. Keep an eye on their Facebook page for upcoming events. The place is becoming a focus for the local community, and Paul is happy to be giving something back to this once-deprived area.

On our visit we enjoyed Electric Bear's Live Wire 5.4%, a USA-style IPA with a citrus flavour, "refreshingly in your face for a summer afternoon", says Paul.

Disabled access ⊗ **Child friendly** ⊗
Dog friendly ✓

THE SILVERBACK ALEHOUSE

Bournemouth, Dorset

ESSENTIAL INFORMATION
Maya Court, 518 Wimborne Road,
Bournemouth, BH9 2 EX
Website: www.silverbackalehouse.co.uk
Facebook: www.facebook.com/
thesilverbackalehousewinton

Opening hours:
Monday-Saturday 1200-2300
Sunday 1200-2200

**Other reasons to go: Bournemouth Beach
Russell Coats Art Gallery and Museum
www.russellcotes.com;
The Bournemouth Aquarium
www.oceanarium.co.uk**

A Silverback is a gorilla 12 years or older who leads and protects his group. He has distinctive silver hair on his back and makes all the decisions on feeding, movement and the wellbeing of the group. A strange name for a micropub, you might think. Well, landlord Derek's (opposite, bottom right) young niece used to say he looked like a fat gorilla, so the name stuck. Derek has had a quirky and varied career - he was a cook on a tall ship for ten years and before that a fireman for 30 years.

Opening in July 2016, this place was one of the newest micropubs as we went to press. Just a 15 minute drive from the sea, it's a perfect place to enjoy a drink after a walk along the coast. Wimborne Road can't be described as pretty but The Silverback Alehouse has provided a much needed drinking place on this busy high street.

Large black flagstones greet you as you enter and high tables and benches surround the edge of the room. Casks and a wooden step provide resting places for your feet. The walls at one end display large blackboards with the day's drinks and a window in a door at the end allows a glimpse into the cooling room where ale is poured straight from the cask by gravity.

The decoration is sparse, with a few canvases on the walls, but pale blue paint contrasts with the dark floor and gives the place a light and welcoming feel. Bare light bulbs hang from the ceiling and pump clips follow the piping. It's a minimalist approach, perhaps old fashioned, and ale is the priority. Like many micropubs in the south there's no bar - your order is taken and brought to the table.

There is a large choice of ales, ciders and gin and a few wines are on offer including a couple that are vegan friendly. You're invited to taste some of the ales before you order. There are four choices, occasionally six. There are never fewer than two local ales and the others are generally from around the Midlands.

Snacks include biltong, Kent crisps, pork scratchings, chilli scratchings and naga scratchings (only for the brave).

Ales they have offered include: Corbel from Eight Arch Brewery, a 5.5% aromatic, hoppy India Pale Ale; 8 Grain Porter from The Brew Shack, a 5% sweet brown porter with roasted malt flavours and a smooth bitter finish; and Infinity from Blue Monkey Brewery, a 4.6% award winning golden ale brewed with Citra hops.

Disabled access ✓ not to WC
Child friendly ✓ until 1900
Dog friendly ✓

WHAT THE REGULARS SAY
'Great selection of drinks. You can have a paddle of three different ales to try. Very friendly staff. Refreshing to have this place in Winton, I hope it stays.'

'A great addition to the area. Might find it hard to stay away.'

THE WIGHT BEAR ALE HOUSE

Bournemouth, Dorest

ESSENTIAL INFORMATION
65 Southbourne Grove,
Southbourne-on-Sea, Bournemouth,
BH6 3QU
Telephone: 01202 433733
Email: hello@thewightbear.co.uk
Website: www.thewightbear.co. uk
www.thebeerbearfamily.co.uk
Facebook: www.facebook.com/
    thewightbear
Twitter: @thewightbear

Opening hours:
Monday 1600-2300
Tuesday-Saturday 1200-2300
Sunday 1200-2230

Other reasons to go: Southbourne Beach,
BH6 4BE
Bournemouth Pier, BH2 5AA
Boscombe Beach and Bouldering (climbing
rocks), BH5 1BN

Micropub names should be local. To 'get' this one, make for Southbourne Beach, a few minutes walk away, when the evening sunlight is on the west end of the Isle of Wight. Only from this spot, with the light in the right direction, can you easily make out the distinct polar bear shape created by the cliffs.

Actually, walking to the beach need not break into good drinking time because a photo hung on one of The Wight Bear's walls (above) also neatly shows the polar bear outline.

David and Nicola Holland, who opened this place in 2015, converting a former greetings card retailer, stand out for being religiously faithful to the micropub core features and values, not just in name but in almost every other way too, and applying them intelligently.

There's no bar ("bars create barriers" says Nicola) – the beer comes instead from a temperature-controlled room at the back – you can see in through windows. Only firkins are used, not pressurized kegs. Staff, who know about ale ('Bear Beer Handlers' is printed on their polo shirts), do swift table service. They are trained.

The tables, and wall seating follow the design of micropubs elsewhere, being raised to ensure those seated are at eye level with those standing. The tables and benches line the walls, leaving open space in the middle, giving easy access for the servers and

WHAT THE REGULARS SAY
'Absolutely lovely atmosphere.'

making backs-out huddles unlikely to form. Conversation is encouraged and mobiles are frowned upon – if yours rings, please put 50p in the charity box.

'Freedom from loud music, mobile phones and children, a huge bonus.'

Traditional ale houses were often no more than front rooms in peoples' houses, notes Nicola, and she's successfully created the same cosy, happy atmosphere here. Success? Indeed so much so that she and David have now opened a second micropub, The Saxon Bear, in nearby Christchurch, strictly following the same formula, down to the etched glass front windows proclaiming 'Just good ale, good conversation and good times.' Is this a bit too brand-conscious for a micropub? The making of a mini chain? While they've done very well to create two such 'pure' micropubs, possibly these are not so completely owner managed as others we've seen. The Saxon Bear (page 317) is almost identical to The Wight Bear.

And then there's the bus stop, right outside The Wight Bear's front, obscuring it from passing traffic. Not ideal, but, this is a bonus because regulars can arrive and leave by bus, drinking as much as they like without a thought for the breathalyzer.

On our visit we drank Wild Beer's Millionaire 4.7% – a sweet and salty stout.

Disabled access ⊗ **Child friendly** ⊗
Dog friendly ✓

CAP AND COLLAR

Bradford, West Yorkshire

ESSENTIAL INFORMATION
4 Queens Road, Saltaire, Bradford,
BD18 4SJ
Email: capandcollarsaltaire@gmail.com
Facebook: www.facebook.com/capcollar
Twitter: @capandcollar

Opening hours:
Monday Closed
Tues-Thursday 1700-2200
Friday 1600-2300
Saturday 1300-2300
Sunday 1300-1800

Other reasons to go:
Natoinal Media Museum
www.nationalmediamuseum.org.uk;
Bradford Industrial Museum
www.bradfordmuseums.org;
Bradford Cathedral
www.bradfordcathedral.org

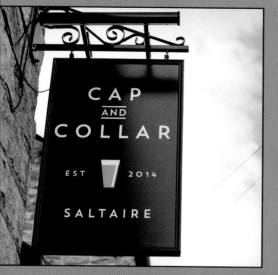

It's unusual for a micropub to be a newbuild, but Phil Garvey got lucky when he came upon this place, built in 2013. The landlord wanted it to be a pizza and curry takeaway, but Phil persuaded him otherwise. In the pleasant Bradford suburb of Saltaire, it's on a semi-residential street.

The frontage and its typography were designed by Phil and a friend for a simple, classic effect. The horizontal lines above and below the word 'AND' is a nod to the similar street signs in Saltaire.

Phil used to be a commercial property lawyer in Leeds. 'Cap' is the amount that rent must not exceed and 'collar' is the amount it mustn't fall below.

Phil and his wife moved to Saltaire in 2012 and loved its sense of community. He's a life-long real ale nut, and as there was nowhere in the area that served the kind of beer he liked, he took the plunge after studying micropubs in Kent.

The interior is carefully designed, with a mixture of low, high and wall bench seating; plus a combination of solidly built square tables and distinctive small round tables. The grey galvanized tubing, rustic sealed concrete floor and solid, pale timber – give an industrial-chic ambience. At the back is an outside seating area that much enlarges the capacity.

Phil runs two key kegs and four real ale firkins, changing them constantly, buying mainly within 25 miles but sometimes further afield. On our visit we drank Eternal from Northern Monk, a 4.1% heavily hopped IPA, light yellow in colour and smelling strongly of tangerines. Your first gulp will drench you with a thirst-quenching citrus explosion.

On the way out we heard someone

on the street singing an opera aria. This turned out to be Singing John, one of the best-known regulars. Some 30 years ago, he had a brain haemorrhage. The operation left a deep furrow on his skull and deprived him of his inhibitions – hence his habit of bursting into song at any moment. He's pictured right performing Adeste Fideles (Come all ye faithful). The operation made him a little forgetful too, and because he shouldn't drink more than two pints, whoever's serving writes 1 and then 2 on the back of a hand as he finishes each pint.

A thoughtful, community-oriented micropub where children are especially welcome (games for all ages, colouring books and crayons); likewise dogs (water bowls and treats).

Disabled access ✓ **Child friendly** ✓
Dog friendly ✓

WHAT THE REGULARS SAY
'Our favourite bar in Saltaire and there's a lot of competition! Great laid back atmosphere, changing selection of beers and lovely wines.'

'Great atmosphere, perfect ales and pies! We will definitely be back.'

'Not your average bar, a local gem in Saltaire.'

© photos top and right by Mark Newton, www.marknewtonphotography.co.uk

THE LITTLE PENYBONT ARMS

Bridgend

ESSENTIAL INFORMATION
11 Penybont Road, Pencoed, Bridgend,
CF35 5PY
Telephone: 07734 767937
Facebook: www.facebook.com/The-Little-
Penybont-Arms-288905297900360

Opening hours:
Monday 1500-2300
Tuesday Closed
Wednesday-Friday 1500-2300
Saturday 1200-2300
Sunday 1500-2300

Other reasons to go: Bryngarw House and
Gardens www.bryngarwhouse.co.uk;
Parc Slip Nature Reserve
www.welshwildlife.org;
Coity Castle www.cadw.gov.wales

This place is exactly what it says it is. It's little, it's on Penybont Road and it's a drinking place. Gareth Roberts felt that the name needed to be simple and easy to understand, just like the micropub concept. He follows all the micropub rules, limiting himself to real ale, cider, a growing selection of malt whiskies and a few wines. There's no music other than the odd sing-song among customers, there's no wifi and no TV.

Gareth is mad about real ale and cider and is a people person who likes little better than having genuine relationships with his customers. Neither are possible in a mainstream pub. So after working in the hospitality industry for 15 years, he decided it was time to work for himself. He opened in early 2015, the first micropub in the area and one of very few in Wales. Gareth has had a varied career: after studying electronic engineering at university he was a teacher before working in hotels and restaurants.

The place has an eclectic feel. One wall is red tiled, almost bathroom style, while the others are simply painted white. The floor is tiled black and white and the lamp shades are red and white. An old map hangs on one wall while a street sign announcing Elvis Presley Blvd hangs on another. The furniture is low tables and chairs with some high chairs at the bar; tables are large to encourage conversation between strangers.

Gareth has a great working relationship with several local breweries including Hopcraft, Mumbles and VOG as well as Gwynt Y Ddraig who produce some of the ciders on offer. Between three and six ales are on sale at a time. There's no key keg but there are a couple of dusty bottles of lager

under the bar for emergencies.

On our visit we enjoyed Grey Trees Brewery's Afghan Pale Ale, a 5.4% dry but crisp ale with three distinctive hop flavours. It's name comes from the fact that IPA was served to British troops during the Anglo-Afghan War in the 1800s; Hopcraft Brewery's It's Probably Going to Rain, a 4% American, golden summer brew; and Shepherds Warning from Wild Weather Ales, a 5.6% pale IPA with a grapefruit, peach and mango flavour.

Disabled access ⊗ **Child friendly** ✓ until 2100
Dog friendly ✓

WHAT THE REGULARS SAY
'An amazing place with an old type landlord who has brought back the art of conversation.'

'Lovely friendly welcome and the ales and cider are second to none, if you like to chat and fancy good company this is the place to go.'

'Great beers, great atmosphere! We love the 'talking pub' concept.'

Bristol

ESSENTIAL INFORMATION
447 Gloucester Road, Bristol, BS7 8TZ
Website: www.thedrapersarms.co.uk
Facebook: www.facebook.com/
    thedrapersarmsbristol
Twitter: @DrapersArmsBris

Opening hours:
Monday-Friday 1700-2130
Saturday 1200-2130
Sunday 1700-2130

Other reasons to go:
Bristol Zoo www.bristolzoo.org.uk;
Tyntesfield
www.nationaltrust.org.uk;
Bristol City Museum and Art Gallery
www.bristolmuseums.org.uk

On Bristol's rather scruffy Gloucester Road, tucked between fast food cafés and computer shops, is this charming micropub painted bright green inside and out. The exterior blends with the surrounding shops, but the interior is a fusion of modern and traditional with a warm and welcoming atmosphere. Garvan Hickey opened it with business partner Vince Crocker (opposite, top) in 2015, the owner of a five-barrel microbrewery – Ashley Down Brewery.

Having heard about micropubs, they decided to look for a place where they could brew and sell the beer from the same premises. They couldn't find anywhere big enough, but they did find this great little place instead.

Garvan used to work in sales and marketing in the hospitality industry, and part time in pubs. He also managed a hotel for a year, so he has experience of consumers and this is obvious from the place's popularity. The name was chosen because for 80 years it was a draper's shop.

Gloucester Road is the longest road of independent shops and restaurants in the UK and The Drapers Arms fits in well, bridging the gap between day-time shopping and an evening meal.

There is no traditional bar, instead there's a bier - a wooden stand for coffins - behind which casks are racked on a stillage. Beer is served by gravity straight from the casks. There is an assortment of low tables and benches with a central high table and some bar-height stools. Bottles and jugs surround the walls and an old standard lamp stands in the corner, reminding one of a cosy living room. The exterior has frosted glass, suggesting to passers-by that they should

come inside to find out more.

There's always one Ashley Down ale on offer as well as three guest ales including one new local beer, plus two ciders and red, white or rosé wine. Pints cost £3.50, a four-pint jug is £12 and CAMRA members get 30p off a pint. They sell cheese and onion rolls at the weekend, 'chicken and chips' (a pickled egg in a bag of crisps) and there are free bowls of nuts. Other than that, this place is for ale and conversation.

On our visit we enjoyed Grey Trees Brewery's Mosaic Pale Ale, a 4.2% single hopped beer with citrus and pine flavours; and Yeovil Ales' Summerset, a 4.1% blonde ale with a fruity tangerine and hop finish.

Disabled access ✓ not to WC
Child friendly ✓ until 1900
Dog friendly ✓

WHAT THE REGULARS SAY
'A great establishment with a knowledgeable and welcoming publican who was able to tell me about each of the local ales.'

'Fantastic! Hats off to the local brewer who has launched not just his beer, but many other local products - not to mention a friendly inviting bar.'

Broadstairs, Kent

ESSENTIAL INFORMATION
1 Sowell Street, St Peters,
Broadstairs, CT10 2AT
Telephone: 07947 062063
Email: mike@thefourcandles.co.uk
Website: www.thefourcandles.co.uk
Facebook: www.facebook.com/Broadstairs,
TheFourCandles

Opening hours:
Monday-Thursday 1700-2200
Friday 1700-2300
Saturday 1200-2300
Sunday and Bank Holidays 1200-1500
then 1800-2200

Other reasons to go: Viking Bay
www.visitthanet.co.uk;
Bleak House Broadstairs
www.bleakhousebroadstairs.co.uk;
Crampton Tower www.cramptontower.co.uk

We don't do prizes or awards - if we did, The Four Candles would get one. It has an outstandingly buzzy, friendly atmosphere; it's quirky and characterful – a true community hang-out; and it has its own microbrewery in the basement.

Owner Mike Beaumont wasn't there when we visited, but Janice Biggs, who helps out regularly, was performing instead, and does a class act. One of those who can make the party go just by being in the room, she's never in one place at a time, darting in and out of the cold room, making everyone feel at home, ensuring everyone has a full glass. We wondered how much beer sales might dip when she's not there. Soon after opening time the place was full, the party rolling, while the ordinary pub on the other side of the road was as quiet as a funeral parlour.

On a corner site in a sleepy residential area of St Peter's village on the edge of Broadstairs (free parking in nearby streets), this looks from the road like a very small, mainstream conventional pub but once inside it's the real micropub deal: a tiny, intimate space with high tables, raised

seating, and a shelf all around the wall for glasses. The hugger-mugger crowd seemed to be thoroughly at home, including one customer who had clearly nipped out for a bit of peace to read his book over a drink – and didn't want to be photographed (opposite left).

On our visit we drank one of Mike's own brews, Triple Hop 4.3% an easy-drinking hoppy session ale. Also much in demand was bottled Citra, made of course with much sought-after Citra hops.

The Four Candles gets its name from one of the best-ever The Two Ronnies (1971-1987) sketches, *The Four Candles* sketch, where a customer goes into a hardware store asking for fork handles. The shopkeeper drives the customer mad by insisting on producing four candles. Of course, there are fork handles on the micropub's back wall and crossed fork handles on the sign hanging outside.

Disabled access ⊗ **Child friendly** ✓
Dog friendly ✓

WHAT THE REGULARS SAY
'You have to go there! We drank amazing ales and ciders and ate Kentish cheeses. My new favourite pub.'

'SUPERB!'

'Just love this place. Great little micropub. Great beer, great people. The best.'

YARD OF ALE

Broadstairs, Kent

ESSENTIAL INFORMATION
61 Church Street, Broadstairs, CT10 2TU
Telephone: 07790 730205-Shawn,
    07792042993-Ian
Facebook: www.facebook.com/Yard-of-
    Ale-248320768663087

Opening hours:
Monday-Friday 1700-2300
Saturday-Sunday 1200-2300

Other reasons to go:
Viking Bay www.visitthanet.co.uk;
Bleak House Broadstairs
www.bleakhousebroadstairs.co.uk;
Crampton Tower www.cramptontower.co.uk

Ian Noble, co-owner with Shawn Galvin, has a family business next door – H. Noble Funeral Directors. As far as we know, alcohol sales in the micropub haven't so far enhanced the undertaker's business and the good-natured Ian certainly wouldn't want them to – the reverse, in fact, because along with nearby The Four Candles (page 58) this place is a life-enhancer, one of the best in the guide.

Its key strength is its eponymous yard: approached through a gate and down a short approach ramp, this is an attractive old walled, unevenly cobbled space at its best on sunny days but which can be covered with an awning. An outside area on this scale, away from a road, is unusual for a micropub.

Step inside from the yard and you enter the atmospheric micropub itself, a former stable, workshop and storeroom formerly belonging to the Noble funeral premises. True to core micropub criteria, cask-conditioned real ales are served from the cold room, tables and seats are high level, and artefacts from the premises's former incarnation make up much of the

decoration. Naturally, two glass yards of ale, (opposite, top), holding 2.5 pints, hang in conspicuous positions waiting for heroes, usually at stag-dos, to drink the contents in one without vomiting or falling over.

They are proud of their food offerings here: £5 buys you an unusually generous cheese board (three big lumps of cheddar, stilton and brie) plus 11 biscuits and chutney. They also sell large pork pies with mustard and pickle, crisps, pickled eggs and a free handful of hay for ponies – a local farmer brings his in for just that. Take-away cartons are also good value at £10 for four pints.

On our visit we drank Stoke on Trent brewer Titanic's Plum Porter 4.9% - plum flavoured, dark, sweet, creamy and moorish.

Every second Tuesday there's a quiz night and the yard makes a great location for their occasional hog-roast BBQs. Music is imported for special occasions. They want their place to be a truly local local as well as worth visiting from further afield and from what we saw the two can live together: the layout allows drinkers to be matey/chatty at close quarters indoors, or several different groups to co-exist outside.

Shawn and his wife Clare run the place with four hardworking staff. They opened a second micropub, Mind the Gap, in Broadstairs in mid 2016 (page 340) it's a one-off, like Yard of Ale.

Disabled access ✓   **Child friendly** ✓
Dog friendly ✓   **Horse friendly** ✓

WHAT THE REGULARS SAY

'Fantastic place to be, best ale house in the area hands down. Beer is always good, and all the staff are friendly, helpful and make the Yard feel like home. Love It.'

'Sat outside on a bale of hay drinking several different types of ale and eating great cheese.'

THE RAMSGATE BREWERY
telephone: 01843 868453
website: www.ramsgatebrewery.co.uk

With the brewery situated just round the corner from the Yard of Ale, GADDS' ales are a regular favourite on the Yard's Beer List.

HIGHLIGHT BEERS:

Black Pearl Oyster Stout 6.2%
Roasted barley, malted oats and Kent grown Fuggles hops combine to create this luscious, bible-black stout.

CASK AND POTTLE

Burton upon Trent, East Staffordshire

ESSENTIAL INFORMATION
2 High Street, Tutbury, Burton upon Trent,
DE13 9LP
Telephone: 07595 423614
Email: gary@caskandpottle.co.uk
Website: www.caskandpottle.co.uk
Facebook: www.facebook.com/
   caskandpottle

Opening hours:
Monday Closed
Tuesday-Thursday 1200-1430
then 1700-2130
Friday 1200-1430 then 1700-2230
Saturday 1300-2230
Sunday 1300-1600

Other reasons to go: Tutbury Castle
www.tutburycastle.com;
The National Brewery Centre
www.nationalbrewerycentre.co.uk;
The Kandy Factory www.kandyfactory.co.uk;
Fauld Crater Memorial, DE13

It's surprising that Staffordshire, which can claim to be one of Britain's brewing capitals, has few micropubs. Owners Gary Hopper (opposite, top left) and Jane Thompson are both retired and used to live in Kent. Their local micropub was The Just Reproach (page 98), and inspired by its success they boldly decided to try their own on virgin territory, opening the Cask and Pottle in 2013. It's been a huge crowd pleaser and has won Burton and South Derbyshire Country Pub of the Year two years running.

At the top of Tutbury's picturesque Victorian high street, a few miles south of the Peak District National Park border, this place has a far more modern feel inside than the exterior might suggest. In a row of shops and surrounded by traditional pubs, it's tiny from the outside and easy to miss. It was formerly a video shop and then a sweet shop.

Inside, it manages to be minimalist but not bare. An ale measure covers one wall and a traditional image of cask carriers covers another and there are a few Second World War propaganda posters. Some board games and books about beer complete the essentially simple ambience.

Gary and Jane have ensured that it's faithful to the micropub concept: there are wooden tables and a continuous bench round the walls, with standing room in the centre. Those standing are at eye level with anyone seated. The bench is scattered with cushions, giving a homely feel, and there are casks on which to rest your feet. There's no bar: a chill room at the back contains the casks and the beer is poured by gravity. You can watch through a small window as your beer fills the glass.

Four ales are usually on offer plus cider,

wine and soft drinks. Crisps, nuts, pork pies and cheese are also available.

We drank Froth Blower's Piffle Snonker 3.8%, a light blonde beer with a sweet start but bitter finish; Springhead's Maid Marian 4.5%, a pale golden beer with an orange flavour and dry peppery finish; and Stroud Brewery's The Last Duel 3.8%, a pale ale with a sherbet finish.

We recommend turning up early if you want a seat: this place fills up quickly.

Disabled access ✓ **Child friendly** ✓
Dog friendly ✓

WHAT THE REGULARS SAY

'Free of all technological noise, it's a great place to talk whilst enjoying excellent beer.'

'Like drinking in someones house.'

'You can never get bored of the ever changing ales they have on offer.'

THE FUGGLE AND NUGGET

Burton upon Trent, Staffordshire

ESSENTIAL INFORMATION
81 High Street, Burton upon Trent,
DE14 1LD
Telephone: 07805 526322
Email: fuggleandnugget@gmail.com
Facebook: www.facebook.com/The-Fuggle-
Nugget-Micropub-711325965647162

Opening hours:
Monday Closed
Tuesday-Thursday 1630-2200
Friday 1630-2230
Saturday 1200-2230
Sunday Closed

Other reasons to go: The National Brewery
Centre www.nationalbrewerycentre.co.uk;
Claymills Pumping Station
www.claymills.org.uk;
National Forest Adventrue Farm
www.adventurefarm.co.uk

You would not think so looking at it, but this place is located in a Grade II listed building – its painted pebbledash doesn't do the place justice. At the end of a row of terraced houses, next-door to Riverside Church, the building was originally the Manse House and was the location of various high street shops before the Fuggle and Nugget arrived. The shop-front window, however, has been well thought through and amusingly done - it displays two smiling hops holding a pint (bottom left). Despite being on a fairly busy road, the place looks out on to a small meadow and the River Trent.

Shaun Rose and Jane Laws loved the micropub concept, especially its community value and weren't the only ones in Burton upon Trent to feel this way – see The Last Heretic (page 66) which is just a 15-minute walk away on Station Street.

Being next door to a church involved some problems with the planning application, but they close on Sundays and as with most micropubs, noise, smoking and drinking on the street outside have

turned out not to be an issue.

The inside is classic, authentic micropub design, and beautifully done: you feel like you're walking into a classic Kent micropub. The tables and benches are high and there are casks to rest your feet on. The wood has been made to look weathered and has a great deal of character. The decoration is simple landscape pictures complemented by pale green walls. Pump clips decorate some of the walls but they don't dominate the place, not yet anyway. Framed blackboards dotted around ensure that you don't have to move far to find out what's on offer. There's no bar - instead drinks are brought to the tables and a small stillage room is visible through a window at the back.

On our visit we enjoyed Ashover Brewery's Milk Stout, a 6% sweet, creamy and rich ale with hints of chocolate, coffee and caramel, brewed with lactose; The Tap House Brewery's Dark and Dangerous, a 5% dark porter with subtle chocolate flavours with a moreish finish; and Nene Valley Brewery's Release the Chimps, a 4.4% everyday crisp IPA.

Fuggles and Nuggets are both varieties of hops.

Disabled access ✓ **Child friendly** ✓ until 1800
Dog friendly ✓

WHAT THE REGULARS SAY

'Fantastic beers, great cheeses and pork pies. Shaun and Jane are lovely and make every customer feel welcome. I love the fact that you can sample local beers, some from breweries I never even knew existed.'

'Run by a truly nice couple. Beer range is ever changing and always in great condition.'

'Always a great relaxed and welcoming atmosphere. Owners come to your table for a chat and there's a good selection of beers and ciders.'

THE LAST HERETIC

Burton upon Trent, East Staffordshire

ESSENTIAL INFORMATION
95 Station Street, Burton upon Trent,
DE14 1BT
Telephone: 07715097797
Email: thelastheretic@outlook.com
Website: thelastheretic.co.uk
Facebook: www.facebook.com/The-last-
heretic-480571588810654

Opening hours:
Monday 1700-2200
Tuesday-Thursday 1600-2230
Friday 1600-2300
Saturday 1200-2300
Sunday 1300-2200

Other reasons to go: The National Brewery
Centre www.nationalbrewerycentre.co.uk;
Claymills Pumping Station
www.claymills.org.uk;
National Forest Adventrue Farm
www.adventurefarm.co.uk

Industry, residential properties and high street shops all mingle on Burton upon Trent's Station Street. Among tall and imposing Victorian buildings this little place is, by contrast, clean and modern.

Peter Spittles worked as cabin crew for 21 years flying from Gatwick Airport as well as having his own business selling organic fruit drinks at country shows and music festivals. The micropub concept appealed to him, so he decided to open his own in May 2016.

Edward Wightman, the last Englishman to be burnt at the stake for heresy, spent most of his life in Burton, so the name is properly local.

The furniture was all bought from churches and consists of long benches set back against the walls with low tables and chairs filling the rest of the space. A corridor leading to a store room also has a high shelf and high stools. The small L-shaped bar stands in one corner – more a place to lean and put drinks than an actual bar - with a large door and window behind it where the casks are visible.

Beer is served straight from the cask and there are five changing ales on at any one time, plus constantly changing ciders. The floor is wooden and the walls are painted pale blue, decorated with a mixture of historical and drink-related pictures and mirrors. Several black boards beside the bar display what's currently on tap and the shelves above the bar display spirits, wines and soft drinks also for sale. A patio at the back provides further seating.

On our visit we enjoyed Tower Brewery's Tower Imperial IPA 5%, a light, golden hoppy pale ale with a citrus flavour and a dry finish; Lymestone Brewery's

Stone Faced, a 4% ale with toffee and berry flavours; and Abbeydale Brewery's Black Mass, a 6.6% dark ruby ale with a chocolate, coffee, raisin and cherry flavour. There's no car park but there are public car parks near the station and there is free street parking on some streets nearby.

Disabled access ✓ **Child friendly** ✓
Dog friendly ✓

WHAT THE REGULARS SAY
'A rather wonderful micropub. Beer is in tip-top condition every visit I have made, the staff are welcoming and Margaux the pub dog is too.'

'The best micropub in Burton! Pete is a top bloke who knows how to run a place.'

'Superb ambience enhanced by the sound of conversation. Love it.'

THE ALE STOP

Buxton, Derbyshire

ESSENTIAL INFORMATION
3 Chapel Street, Buxton, SK17 6HX
Telephone: 07403 528605
Facebook: www.facebook.com/The-Ale-
    Stop-1494140147497459

Opening hours:
Monday 1200-2200
Tuesday-Thursday 1100-2200
Friday 1100-0000
Saturday 1100-2200
Sunday 1200-2100

Other reasons to go: Poole Cavern
poolescavern.co.uk;
Buxton Opera House
www.buxtonoperahouse.org.uk;
Buxton Museum
www.derbyshire.gov.uk

The outside doesn't do it justice, but as soon as you're inside you'll appreciate the enthusiasm and effort that has gone into creating this micropub. The walls are plastered with an amazing combination of musical items and pump clips: it's so dizzying and colourful, you could spend hours taking it all in.

Dan Hawtin worked in several other pubs in the area until he got fed up of the sheer quantity of food that had to be produced. He wanted to focus on beer, so turned to the micropub concept. He happened to move into a flat above a wine shop, whose potential he recognised when it became vacant. Not much needed doing: the furniture came from ebay and friends - essentially low tables and chairs with a few high stools. A ledge around the edge of the room provides a useful space on which to stand drinks. Around 40 people can fit in.

A side room holds an ever-growing collection of vinyl records donated by customers along with a sound system only used for special occasions. There's also a record player on the bar.

In the North and the Midlands

micropubs are less faithful to the core micropub values pioneered in Kent, but of the several micropubs in this area, The Ale Stop stands out as being one of the 'purest'. There's no lager other than speciality bottles; there's no TV; and the only music is either live or vinyl. The bar offers three beers from handpumps and there are always three ciders on offer. Under a hatch in the corridor is a cellar – an unusual bonus.

The beer is sourced as locally as possible, but they stock several from further afield especially Scotland.

On our visit we enjoyed Under Current's Oatmeal Pale Ale, a 4.5% part pale, part oats and part caramel barley. Also going well were Abolition's Amber Ale 3.8% and Atom's Uncertainty Principle 6%.

Disabled access ✓ Child friendly ✓
Dog friendly ✓

WHAT THE REGULARS SAY
'Great venue with a fantastic atmosphere and lovely people.'

'Unusual quality cask ales, great for lover of hops.'

'A fabulous little place, unique to the town.'

Carnforth, Lancashire

ESSENTIAL INFORMATION
Unit 6, Carnforth Gateway Building,
Carnforth, LA5 9TR
Telephone: 07927 396861
Email: The.Snug.Carnforth@gmail.com
Website: thesnugmicropub.blogspot.co.uk
Facebook: www.facebook.com/
   TheSnugMicropub/?fref=ts
Twitter: @TheSnugMicropub

Opening hours:
Monday Closed
Tuesday-Saturday 1200-1400
then 1700-2100
Sunday 1230-1630

Other reasons to go:
Leighton Hall www.leightonhall.co.uk;
Lancaster Castle www.lancastercastle.com;
Lakeland Wildlife Oasis wildlifeoasis.co.uk

Film buffs may recognise this micropub. It's in Carnforth Railway Station, used as the location for the poignant meetings in Brief Encounter (1945). It's worth watching in order to appreciate The Snug's iconic surroundings. The station was closed down in 1970 and went into disrepair until 2000 when a three year restoration project was started. It has now been converted into a heritage centre, a cafe (re-created to be identical with the film) and this cosy micropub.

Julie and Gregg, inspired by the success and ethos of other micropubs, decided to open their own. Both gave up their jobs to pursue this venture. They have to employ several bar staff to help out; when we visited it was so full that we had to claw our way to the bar. Don't let this put you off, the atmosphere is genuinely friendly and the locals are up for a good chat. Some of them have even contributed to the decoration for example Paul, a regular who is responsible for much of the Banksy-esque art work on the walls. There is a well-stocked bookshelf, more for decoration than for reading.

The lovely old station building gives the pub, a unique ambience. It has high ceilings but its floor area is only 300 square feet. There's a conventional wooden bar and 16 bar stools plus tables. Outside, there's seating on the old station platform, now separated from the trains by railings. If you're lucky, you might see a steam train puff by.

The bar has five hand pumps and behind, in an air-conditioned glass-fronted cupboard, are the casks. They stock a range of English craft beers in bottles and cans, also, Swedish beers from Gotlands

Bryggeri and around ten different gins.

On our visit we drank Conqueror Black IPA 5.0%, from Windsor and Eton Brewery, with a dark stout colour, and a strong hoppy flavour - thoroughly enjoyable. We also tried Earl Grey IPA 6.8%, from Marble Brewery which was citrusy and smooth.

For keen beans The Snug offers a loyalty card: buy nine pints and get one free. We picked one up as a souvenir, thinking the offer was a bit of a challenge for one night.

Disabled access ✓ **Child friendly** ⊗
Dog friendly ✓

WHAT THE REGULARS SAY
'Great pub, captures the essence of the old-fashioned real ale establishment.'

'The thrill of an express thundering past a perfect pint has always added value to any afternoon or evening.'

'The size of the welcome is surpassed only by the quality of the beer.'

Castle Donington, Leicestershire

ESSENTIAL INFORMATION
32 Borough Street, Castle Donington,
DE74 2LA
Telephone: 07841374441
E-mail: rasmad4@gmail.com
Website: www.chequered1.com
Facebook: www.facebook.com/The-
   Chequered-Flag-567890109993579

Opening hours:
Monday Closed
Tuesday-Thursday 1500-2230
Friday 1500-2300
Saturday 1200-2300
Sunday (and Bank Holidays) 1200-1600
New Years Eve 1200-0030

Other reasons to go: Castle Donington
Museum www.castledonington museum.
org; Download Rock Festival
www.downloadfestival.co.uk;
The Ron Haslam Race School
www.haslamraceschool.com

There is plenty of high-octane fuel here to keep your engine faring. The Chequered Flag opened in April 2014 and was the 51st micropub in England. Initially owned and run by Michael Willies and Caroline Campbell, it is now under the careful management of Robert Sandham.

Given its location near Donington Park motorsport circuit, this place has an appropriate name and appropriate decoration. Motorsport memorabilia adorn the walls with autographs from different racers and photos of cars and motorbikes. Bert had previously worked in the metallic paint industry, specialising in drag reduction coatings for racing cars.

It's small, with contemporary-style bright, clean walls, a nice dark wooden floor and a smart wall-mounted electric fire. The atmosphere is hugely inviting; you can relax and enjoy great company and quality beers even if not a racing fan.

The furniture consists of wrap-around leatherette padded benches, some small circular tables and high tables and chairs. There are also, towards the back, long wall-mounted shelves with several bar stools. Photos and pictures, grouped according to size, plus exposed brickwork and white plaster walls contrast nicely.

The serving counter is decorated with leatherette squares set out in a chequered flag pattern. A couple of small shelves behind hold a stock of wine and soft drinks. Overhead chalk boards advertise what's on offer.

The beer casks and cider polypins are kept in a temperature-controlled cool room just beyond the bar visible through a small window. Usually, six beers are on at a time. The house beer is Flag Ale,

a 4% copper bitter brewed specially for the micropub by Derby-based Dancing Duck Brewery. Other beers they've offered include: Nene Valley's DXB, a 4.6% chestnut-coloured spicy hoppy ale; and Falstaff's 3 Faze, a 3.8% session ale, with a full, traditional bitter taste. There are usually six ciders (but sometimes up to eight or nine); a selection of wines; a range of soft drinks from Fentimans and Frobishers and a small selection of gins and whiskies.

Snacks include nuts, crisps, pork scratchings and pork pies supplied by Smith Hall Farm, Hulland Ward.

Disabled access ⊗ **Child friendly** ✓
Dog friendly ✓

WHAT THE REGULARS SAY
'Absolutely fabulous. Best gin and tonic, great ale, great atmosphere and amazing pork pies. Make time for a visit.'

'A must for any ale fan. I order a half of each ale with one of their award-winning pies as a palate cleanser.'

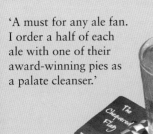

Chelmsford, Essex

ESSENTIAL INFORMATION
173 Moulsham Street, Chelmsford, Essex
CM2 0LD
Telephone: 01245 353570
Email: Info@thehopbeershop.co.uk
Facebook: www.facebook.com/pages/The-
    Hop-Beer-Shop/157869069568322
Twitter: @HopBeerShop

Opening hours:
Monday Closed
Tuesday-Saturday 1200-2100
Sunday 1200-1600

Other reasons to go: Chelmsford Museum
www.chelmsford.gov.uk;
Hylands House and Park
www.chelmsford.gov.uk;
Tropical Wings World of Wildlife
www.tropicalwings.co.uk

Formerly a music store and located next to Stuffsamust, which sells peculiar lifestyle gifts, The Hop Beer Shop is devoted to craft and alchemy of a different nature. It is both a shop and a micropub, and has a bright green store sign with a cheerful cartoon beer-hop man. Buyers beware – once you step in, there are offers here you cannot resist.

The Hop Beer Shop is an Aladdin's Cave of liquid gems, and silver-haired proprietor, John Prior, stocks over one hundred bottled beers from local and international breweries. All tastes are catered for. John put in all the fixtures and fittings himself, including the bar counter, the wooden framing for the stillage room, the long wall bench and high tables, and of course the shelves for his bottled stock.

The Hop Beer Shop seats about fourteen people inside, with room to stand here and there, plus a couple of tables outside. The atmosphere is far more intimate and cosy than your regular pub. It promotes conversation – not just between friends but with the other customers – creating

the vibrancy and friendliness for which micropubs are becoming increasingly known.

The place could feel small, but it follows the standard micropub model of high tables and simple decoration, and does not feel cluttered or confined. The walls are light cream and mint, and the room is bright and warm.

Hop bines encircle the ceiling, a fine selection of Belgian beer glasses sit on a high shelf, and old pump clips decorate the ceiling beams. An attractive wall clock opposite the bar counter is made from a wooden barrel top.

Aside from the extensive bottled selection, four or five guest beers are served from the cask by gravity from the stillage room – some come from local breweries, as well as interesting beers from further afield. This usually includes stout, porter and a golden beer. Whilst visiting, we sampled Wantsum Brewery's Imperium, a 4% amber Best Bitter with biscuit malts; and RCH Brewery's Blackberry Slug – 4.5%, full bodied and aromatic. If you're not a beer type, there are four draught ciders, wine or soft drinks.

Disabled access ⊗ **Child friendly** ⊗
Dog friendly ✓

WHAT THE REGULARS SAY

'I like real ale. Micropub owners are more knowledgeable about the beer they keep — it's more passion than business'.

'It's how pubs used to be. I like the fact you end up talking to complete strangers and often from different age groups'.

Chesterfield, Derbyshire

ESSENTIAL INFORMATION

37 West Bars, Chesterfield, Derbyshire,
S40 1AG
Email: chesterfieldalehouse@gmail.com
Website: www.chesterfieldalehouse.co.uk
Facebook: www.facebook.com/
   ChesterfieldAle
Twitter: @ChesterfieldAle

Opening hours:
Monday-Sunday: 1200–2200

Other reasons to go: Chesterfield Museum
and Art Gallery
www.chesterfield.gov.uk
Hardwick Hall
www.nationaltrust.org.uk
Bolsover Castle
www.english-heritage.org.uk

The ever tempting offer of 'Free Beer Tomorrow' (but never today) is displayed next to the bar in this truly micro micropub. It's a quiet refuge from the busy main road just outside and it's on two mini levels with the bar on the upper one and the seating on the lower one.

Alun Waterhouse and Trevor Maris opened Chesterfield Alehouse together in 2014 and work alternate shifts throughout the week. They met as volunteers at CAMRA beer festivals before deciding to go it alone and make their hobby a permanent career.

Alun, who worked for the county council for 25 years, describes this place as 'a village pub in a town', and it certainly feels like that. Small and friendly, it encourages anyone and everyone to come in, whether alone or in a group.

The bar offers six rotating ales. Pump one is always below 4%, two is below 5%, three is above 5%, four is a bitter or a red, five is dark and six is a wild card, often a beer with fruit. The glasses are oversized and marked with a line to show you've been poured more than a full pint. Prices are reasonable. More than 60 bottled beers are available including a low alcohol one.

Besides beer they have a large range of ciders - up to 12 choices. There are also fruit wines and bottled lagers. Soft drinks are priced low for drivers at only £1.

Upstairs is a TV room, this is a separate space which doesn't interfere with the micropub atmosphere downstairs.

The ground floor is furnished with five low tables with benches and chairs. Bar stools are out "because they get in the way". The walls are sparsely decorated with pictures and a mirror: Most of

the space is given over to blackboards displaying everything on offer.

This place can't be faulted for its emphasis on providing new and excellent drinks - "people like brand new breweries and brand new beers" says Alun.

Tuesday night is cheese night and on bank holidays they have a 'tap takeover' - all the handpumps offer beers from just one brewery.

On our visit the Alehouse was offering Weetwood's Bitter 3.8%; Saltaire Brewery's Raspberry Blonde 4%; and Vog Brewery's Dark Matter, a 4.4% blackcurrant porter.

Disabled access ✓ not to bar
Child friendly ✓
Dog friendly ✓

WHAT THE REGULARS SAY
'A unique place to come and enjoy a drink.'

'Simply excellent all round.'

'Great service, great beer and great snacks.'

BOB INN

Chorley, Lancashire

ESSENTIAL INFORMATION
24 Market Place, Chorley, PR7 1DA
Telephone: 07767 238410
Facebook: www.facebook.com/thebobinn

Opening hours:
Monday-Saturday 1000-1800
Sunday Closed

Other reasons to go: Astley Hall
chorley.gov.uk;
Heskin Farmers Market
www.heskinfarmersmarket.co.uk;
Chorley Market www.chorley.gov.uk

Chorley is famous for its markets with the earliest known dating back to 1498. It's here, in the covered market, that this micropub is located.

Landlord Stephen Cooney was a Cellar Service Engineer before working in a number of sales roles for several breweries. He then established the Merseyside-based events company, The Occasional Drink Ltd. Following this he decided to branch out alone and open his own micropub with his wife Jill in 2014.

This place is one of the smallest bars in Lancashire at 11' by 9', and its not hard to believe. The premises is a tiny market stall and used to be a wool stall, giving The Bob Inn its name, as well as the fact that customers bob in and out. This gives it an almost unique feel.

There is very limited seating inside, but it spills out on to both sides of the covered market. There are a few chairs on the outside and on the inside there are a few casks and stools to sit on by a counter-style wall. A next door stall has a further seating area which is separate from the main bar.

The walls are all exposed brick and minimally decorated. Amusing signs hang

on the end of the bar: 'When I die, bury me under the pub so my husband will visit me 7 times a week.' and 'Alcohol is the answer...Sorry I can't remember the question.'

Shelves behind the bar are full to bursting with bottles and a small fridge holds yet more. The bar has five handpumps, three of which are ever changing ales and two of which are ciders. Unusually for a micropub there are numerous spirits on offer as well.

A few ales that have been on offer are: Springhead's Outlawed, a 3.8% triple hopped, golden ale with a citrus aroma; Tiny Rebel's Cwtch, a 4.6% Welsh Red Ale. Cwtch means cuddle or cubbyhole. This ale is made up of six caramelly malts and three citrussy American Hops; and Lytham Brewery's Top Dog, a 4.4% ruby ale with roasted malts and solely British hops.

Disabled access ✓ to some areas
Child friendly ✓
Dog friendly ✓

WHAT THE REGULARS SAY
'You just can't go in there and not chat to somebody.'

'It's nice that you can eat a pizza or fish and chips with your drink outside on the tables'

'Superb! Ale and conversation. No other distractions. What more do we need?'

SHEPHERD'S HALL ALE HOUSE

Chorley, Lancashire

ESSENTIAL INFORMATION
67 Chapel Street, Chorley, Lancashire,
PR7 1BS
Telephone:07412 584907
Website: shepherdshallalehouse.
   wordpress.com
Facebook: www.facebook.com/
   shepshallalehouse
Twitter: @ShepsAleHouse

Opening hours:
Monday Closed
Tuesday-Thursday 1400-2200
Friday 1400-2300
Saturday 1200-2300
Sunday 1400-2100

Other reasons to go: Astley Hall
chorley.gov.uk;
Heskin Hall
www.heskinhall.com;
Heskin Farmers Market and Craft Centre
www.heskinfarmersmarket.co.uk

Shepherds' Hall Ale House is a family-run business opened by three brothers in 2014, when Graham, Stuart and Tom Hardyman (opposite, bottom) made the decision to work together and turn an old florists into Chorley's first micropub. Located in the imposing Victorian building of Shepherds' Victoria Hall, the name came on a plate.

The three brothers, inspired by the micropub concept and by the successful opening of The Market Ale House (page 156), launched their own. Apart from a stint in the Chorley Rugby Union Club, none had any experience of running a bar, but this hasn't held them back. They mugged up on how to look after cask-conditioned beer from numerous books and haven't looked back since. Graham and Stuart both work part time alongside other jobs while Tom, at only 25, works full time.

The walls are decorated with landscape photographs and above the picture rail are numerous rows of beer clips. All the furniture has been rescued from old pubs, most notably an L-shaped bar holding five handpumps which serve four local ales and one from further afield. They also offer bottled continental beers and wine and if there's a beer you want them to serve, there's

a beer suggestion box.

We drank Ossett Silver King 4.3%, a very pale beer with a crisp, dry flavour; Banktop Sweeney's 3.8%, a toffee and caramel flavoured beer with a bitter finish; and Monty's Mischief 5.0%, a golden beer with a slight sweet finish.

The one drawback to this place is its location on the corner of a main road.

Disabled access ✓ **Child friendly** ⊗
Dog friendly ✓

WHAT THE REGULARS SAY
'This is the one and only place to go in Chorley for a proper pint of beer.'

'A spot on place to drink real ale.'

'Cracking little boozer. Looking forward to my next visit.'

'I am never disappointed with the range and quality of the ales. Always greeted with a warm welcome.'

PLATFORM 3

Claygate, Surrey

ESSENTIAL INFORMATION
37B The Parade, Claygate, Esher, KT10 0PD
Telephone: 01372 462 334
Email: alex@brightbrew.co.uk
Website: www.brightbrew.co.uk
Facebook: www.facebook.com/
Platform3SmallestPubinUK

Opening hours:
Monday-Wednesday Closed
Thursday-Friday 1130-2200
Saturday Closed
Sunday 1230-1900

Other reasons to go: Chessington World of
Adventures www.chessington.com;
Sandown Park Racecourse
www.sandown.co.uk;
Surbiton Golf Club
www.surbitongolfclub.com

It can claim to be the smallest micropub in the country, definitely in Surrey: there's room for the bar, the barman, and at most two thin people in this former cab office on Claygate Station's Platform 3. Locals enjoy hopping off for a quick one, then back on the Waterloo-Guildford trains that stop at Claygate. Or they arrive by car, using the station car park.

So how can it possibly survive serving two people at a time? Answer, of course, by having an adjacent outdoor drinking area which is covered by an awning in winter months and warmed by patio heaters. Here there's room for around 25 people – still huggermugger – but it works – and the only drawback is the plastic glasses which the police insisted on when the licence was granted. Good beer, just like good wine, tastes best in the right sort of glass, so plastic is a shame when it comes to cask-conditioned real ale.

This is the brewery tap for Brightwater Brewery started by Alex Coomes and his partner Sue in 2012. They serve rotating Brightwater ales with one guest ale. A pint cost £4 as we went to press and a half pint £2 - over the odds compared with most micropubs. A two-pint takeaway cost £6. In other words, this is not a charity and the commercial ambience is further underlined by the Platform 3 merchandise they sell – pint glasses, baseball caps and tote bags.

On our visit we tried Brightwater's Daisy Gold, one of their enduring favourites. It's a 4 % quaffing beer, ie session ale, golden coloured with a bitter-sweet aftertaste. We followed up sensibly with their low-alcohol 3.1% Little Nipper, a dark chestnut-coloured bitter with a chocolate aftertaste.

Alex and his helpers, who are all

knowledgeable ale enthusiasts, create an informal community atmosphere where all ages (six to 80) can feel at home, including single women and couples. Alex is usually there to pour your pint on a Friday or Saturday.

Disabled access ✓ **Child friendly** ⊗
Dog friendly ✓

WHAT THE REGULARS SAY
'Absolutely fantastic.
What a gem of a place.'

'The perfect watering hole and meeting place. Claygate wouldn't be the same without it. We love it!'

'Great location, even better beer.'

5 LITRE MINI KEG TO TAKE HOME

THE TAP ROOM

Cliftonville, Kent

ESSENTIAL INFORMATION
4 Northdown Parade, Cliftonville, Kent,
CT9 2NR
Telephone: 01843 280322
Facebook: www.facebook.com/
   TapRoomAleHouse

Opening hours:
Monday-Friday 1200-1500
then 1630-2200
Saturday 1200-1500 then 1630-2300
Sunday Closed

Other reasons to go:
Cliftonville Farmer's Market, CT9 2HL
Quex Barn Farm Shop quexbarn.com;
Viking Coastal Trail explorekent.org;
The Micro Museum,
www.themicromuseum.org

One of the cluster of micropubs at the eastern tip of Kent, this is in Cliftonville on the edge of Ramsgate. You could sample them all using the bus service (every seven minutes) connecting Margate, Cliftonville, Broadstairs, Westwood Cross and Ramsgate.

Phil Leader would have been the seventh to open a micropub in the UK but deaths in his family sadly delayed opening until April 2015. His place holds its head up among the excellent nearby micropubs as cosy, friendly and personal. Phil's main helper is his son Edward, but partner Sandra also plays her part.

He says: "There are good and bad things about the micropub craze. Some people don't have the passion for real ale but jump on the bandwagon and the ale isn't as good as it should be." This is one reason why he buys the expensive ales, despite the profit margin being tighter than on cheaper ones.

Although there's a bar, and background music, we still rate this a genuine micropub because of Phil's uncompromising focus on quality real ales, and because his personal approach to customers creates an atmosphere in which friendships are made. He makes no apology for selling bottled lagers – "We are not anti anything."

The exterior is simple and inviting – painted dark grey with the name picked out in bright green using a non-standard modern typeface. Inside the decoration is advertising posters from the past, either framed or enamel. Five quarter-turn taps mounted on a wall are directly connected to casks behind the wall in a temperature-controlled area.

WHAT THE REGULARS SAY

'Great little micropub with excellent beers on tap that are well kept, pleasant decoration and atmosphere.'

'The Jewel in the Cliftonville crown. Amazing beers, always have a good stout or porter on and super friendly to boot. Why go anywhere else?'

'Fast becoming the embassy of good conversation, laughs and of course cracking ale in Cliftonville.'

On our visit we tried Hophead from Dark Star Brewery – a 3.8% pale golden ale with a flowery aroma and distinct taste of elderflower from Cascade hops. Later, in the mood for something stronger, we drank Jaipur from Thornbridge, another pale ale, but complex. At first the impression is of softness and smoothness, but then you are blown away by a tidal wave of hoppiness, plus some honey-sweetness. The aftertaste is long and bitter. Phil tries to keep these two as staples. He also serves wine, Prosecco, crisps and nuts.

In the evening he turns down the lights and increases the music volume – lunchtime is lower key. Cliftonville has one mainstream pub, the Bellevue, which is a complete contrast to The Tap Room – a big space, with Sky TV and loud music.

Disabled access ✓ **Child friendly** ✓
Dog friendly ✓

THE DOG HOUSE

Coleford, Gloucester

ESSENTIAL INFORMATION
13 - 15 St. John's Street, Coleford,
Gloucester, GL16 8AP
Telephone: 07442787015
Website: www.thedoghousemicropub.co.uk
Facebook: www.facebook.com/
   Thedoghousemicropubcoleford

Opening hours:
Monday-Friday 1700-2200
Saturday 1200-2200
Sunday 1200-1500

Other reasons to go:
Royal Forest of Dean
www.wyedeantourism.co.uk;
Clearwell Caves www.clearwellcaves.com;
Hopewell Colliery
www.hopewellcolliery.co.uk

This place was the second of the three Cobblers micropubs in this area (see also page 210), before Greg Daniel took over and changed the name along with the atmosphere. Coleford is a small market town on top of a hill in Monmouthshire and is the geographical centre of the Forest of Dean as well as the administrative centre of the Forest of Dean district.

Greg, who opened in 2014 after working 15 years for Severn Trent Water, wanted a change of career and had always thought about running a pub. He was put off by the horror stories about big chains, and the micropub model seemed the obvious answer. He says he doesn't compete with other pubs in Coleford, but offers instead the unique experience of having a conversation without needing to shout.

There are three small seating areas. The furniture is not what you would expect in a pub, and it lacks character, as does the decoration generally. The only relief is the original woodcut designs covering some of the walls and a quote from Frank Sinatra: "I feel sorry for people who don't drink. They wake up in the morning and that's the best they are going to feel all day." The real log fire is a welcome feature, the first we have come across. The place is always lively, full of regulars, and encourages local community spirit.

There's a traditional bar, which dominates the right hand side of the pub, with two handpumps and further choices of ale served straight from casks sitting on a single-tier wooden stillage behind the bar. Greg uses local breweries as much as possible, always offering at least one local beer. A large fridge displays other choices including ciders, wines and spirits.

On our visit we enjoyed Goffs Brewery's Lancer, a 3.8% light golden ale with citrus elements; Otter Brewery's Otter Amber 4%, tasting of citrus, spice and tropical fruit; and Bath Ales' Summer's Hare, a 3.9% light and hoppy ale with a full malt flavour and fruity bitterness.

There is a regular quiz night followed by supper with the money raised going to a different charity each time.

Disabled access ✓ **Child friendly** ⊗
Dog friendly ✓

WHAT THE REGULARS SAY
'A friendly local with a good selection of ciders, real ales and local characters.'

'Great pub. Best in Coleford. Great atmosphere. Great people.'

'The dog house is the best pub in Coleford. Great place to make new friends.'

'So much character in this place, who can complain about real ales and dogs eh?'

BOYCE'S BARREL

Colne, Lancashire

ESSENTIAL INFORMATION

7 Newmarket Street, Colne, BB8 9BJ

Telephone: 07736 900111

Facebook: www.facebook.com/
    boycesbarrelcolne

Opening hours:

Monday Closed

Tuesday-Friday 1600-2100

Saturady 1300-2100

Sunday 1600-2100

Other reasons to go: Wycoller Country Park
www.friendsofwycoller.co.uk;
The Muni Theatre www.themuni.co.uk;
Pendle Village Mill
www.pendlevillage.co.uk;
Towneley Hall www.burnley.gov.uk

Our guest contributor Richard Reeve visited here. It opened in 2014 and occupies a narrow shop unit on a quiet side street near the centre of Colne. There are three partners: Andrew Turner (aka 'Smiler') and Carl (opposite, bottom right) and Nina Pawson. Nina also works for the Flying Firkin Beer Distribution Company, a very handy connection to have. 'Boyce' came from the name of an unrelated business run by several generations of Carl's family.

As is often the case with micropubs, the outside appearance is deceptively small, however, the inside stretches back further than you would imagine. The furnishings are the most striking aspect of Boyce's Barrel, which are dark but warm and retro, something like an old railway waiting room. The dominant colours are burgundy and cream – the livery of the old Midland Railway.

Handmade bar-height tables and fitted benches built from railway sleepers are set back against the walls, they are clearly a solid investment built to last. The arrangement is similar to many a micropub down south – I haven't found it much in evidence north of the Watford Gap, and it made a refreshing change. Waiter service is often available: just ring one of the various types of bell placed on the tables and Andy or Carl will appear resplendent in their serving aprons.

On the walls and in the loos, memorabilia are in no short supply. Fans of Minder (1979-1994) and the legendary Arthur Daley played by George Cole will not be disappointed. There are also street signs, and the almost obligatory "KEEP CALM' poster. The bar is set right at the

back of the room with a hatch behind it leading to the cellar – an unusual perk for a micropub and one that makes storing the beer that much easier.

There are five hand pumps and they come with an unusual twist. Most micropubs offer local beer supplied by local microbreweries. Andrew's philosophy, however, is the opposite. Explaining that many other pubs in the area stock local ale he wanted to offer his customers something different. Following this theory I drank Houston Brewery's Killellan 3.7%, an amber ale 'brewed with pride in Scotland'. Other customers told me they had enjoyed Loch Ness Brewery's Loch Ness 4.4%, a malty brown ale. I was told that while lunchtime tends to be quiet, the evenings get very busy.

Disabled access ✓ **Child friendly** ⊗
Dog friendly ✓

WHAT THE REGULARS SAY
'This is an absolute gem of a micro pub.'

'Reminiscent of the beer houses in Prague and Belgium.'

'Can't even begin to describe how much I love this place!'

THE PENNY FARTHING

Crayford, Kent

ESSENTIAL INFORMATION
3A Waterside, Dartford, DA1 4JJ
Telephone: 07772 866645
Email: bob.1@ntlworld.com
Website: pennyfarthingcrayford.co.uk
Facebook: www.facebook.com/Penny-
   Farthing-777562915621454

Opening hours:
Monday Closed
Tuesday to Thursday 1200-1500
then 1700-2130
Friday and Saturday 1200-2230
Sunday 1200-1500

Other reasons to go: Barnehurst Golf
Course www.mytimeactive.co.uk;
Hall Place and Gardens www.
bexleyheritagetrust.org.uk;
JJ's Clay Shooting Club www.jjscsc.co.uk;
The Manor Gatehouse
www.akentishceremony.com

Husband and wife Bev and Bob used to manage The One Bell pub in Crayford, but gave it up when they started a family, beginning new careers as a rehab assistant and driving instructor. They were both keen to go back into the pub trade but had to do their homework because they didn't like the way pubs had changed. A micropub seemed the obvious way to go as the concept was so clear cut and the start-up cost low.

They opened The Penny Farthing in 2014 on a site that used to be a bicycle shop where Bev and Bob had bought bikes for their children. The site is on a small pedestrianised part of Waterside – so there's plenty of room to drink outside in warm weather. It's opposite a small park.

As with most Kent micropubs, there's no bar, instead you order your drink and wait for it to be brought to your table. Benches line the walls, chairs and tables are high, and there's standing space in the middle. There's no seating at the ends of the tables, which helps conversation, and table sharing is encouraged. At the back is a cool room with a window allowing a view of the casks. Pump clips from ales they have sold cram every inch of wall leaving little space for anything else other than a few photos of penny farthings.

Although there are six mainstream pubs within walking distance, none cater for the real ale drinker, so this place has found a niche and is thriving. The ales are constantly changed - one customer said he "felt like a kid in a sweet shop, not knowing what to choose."

They offer six traditional ciders, red, white and rosé wines and Prosecco. There's a selection of soft drinks, tea, coffee, snacks and pies. On our visit we enjoyed

Bexley Brewery's Golden Acre, a 4% single malt golden ale named after the green in Bexley Village; and Mad Cat Brewery's Educated Guess, a 4.7% full-flavoured dark bitter with a fruity finish.

Disabled access ✓ **Child friendly** ✓
Dog friendly ✓

510 Different Beers Since 11th Sept 2014

WHAT THE REGULARS SAY

'A real ale pub with a good selection served to your table, there's also cider and wine available. Free parking, close to Crayford station and bus routes as this is not the place for a swift pint.'

'One of our regular haunts. Always a good selection of ales.'

'By far my favourite place to drink great beer and great cider. Lovely atmosphere, friendly people, 100% recommended.'

LIVERPOOL PIGEON

Crosby, Merseyside

ESSENTIAL INFORMATION
14 Endbutt Lane, Crosby, L23 0TR
Telephone: 07766 480 329
Email: j.moore2012@btinternet.com
Website: liverpoolpigeon.co.uk
Facebook: www.facebook.com/
    liverpoolpigeon

Opening hours:
Monday Closed
Tuesday-Friday 1600-2100
Saturday 1300-2100
Sunday 1300-1700

Other reasons to go: World Museum
www.liverpoolmuseums.org.uk;
Black Pearl Pirate Ship www.facebook.
com/TheBlackPearlNewBrighton;
Antony Gormley's Another Place
www.antonygormley.com

Pat Moore spent 13 years as a primary school teacher, before deciding to turn his passion for beer into a career. He was very excited by the micropub concept and after reading an interview with Martyn Hillier, who opened the first micropub in Kent (page 140), he realized that it was possible to go it alone without the help of any large pub chain or brewery.

Opening his doors in 2013, he has transformed this old children's clothes shop into Merseyside's most original place to drink. He now runs it with his wife Jacky.

It's named after the now-extinct pigeon known as the Liverpool or Spotted Green Pigeon. The last remaining specimen can be seen in Liverpool's World Museum.

Green is the colour scheme throughout. The exterior is dark green, with essential information displayed in the window. Inside, the same colour scheme continues with dark green walls and stool cushions. The colour gives a countrified vibe, and the atmosphere is certainly relaxed, warm and welcoming. The furniture consists of traditional wooden chairs and round tables. The walls are decorated with cartoon images of Liverpool Pigeons and old brewery trays. There are board games, and a library of beer books.

Despite being a little way out of Liverpool, hidden down a side street, there is no shortage of drinkers. Word of mouth and two Liverpool and District CAMRA awards has put the Liverpool Pigeon at the heart of the Merseyside drinking scene. A notable feature is the oversized glasses, loved by the locals and guaranteeing a full pint every time.

The L-shaped bar has five hand pumps, all with rotating beers. The beers include:

Exit 33's Thirst Aid, a 4%, light and fruity
beer; Blackjack Beers' Jabberwocky, a
4.1% golden ale with a bitter aftertaste.
They also often stock Hawkshead and
Salopian beers. There are also two ciders,
along with bottled British, Belgian and
German beers.

Disabled access ✓ **Child friendly** ✓
Dog friendly ✓ only if well behaved

WHAT THE REGULARS SAY
'Lovely atmosphere, great ales – heaven.'

'Wonderful beers and very knowledgeable
staff.'

'Exemplary beer – other pubs could learn
from this little bar.'

Daventry, Northamptonshire

ESSENTIAL INFORMATION
3 Prince William Walk, Daventry, NN11 4AB
Telephone: 077072 99959
Email: carolinelanglands@yahoo.co.uk
Facebook:
www.facebook
com/Early-Doors
Daventry
Twitter:
@EarlyDoorsDav

Opening hours:
Monday Closed
Tuesday- Saturday
1200-2100
Sunday Closed

Other reasons to go:
Canons Ashby House
www.nationaltrust.org.uk;
Coton Manor www.cotonmanor.co.uk;
Daventry Country Park
www.daventrydc.gov.uk

This gorgeous little place was opened in February 2015 by Caroline Langlands and Neil Hawkey, hoping to bring a sense of community back to an area dominated by large pubs. Like many micropub owners, they were looking for a new direction, Caroline from her job as a warrant officer, and Neil from working as an electrician for Northamptonshire County Council. He still works for the council, but is a regular presence behind the bar, and is responsible for most of the wiring, fixtures and fittings.

'Early Doors' refers to the time between 4 and 8pm when people come from finishing work to have a drink – a steady stream of customers but not too hectic. Caroline once worked in a mainstream pub and this was her favourite time as it gave her extra freedom to interact with customers. The name fits with Early Doors' focus on quality customer service and genuine hospitality.

At first glance, the pub looks rather like a café, with patio-seating and floor-to-ceiling windows. It is smart, simple and appealing. Inside the theme is shabby-chic. The walls are painted a light teal, contrasting with the velvet curtains and purple furniture. There is a comfy leather sofa and a reclaimed pew. The bare concrete floor gives the place a lived-in feel, and is perfect for their regular 'dog nights' when owners can bring their dogs. A few attractive pictures hang on the walls, but a First World War Bristol Biplane propeller blade salvaged from an old Officer's Mess is the most interesting feature. A gong is attached to it which was used to sound the dinner bell – today it marks last orders.

The bar counter is full of character and made from recycled doors – as is one of the picture frames and the drinks board is made from old wardrobes. The stillage facility was hand built by Neil and the wooden frame serves as a cooling cabinet with the casks on traditional chocks - there are six ales to choose from. I enjoyed Val Brewery's Gravitas, a 4.8%, citrusy Golden Ale and Stratford-Upon-Avon Brewery's Malty Pig, a 4.4% full-bodied bitter with a caramel flavour. Hart Family Brewers supplies the house session ale – 'Early Doors'.

There is a selection of Fentimans' soft drinks and teas, and coffees are available with or without liqueur. Snacks include Piper's crisps, local, handmade Moulton Pie Company pork pies, nuts, and pork scratchings.

WHAT THE REGULARS SAY

'Takes me back to when I first drank real ale and there is a great revival in good ale now.'

'Small breweries are strongly represented and the emphasis is on quality, not quantity.'

'The concept is brilliant and I love the civilised opening hours.'

WHO BREWS THE BEER?

STRATFORD UPON AVON BREWERY
telephone: 07866 495232
website: www.sua-brewery.co.uk

The UK's most eco-friendly brewery. There are six varieties of hops grown on the brewery's land, the brewery is powered by solar energy and the water comes from their own well.

Disabled access ✓
Child friendly ⊗
Dog friendly ✓

Daybrook, Nottingham

ESSENTIAL INFORMATION
89 Mansfield Road, Daybrook, Nottingham,
NG5 6BH
Telephone: 07852862275
Email: matt@theabdication.co.uk
Website: www.theabdication.co.uk
Facebook: www.facebook.com/
   theabdicationmicropub
Twitter: @theabdication

Opening hours:
Monday-Tuesday Closed
Wednesday-Saturday 1600-2130
Sunday 1400-1800

Other reasons to go: City of Caves
www.cityofcaves.com;
Escapologic www.escapologic.com;
Galleries of Justice Museum
www.galleriesofjustice.org.uk.

This pleasant little micropub is situated in the Grade II-listed Coronation Buildings, which were built by the Home Brewery (across the street) to commemorate George VI's accession to the throne following his brother Edward's abdication. This is the abdication to which the pub's name — unsurprisingly — refers. The Abdication further honours its heritage with a tagline on the frosted-glass window which reads 'Where beer is king'. Intentional or not, The Abdication's name is also an apt metaphor for the micropub revolution — the movement away from the attitudes and practices of mainstream pubs. And long may it live.

Owner and former rail maintenance worker Matt Grace harbours a keen interest in home brewing. He had originally planned to open his own microbrewery, but with so many already established he looked instead to the micropub scene. After reading an article about them in 2012 he caught the bug and opened up shop with his partner Lucy Simons in August 2014. They have not looked back since.

Over the years his chosen site was a sweet shop, a cake decorator's shop, an appliance repair facility and a second-hand jewellery shop. Today the place has a lived-in quality more like a home than a business: it is almost like having a drink in someone's living room. The back room has a grandfather clock which ticks steadily and chimes on the hour, a roaring fire and a mantlepiece adorned with trinkets. From the moment you step through the door you are welcomed into hearth and home.

Rough round the edges, the interior is rudimentary but comfortable. The floor tiles, worn and chequer-patterned, may well

TOTALLY BREWED
telephone: 0115 9984635
website: www.totallybrewed.com

A progressive brewery established in 2014. Located in the heart of Nottingham on the old fruit and flower market and making a wide range of beers from dark, rich stouts to hop forward IPAs. They have been winning awards from the very start and are going from strength to strength with a continually growing range of interesting and flavourful beers.

HIGHLIGHT BEERS:

The 4 Hopmen of the Apocalypse 5.2%
Our flagship IPA and SIBA midland gold winner 2014.

have a tale or two to tell. Seating around 26 with three cushioned benches and plenty of chairs and stools, you are never far from the action, or indeed the bar. Conversation flows as smoothly as the ales. The serving area itself is a simple wooden affair with four hand pumps – there are four beers at any one time. These include a bitter, a blonde/pale ale, a dark stout/porter and a strong IPA or a wheat beer. During my visit I sampled Scribbler's Ales Rubecca — a 4.8% ruby ale — smooth, nicely malted and slightly chocolatey, and Red Squirrel Brewing Co Conservation Bitter, a 3.7% amber bitter with a lovely fruity bitterness which complemented the malt. There is also cider, wine (red, white, rosé) and a selection of soft drinks available, as well as the standard pub snack fare.

The large main room has a quirky feel with an eclectic mix of items. Two bookshelves feature books on an assortment of topics, but the most interesting display is a wall-mounted racing bike complete with skeleton rider – recalling the time our guest contributor Richard Reeve undertook the Alzheimer's charity bike ride. As random as all this seems, The Abdication is a lovely venue for a relaxing drink, with a genuine ambience. The place's service matches its charm.

Disabled access ✓ **Child friendly** ✓
Dog friendly ✓

WHAT THE REGULARS SAY
'Mainstream pubs are now too generic. Here is more personal, individual and intimate.'

'Much friendlier, a more cosy attitude and no pretentiousness.'

'There is a sense of community and they listen to what the public wants.'

THE JUST REPROACH

Deal, Kent

ESSENTIAL INFORMATION
14 King St, Deal CT14, 6HX
Email: mark.robson@btinternet.com
Facebook: www.facebook.com/
   The-Just-Reproach-Deals-
   Micropub-214290775307658

Opening hours:
Monday 1200-1500 then 1700-2000
Tuesday-Thursday 1200-1400
then 1700-2100
Friday 1200-1400 then 1700-2300
Saturday 1200-2300
Sunday 1200-1600

Other reasons to go: Deal Castle
www.english-heritage.org.uk;
Walmer Castle
www.english-heritage.org.uk;
Royal Cinque Ports Golf Club
www.royalcinqueports.com

One hundred per cent in its skin: everything feels just right. It's solidly built, in a pleasant corner site with bus stop, train station and car parking two to three minutes away; the beach is 100 yards off; inside it's just the right size and decorated – but not cluttered - with interesting memorabilia hung on cream painted tongue and groove; the layout is classic Kent micropub - chunky high wooden tables round the edge of the room with high seating. Deal is a more attractive seaside town than its neighbour Dover.

The name is properly local – see the poem mounted on the wall. "Defoe alleges that the local inhabitants were reluctant to put to sea to rescue sailors in trouble from the hurricane, though were not averse to plundering boats when the opportunity arose. Locals still resent this assertion!"

Affable owner Mark Robson (below middle) who runs the place with his daughter Bronwen is a fan of Defoe, admiring his nonconformism. He was a head teacher in a Kent special school for children with autism. When our reporter said he guessed that running a micropub must be easy compared with that, he replied "On the whole, but with a few of the customers it's a close-run thing."

Like many another micropub, The Just Reproach was inspired by visits to The Butcher's Arms, page 140, but opening wasn't a snap decision. It took Mark five years to take the plunge – "I waited til the children had grown up and the mortgage was paid off."

Everyone really does talk to each other in this place – the buzz of conversation can be heard down the street. Many micropubs believe they've created a community, but

here it's no idle claim, and is supported by the micropub's success in fundraising. Mark operates a zero tolerance mobile policy – witness the phones nailed to the wall.

Four real ales (five at weekends) are served by hand from the cold room, plus local wine, a house wine and four ciders. On our visit we enjoyed Wantsum Brewery's 4.2% Challenger Green Hop – fruity with a depth of flavour combined with freshness.

We rate this place one of the best in the guide. Mark also owns The Thomas Tallis in Canterbury, page 134.

Disabled access ✓ not to WC and small step at entrance
Child friendly ✓
Dog friendly ✓

WHAT THE REGULARS SAY
'I just love this micropub. Superbly friendly staff and such a relaxed and friendly environment.'

'There is no bar, take a seat and check out the list of beers available. The beer is well kept and local and is very reasonably priced. So onto a winner there.'

WHO BREWS THE BEER?
KENT BREWERY

KENT BREWERY
telephone: 01634 780 037
website: www.kentbrewery.com

HIGHLIGHT BEERS:

Brewers Reserve 5%
This hoppy and fruity strong Pale Ale is a customer favourite, especially with the legendary brothers!

LITTLE CHESTER ALE HOUSE

Derby, Derbyshire

ESSENTIAL INFORMATION
4a Chester Green Road, Derby, DE1 3SF
Telephone: 07584 244726
Email: hartshornsbrewery@gmail.com
Facebook: www.facebook.com/
  LittleChesterAleHouse

Opening hours:
Monday-Thursday 1500-2230
Friday-Sunday 1200-2230

Other reasons to go: Kedleston Hall
www.nationaltrust.org.uk;
Derby QUAD www.derbyquad.co.uk;
Little Chester Heritage Centre
www.littlechesterhistoryderby.btck.co.uk

Along with The Last Post (page 102), this micropub was opened by Wentwell Brewery in 2012 before Darren Hartshorn bought it. Many changes have been made and when we visited more were imminent. The bar was about to move, more loos were being built and the exterior was about to have a complete makeover.

The premises used to be a laundrette and before that it sold car parts. For more than four years before this guide went to press, it has been a micropub, and since November 2015 it has been run by Richard Swanwick and Darren Hartshorn. It certainly is small, looking larger from the outside than it is inside. It can fit around 30 people, making it Derby's smallest drinking place. There are several traditional pubs and micropubs in the Derby area, but, Richard and Darren aren't worried. They say it makes everyone up their game and they certainly work at keeping their ale in best possible condition.

Before the place opened there were concerns among locals about noise and anti-social behaviour, but the council gave the go-ahead and the locals' attitude soon changed. It's a hugely popular place, a great addition to Little Chester, a suburban, mainly residential area of Derby. It's the oldest inhabited part of the city, located on the conservation area known as Derventio Coritanorum, a Roman fort which went in and out of use over a period of 300 years. Little Chester Ale House sits on the edge of the ancient site. There is much more history hereabouts than you might think – for more information about the area visit the Little Chester Heritage Centre.

The bar has four handpumps, each delivering a stronger ABV than its neighbour. There is always at least one

PIES

Quality, Locally-Sourced Pies:
* Pork
* Pork n' Stilton
* Huntsman's

BAR SNACKS

* Home-Made Pickled Onions
* Crisps N' Nuts
* Sandwiches (Various)
* Pork Scratchings

CHEESE-NIGHT

EVERY MONDAY
FREE!! FROM 7:30 p.m.
· 10 Different Cheeses
· Crackers
· Pickles

dark beer. Because of the strong connection with Hartshorns Brewery you'll often find a choice from there. Every Monday there's a cheese night and at other times they serve simple bar snacks.

On offer on our visit were The Great Yorkshire Brewery's Yorkshire Blackout, a 5% black porter with chocolate and vanilla flavours; White Horse's Wayland Smith, a 4.4% ale full of aromatic hops; and Blue Anchor's Spingo Middle, a 5% ale originally brewed to welcome home men who fought in the First World War.

Like The Last Post, this is a great place for tickers to start a visit to Derby, before working their way into town.

Disabled access ✓
Child friendly ✓ until 1900
Dog friendly ✓

WHAT THE REGULARS SAY
'No lager, no spirits, proper beer and cider with wine and soft drinks. No music, the clientele talk to one another.'

'Lovely little pub, everyone is made to feel welcome, fantastic landlords and most importantly excellent beer.'

'Great pub, five cracking beers, lovely atmosphere, what more can you want?'

Bottled Ales Drink in or Take Out £2·80 a Bottle

Derby, Derbyshire

ESSENTIAL INFORMATION
1 Uttoxeter Old Road, Derby, DE1 1GA
Telephone: 01332 296737
Email: thelastpostderbyltd@gmail.com
Website: www.thelastpostderby.pub
Facebook: www.facebook.com/The-Last-
    Post-463961820371769

Opening hours:
Monday-Wednesday 1100-2000
Thursday-Sunday 1100-2300

Other reasons to go:
Derby Museum and Art Gallery
www.derbymuseums.org;
Pickford's House www.derbymuseums.org;
Derby Gaol www.derbygaol.com

Painted as red as the postbox on its sign, this micropub is proud of its former incarnation- a post office, of course. Chris and Karen O'Brian, partnered by Muirhouse Brewery, bought the place in 2015 from Wentwell Brewery, which incidentally owned the Little Chester Alehouse (page 100). Chris and Karen have now bought out Muirhouse Brewery, but they still maintain close ties with the brewer, which still makes beers especially for them.

Chris used to be a financial consultant, then worked at bars during beer festivals until he decided he needed a long-term project. With regular pubs on the decline and with micropubs being similar to festival bars, the progression came naturally.

Before Chris took over from Wentwell Brewery, the place only sold real ale. Chris soon found this was putting off potential customers. "If a group of ten walk in and three don't want beer you loose the lot." So now he sells 23 single malts, plus a few other spirits, three ciders and one permanent speciality lager – Vedett. This means that the place is not a pure micropub, however, it does enable him – so he claims – to offer really great speciality ales. The need to sell spirits alongside real ale is more common in the Midlands and the North than in the South-East.

All the low tables and chairs were inherited from the previous owners along with some of the decoration. Wooden ducks on the mirror mantle piece were given by a customer, as was the old post office bag you see hanging on the wall. The bag was used in this very post office. The shovel above the bar was a gift from Richard at the Muirhouse Brewery.

A hatch door behind the bar leads down

to the cellar – a luxury in the micropub world – and at the back is a small yard with a table and several benches and chairs. The yard is partially divided and shared – apparently without problems - by the residents on one side and a chemist on the other.

The bar has four handpumps, one of which always provides a dark beer. In quiet periods only three are on offer. The sandwich shop next door makes fresh rolls for the micropub customers, while pork pies, crisps and pork scratchings are on offer at the bar. Four pint carryout cartons are available for £1.50 plus the cost of the beer and there are discounts for CAMRA members. Chris also runs private whisky tasting sessions.

On offer when we visited were: Coastal Brewery's Springfire Blonde, a 4.2% golden citrus beer; Lytham Brewery's Lytham Blonde, a 3.8% pale golden beer with a smooth dry finish; and Raw Brewing Company's Dark Peak Stout 4.5%.

Being in the suburbs of Derby, The Last Post is a popular place to start a micropub crawl of the many in the area as people work their way back towards the station.

Disabled access ✓ not to WC
Child friendly ✓ until 2000
Dog friendly ✓

Dorking, Surrey

ESSENTIAL INFORMATION
23 West Street, Dorking, RH4 1BY
Telephone: 01306879877
Email: info@cobbettsrealales.co.uk
Website: www.cobbettsrealales.com
Facebook: ww.facebook.com/Cobbetts-
   Real-Ales
Twitter: @CobbettsRealAle

Opening hours:
Monday-Thurursday 1200-2000 Friday-
Saturday 1000-2000, Sunday (& Bank
Holiday Mondays) 1200-1800

Other reasons to go:
Box Hill www.nationaltrust.org.uk;
Dorking Halls www.dorkinghalls.co.uk;
Dorking Museum and Heritage Centre
www.dorkingmuseum.org.uk

Cobbett's Real Ales is a family business started by Tim and Helen Sullivan with a focus on selling quality ales and ciders. Their shop and micropub that followed are named after William Cobbett the famous radical and reformer, who may have been an ancestor of Helen's. He wrote numerous publications including Cottage Economy which amongst other things, gave practical advice on how to brew good beer. Cobbetts Real Ales is almost a modern variant of the cottage industry concept. Tim and Helen very much appreciate and respect traditional values and reflect this in the beer shop and micropub they proudly and successfully run.

The micropub was born after a regular customer suggested that the back room could be used as a micropub. In July 2014 it opened for the first time in a somewhat tight space. A tiny room houses high stools by a long shelf on one side with padded leather seats and small wooden tables on the other side. Around 13 people can fit in but on my visit the seven there made it feel a little cramped. An outside seating area can seat around six to eight more on simple patio chairs. Compared to the beer shop with its attractively stained wooden shelving and hop-bine garlands, the micropub is basic and somewhat resembles a mainstream pub snug bar.

Most of the decorations are typical breweriana accessories. A bookshelf holds a small selection available for 'bookswaps' for those who don't wish to talk. However, it is a great place to enjoy good beer and great company. I had a good conversation with a couple of regulars and the atmosphere was genuinely friendly. Whilst there I enjoyed Big Smoke Brew Co.

Solaris 3.8% ABV Pale Session Ale which was crisp, dry and citrusy and Tiny Rebel's FUBAR 4.4% ABV Pale Ale - moderately sweet and floral with a pleasant spicy bitterness to finish.

The micropub was nominated Pub of The Season Summer 2015 by CAMRA and enjoys a loyal following.

Cobbett's sell a range of Draught Ales, ciders and beers, from local breweries from further afield. At least two beers are sold straight from cask during the week and a further four to five on Fridays and Saturdays. Other beers are sold by keg. At least one draught cider and Perry are available in summer and one cider in winter. A small selection of wines and soft drinks are available as are basic pub snacks. If taking out, the beers are available in two or four pint containers for same (or next) day drinking. The cider should be fine for three to five days in a fridge. If drinking in, then add 30p per pint.

Disabled access ⊗ **Child friendly** ✓
Dog friendly ✓

WHAT THE REGULARS SAY
'I live over a pub but enjoy Cobbett's because of the good selection of beers.'

'I love the beer, it's well kept.'

'Enjoyable and more importantly, it's local.'

THE LANES

Dover, Kent

ESSENTIAL INFORMATION
15 Worthington Street, Dover, CT17 9AQ
Telephone: 07504 258332
Email: debbie.lane1@ntlworld.com
Facebook: www.facebook.com/
   TheLanesMicropub
Twitter: @TheLanesMicropub

Opening hours:
Monday 1200-1800
Tuesday-Saturday
1200-2300
Sunday 1300-2300

Other reasons to go:
White Cliffs of Dover;
Dover Castle www.english-heritage.org.uk;
Deal Castle www.english-heritage.org.uk

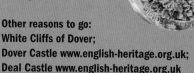

Of Dover's four micropubs, this and The Mash Tun are the most similar – well presented and clubby, while the other two might be described as gritty. At The Lanes more or less everyone is greeted by a kiss on the cheek from Debbie and a friendly 'Can I get you a drink?" from Keith. They are very much the married couple (below left), together 35 years as we went to press, creating an enveloping atmosphere.

Gentle-mannered Keith was a train driver and Debbie had several jobs including a spell in social care. They work at creating a stable, home-from-home atmosphere for ordinary folk who want quiet enjoyment of good beer, and no gimmicks. Swearing is not encouraged, and unlike some, this micropub is not too blokey, women of all ages feel comfortable here. The entrance lobby traps the draught and noise from the street so it feels at one remove. It's hard to believe that this was an amusement arcade before conversion to a micropub. There's a mixture of high and low seating.

Keith takes good care of the beer, letting new firkins rest on the bottom rack then hoisting it gently, to avoid stirring it up, to the next level for pouring. On the rare occasions a firkin goes off, he doesn't sell it.

The place is smartly carpeted throughout and the decoration is pleasant but restrained, with green man faces as a dominant theme (opposite, bottom right).

On our visit we enjoyed Green and Gold from The Canterbury Ales – a very smooth 5.1% golden ale – hoppy heaven. Eighty per cent of what they sell is Kentish ale and cider, because it means they keep faith with the county, they get to know the brewers and transport costs are kept low. They particularly favour Kent Brewery.

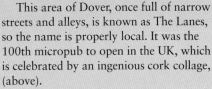

This area of Dover, once full of narrow streets and alleys, is known as The Lanes, so the name is properly local. It was the 100th micropub to open in the UK, which is celebrated by an ingenious cork collage, (above).

Disabled access ✓ **Child friendly** ⊗
Dog friendly ✓

WHAT THE REGULARS SAY
'The best. Keith and Debs are brilliant, the beer is always good, the selection is always changing and there's beer to suit everyone.'

'Excellent welcome, warm, friendly atmosphere made even better by the qualities ales.'

'Great location, great micropub. Always a friendly welcome from Debbie and Keith and the ales and ciders are spot on.'

THE MASH TUN

Dover, Kent

ESSENTIAL INFORMATION
3 Bench Street, Dover, Kent, CT16 1JH
Telephone: 01304 219590
Facebook: www.facebook.com/The-Mash-
   Tun-813044678727270
Twitter: @MashTunDover

Opening hours:
Monday-Tuesday Closed
Wednesday-Saturday 1200-2200
Sunday 1200-1600

Other reasons to go:
White Cliffs of Dover;
Dover Castle www.english-heritage.org.uk;
Deal Castle www.english-heritage.org.uk

Owner Peter Garstin (opposite, bottom left) had classical music playing in the background when we visited, adding to the mellow, clubby atmosphere of his micropub created by buttoned leather sofas and armchair; a mantelpiece and a grandfather clock (opposite, bottom right); and a pulpit (opposite, bottom left) salvaged from a church which is still used for preaching – "Anyone who feels the need gets up there and pontificates."

This is the most upmarket of Dover's four micropubs (the clientele includes retired professionals) and we imagine that while the atmosphere of the leather sofa area at the front is distinctly well mannered, with both sexes equally at home, things get more relaxed at the back where the room narrows and the posh furniture gives way to traditional Kent micropub high tables and stools. Beyond that there is a substantial outdoor drinking area and beyond that a low building where Peter has got planning permission to run a microbrewery.

Peter has known Martyn Hillier of The Butcher's Arms, page 140, for 30 years, so witnessed the micropub movement from its birth and has always loved real ales. He worked in the banking industry, and then as a manager of large pubs where he experienced among other drawbacks their staffing problems. He says that the decision to open a micropub bought him a simpler life and better financial returns. The premises were semi derelict when he took them over – it was a bistro bar and before that a green grocer - and he has spent money to get a good finish. There are some nice homely touches here, such as the fresh free range eggs for sale on a dresser; a guitar and upright piano for anyone to

play, plus embroidered piano stool; a framed poster announcing 'Grumpy old mens' club'; Scrabble and chess boards.

On our visit we drank Peter's own house bitter blended for him by Hopdaemon. This is a 3.9% traditional Kent session bitter with extra hops to give it fresh, pure hoppy flavour and it's keenly priced at £2.80 a pint.

The Mash Tun is on the edge of the town centre, near the pedestrian zone, on the main walking route from the centre to the sea front, which helps provide passing trade. A major commercial property development nearby will bring extra people into Dover, which we hope will benefit all the town's micropubs.

Disabled access ⊗ **Child friendly** ⊗
Dog friendly ✓

WHAT THE REGULARS SAY
'Nice friendly micropub in the centre of Dover. Ales kept in excellent condition. Pork scratchings the best I have had in a long time.'

'Genuinely lovely place with a relaxed atmosphere that attracts great company. Good quality ales.'

'Very friendly, cozy and homely feel with a great selection of drinks.'

RACK OF ALE

Dover, Kent

ESSENTIAL INFORMATION
7 Park Place, Dover, CT16 1DF
Telephone: 07703 059201
Email: rackofale@live.co.uk
Facebook: www.facebook.com/RackofAle-
Micropub-Dover-779200715467574
Twitter: @Rackofale

Opening hours:
Monday 1400-1700
Tuesday-Wednesday 1600-2100
Thursday 1400-2100
Friday-Saturday 1200-0100
Sunday 1400-1900

Other reasons to go: Dover Castle
www.english-heritage.org.uk;
St Augustines Abbey
www.english-heritage.org.uk;
Dover Museum
www.dovermuseum.co.uk;
White Cliffs of Dover

Of Dover's four micropubs (see also pages 106, 108 and 112), this was the first and is the earthiest – or as owner Trish Gulliford puts it, "spit 'n sawdust". Not that the word rough could ever enter into it – Trish is too strong a personality to put up with any rubbish from customers, which is not to deny that sometimes things get lively here. By the way, Trish is one of two characterful female micropub landladies in the Dover area – see also The Wrong Turn, page 26.

Besides the no-frills decoration, more or less confined to prints and photographs of cross Channel ferries, this place stands out for its exclusive ales – you can't drink Trish's selections anywhere else in Dover. It also offers 14 gins and 14 rums, again unique in Dover, a unique selection of Belgian beers, and every autumn an 'Oktoberfest', again the only one in Dover, inspired by the Munich beer festival. Something else which we guess is unique in any micropub anywhere in the country: she has a loyal following of around thirty customers who help her out when things get busy by serving themselves to beer in the cold room and putting their cash straight in the till. The books always balance.

Trish's individual approach continues with serving food, typically paella, in waiving the usual no mobile phone rule and in playing background music. None of these

stop the place being a 100 per cent genuine micropub – there's no key keg and the four or five real ales served on weekdays can increase to ten at weekends.

Her front space, a former optician's, is long and thin with high tables and seats down the sides. At the back there's a larger area done out in a nautical theme where you can play darts.

Trish worked at Ripple Steam Brewery before opening here in 2012, naming the place after the racks on which firkins of ale are stored.

She says that 2015 was a tough year commercially, but her continually changing attractions plus the extra room at the back have made the difference. She's the sole owner - "hard work" - and says "I may own it, but it's the customers' pub."

On our visit we enjoyed Lymestone Brewery's 4% Stone the Crows, which is dark and malty with a bitter finish.

Disabled access ✓ **Child friendly** ⊗
Dog friendly ✓

WHAT THE REGULARS SAY
'Comfortable environment to quaff quality beer.'

'It may be called the rack but it's a long way from the Spanish Inquisition.'

'It's like being invited to a party where you didn't know anyone but everyone was super cool and friendly so you felt right at home.'

Dover, Kent

ESSENTIAL INFORMATION
107 High Street, Dover, Kent, CT16 1EB
Telephone: 07454 934833
Facebook: www.facebook.com/
   TheThirstyScarecrowDover
Twitter: @TheThirstyScarecrowDover

Opening hours:
Monday Closed
Tuesday-Thursday 1200-2200
Friday-Saturday 1200-2300
Sunday 1300-2100

Other reasons to go: Dover Castle
www.english-heritage.org.uk;
St Augustines Abbey
www.english-heritage.org.uk;
Dover Museum www.dovermuseum.co.uk;
White Cliffs of Dover

This is unique twice over (or was when we went to press): the only cider micropub in Britain and the only micropub to have a joint-venture hairdressing salon on the premises. Kieran Redmond sells an amazing 40 ciders (plus one real ale) while his partner Katy Tatham (pictured above) has a small room out the back where she does hair-dos. While the bloke takes his mind off waiting over a few drinks, the other half gets dolled up – chances are everyone will end up happy.

Dover has three other micropubs (The Lanes, The Mash Tun and Rack of Ale pages 106, 108 and 110) all doing real ale, so The Thirsty Scarecrow's niche makes sense. Kieran worked at Rack of Ale for Trish Gulliford before setting up here in late 2015 and it's nice that their businesses complement each other rather than compete. The Thirsty Scarecrow name came easily: scarecrows are seen all round rural Kent, and always need a hairdresser.

In some places cider drinkers have a reputation for getting hammered, but Kieran says his regulars are no different from ale drinkers. They are all ages, perhaps with a bias towards 25-40.

This is a very homely place – some might say distinctly home made. The sitting area by the entrance (see left) could be your front room – sort of. It's been done on a budget and there's nothing wrong with that if the atmosphere is right. Kieran manages

to chat with most of the customers as he delivers orders from the cold room.

From the entrance you climb some steps to a second drinking area by the cold room and then down a passage, past the hair dressing room, is a garden where you find more seating and yet more scarecrows.

Kieran follows micropub rules by serving simple bar food, wine and soft drinks. On our visit we tried two contrasting ciders: first, Devon cider maker Annings's Pear and Peach 4% whose fresh, natural flavours complement each other; then Kent Cider Company's Blend 23, a dark and fruity medium sweet still cider.

Disabled access ⊗
Child friendly ✓ until 1800
Dog friendly ✓

WHAT THE REGULARS SAY
'It's always good at the Thirsty Scarecrow, good company, good beer. And it's entirely possible to have your hair, phone, or computer fixed at the same time.'

'One of the best cider houses I've been to! Good company, lovely atmosphere and kick ass ciders.'

'Such a welcoming cider house, ales available too, great atmosphere and Katy is the best hair magician in the world.'

Driffield, East Yorkshire

ESSENTIAL INFORMATION
24, Middle Street South, Driffield,
YO25 6PS
Telephone: 01377 254032
Website: www.thebutchersdog.com
Facebook: www.facebook.com/
thebutchersdogdriffield
Twitter: @
thebutchersdog

Opening hours:
Monday 1200-1800
Tuesday-Wednesday
1200-2200
Thursday-Saturday 1200-2300
Sunday 1200-2200

Other reasons to go: The Singing Barber
themed hairdresser next door at 23a
www.facebook.com/thesingingbarber2014;
Burton Agnes Hall www.burtonagnes.com

Natalie Briglin is only 26 but she runs her micropub as if to the manor born - not surprising since she has managed pubs most of her working life.

When the time came for her own venture, she wanted somewhere easy to run, and faithful to traditional pub values. To fit it out she begged, borrowed and talked nicely to her dad, who lives locally and is good with his hands. The result is restful, comfortable and homely, with pleasing old wooden high-backed seats and plenty of quirky decorations, chief of which is the whacky butcher's delivery bike, found by Natalie's boyfriend Tim. It hangs in the front window, a focal point from inside and out and is colourfully decorated with beer mats from here, there and everywhere.

You pick up the friendly atmosphere almost before you're through the door. We visited early on a cold February afternoon and the mainly local crowd were hanging out without a care in the world. The layout, with the bar at the back and seating round the edges is nicely inclusive, and Natalie makes it all happen by chatting and introducing.

She'll encourage you to sample the beers by offering, for the price of one pint, three thirds-of-a-pint of different beers each in its own glass served on a tapas tray. She also sells beer to take home in specially designed two-pint paper cartons.

Next door she and Tim have opened The Butchers Dog bottle shop selling real ales, specialist ciders and wine. Also in town is their own microbrewery (opened February 2016) selling beers across the north-east and concentrating on quality, flavour and best brewing technique.

On our visit we especially enjoyed

drinking their own brew, Butchers Dog Stout (4.6%) – dark, smooth and flavoured with liquorice and coriander; and the more summery Lunar (5.5%), a refreshing, fruity, very hoppy India pale ale.

Driffield had several traditional pubs until some of them closed in recent years. Natalie and Tim hope that an enterprise such as theirs, concentrating on the basics - real ale in a real pub -can survive in today's climate – so far it is.

Disabled access ✓ **Child friendly** ✓
Dog friendly ✓

WHAT THE REGULARS SAY

'Nat and Tim know <u>their stuff</u> about beer.'

'Home from home.'

The Butchers Dog

THE BUTCHERS DOG MICROBREWERY
telephone: 01377 254032
website: www.thebutchersdog.co.uk

An independently owned, one barrel plant microbrewery. We promote traditional real ales within a 30 mile radius of Driffield, producing and delivering the beers ourselves.

HIGHLIGHT BEERS:

Peppa's Pawter 4.7%
A unique dark red ale combining fine malts with black treacle and first gold hops.

Black Spot Stout 4.6%
A complex dry stout made with a unique blend of seven malts.

Yorkshire Tyke Bitter 3.8%
A true session ale for the real ale fanatic.

Kukar IPA 5.8%
A traditional IPA complimented with an abundance of early cascade and late galaxy hops.

One-O-One Pale Ale 4.6%
With citrus notes made from east kent goldings, agnus and bobek hops.

THE ROUND ROBINN

East Leake, Nottinghamshire

ESSENTIAL INFORMATION
54 Main Street, East Leake,Loughborough,
LE12 6PG
Telephone: 0115 7788168
Email: ale@theroundrobinn.pub
Facebook: www.facebook.com/pg/
theroundrobinn/about/?ref=page_
internal

Opening hours:
Monday Closed
Tuesday-Thursday 1700-2300
Friday 1600-2300
Saturday-Sunday 1200-2300

Other reasons to go: Rushcliffe Golf Club
www.rushcliffegolfclub.co.uk
Donington Park Circuit,
www.donington-park.co.uk
Ragdale Hall Health Hydro and Thermal
Spa, www.ragdalehall.co.uk

Co-owners and partners Rachel and Darren (opposite, top and bottom) made their micropub's name work nicely in several ways. Darren's dad ran a local betting shop on these same premises for 40 years and was an inspiration because he was an ethical bookmaker – for example, getting rid of casino-style fruit machines when he realized the damage they were doing to the lads in the village. A round Robin is a type of bet. Darren's dad was named Rob.

Rachel was a business analyst for eight years and before that enjoyed working in pubs and restaurants. Darren still runs a software business alongside the micropub. They noticed how East Leake was rapidly expanding, and that the local pub owners were not investing in their premises: an opportunity to compete and to do something for the community by keeping an independent business open on the high street, supporting local microbreweries and providing a friendly place where people could socialize. There's a large number of regulars who know that if they pop in on their own there will always be someone to whom they can talk.

There's seating for around 45 people on

high stools and conventional chairs and tables. Decoration is plain. The firkins are on display behind the bar at the back.

They offer five to seven rotating real ales poured by gravity. On our visit we enjoyed Lincoln Green Brewing's unusual Josef Keller 4.8% chocolate cherry stout. Every pint is served with a chocolate that brings out the chocolate and cherry flavour. Josef Keller invented the Black Forest gateau.

Six months after opening they won the Nottingham CAMRA Village Pub of the Year award because they encouraged a diverse mix of customers, always had smile, acknowledged everyone who walked through the door and had a genuine passion for all things ale. Of course, all true micropubs aim to do this, but a measure of how well they do it here is neatly summed by social media comment: 'Just like arriving at a party with all your friends, only you never met any of them before.'

Disabled access ✓ **Child friendly** ✓
Dog friendly ✓

WHAT THE REGULARS SAY
'Great to have a place which really cares about the produce it sells.'

'Lovely addition to the village. Strong selection of cask ales in good condition.'

Eastwood, Nottingham, Nottinghamshire

ESSENTIAL INFORMATION
Hilltop, 209 Nottingham Road, Eastwood,
Nottingham, NG16 3GS
Telephone: 07837 386798
Website: www.tapandgrowler.co.uk
Facebook: www.facebook.com/pg/
tapandgrowlermicropub

Opening hours:
Monday-Wednesday Closed
Thursday-Saturday 1200-2230
Sunday 1200-2200

Other reasons to go:
Wollaton Hall Gardens and Deer Park
www.wollatonhall.org.uk;
Codnor Castle www.codnorcastle.co.uk;
Beauvale Priory www.beauvalepriory.co.uk

Growler is American slang for a container that holds draft beer. The term has several other slang meanings too, some of them highly inappropriate to a pleasant place like a micropub devoted to good conversation and good beer. However, while converting the premises, Aaron Butler and his wife Carrie came upon a ceramic lion which is now prominently on display, providing a respectable alternative 'growler'. 'Tap' is self explanatory.

We like the narrow, neatly designed plain grey exterior on a corner in a row of shops on Nottingham Road.

Inside it's long and thin, with a bar to the left and a cold room at the back behind glass doors. Tables and chairs are low. The decoration is simple, relying on the textures and natural colours of tiles on the floor, exposed brick walls and timber planks of varying shades on the bar front and ceiling. They have gone, in other words, for the uncluttered style which although not always ideal acoustically gives the calm, relaxed ambience they want to achieve.

Aaron, who used to be in IT, is a lifelong real ale lover who still does homebrewing in his garden shed – though would not dream of serving it. He and Carrie offer a generous choice of often-changing ales – up to four on handpump and four by gravity from the cask, plus a real cider. On our visit we enjoyed one of Grafton Brewing Company's fruit beers: 4.8% Apricot Jungle brewed with English Beata hops that give it an apricot, honey and almond flavour.

Aaron and Carrie are community minded and thinking about becoming part of the Greasley Gathering – a local annual day of family events, and perhaps the Beauvale Priory Beer Festival too. Their ambition

for the Tap & Growler is to make it a community hub for people who like the social atmosphere of traditional pubs but want a quieter, less busy (or less rowdy) environment.

Disabled access ✓ step at entrance
Child friendly ✓ until 2000
Dog friendly ✓

WHAT THE REGULARS SAY
'I find it hard to take my custom elsewhere...so I don't!'

'Totally fabulous friendly pub, you only have to be there one minute and someone talks to you.'

'Best pub in area, great atmosphere, great beer. Great staff.'

THE LONG POND

Eltham, London

ESSENTIAL INFORMATION
110 Westmount Road, Eltham, SE9 1UT
Telephone: 020 8331 6767
Email: mwren4965@gmail.com
Website: www.thelongpond.co.uk
Facebook: www.facebook.com/
   thelongpond
Twitter: @thelongpond

Opening hours:
Monday 1700-2200
Tuesday-Wednesday 1130-1430 then
1700-2200 Thursday-Friday 1130-1430
then 1700-2300 Saturday 1100-1500 then
1830-2300 Sunday 1200-1430

Other reasons to go: Severndroog Castle
www.severndroogcastle.org.uk;
Eltham Palace & Gardens
www.english-heritage.org.uk;
The Bob Hope Theatre
www.bobhopetheatre.co.uk

In a small parade of shops, The Long Pond occupies the old premises of a plumbing merchant. Its namesake — a local ornamental pond and former boating lake in Eltham Park — is home to tame ducks, wildfowl and a handful of terrapins which can be seen basking in the sun on a warm day. The Long Pond's own clientele is equally diverse. During our visit on a bank holiday Monday afternoon, we were pleased to see a bright-eyed young couple enjoying a drink in what is one of the more unusual features of this particular micropub — the intimate anteroom off the main body of the pub. The notion that specialist ale houses are exclusively for the bearded old gent is clearly outdated.

Combined with the large main seating area, it is obvious that The Long Pond is larger than the micropub norm, and deceptively so given its rather modest exterior. The proprietor is local man Michael Wren (opposite, bottom), who named his pub after what is a popular gathering spot in the park — here is yet another micropub with a conceptual, inventive name.

WHAT THE REGULARS SAY
'As an Eltham resident for 35 years this
is the first pub I have been happy to call
my local, it ticks all the boxes, with an
excellent range of ales, all dispensed
impeccably in a pleasant and friendly
environment'.

The decoration is understated and tidy.
The main room has bench-seating around
elevated tables. More conventional pub
furniture can be found in the smaller 'snug'
room. There is a small bar-counter, behind
which is the door to a chilled tap room.
Here, four to six cask ales (mainly from
Kent-based breweries) are served by gravity
dispense on auto-tilt stillage.

The house beer, Pond Life, is a
refreshing, light and fruity 3.6% traditional
English-style session bitter from Tonbridge
Brewery. Also on offer is a selection of
ciders and perry, as well as wine and
soft drinks. In keeping with micropub
principles, no lager, spirits or alcopops are
served. Likewise, the use of mobile phones
is frowned upon, with a £1 'fine' donated
to charity as atonement for any babbler's
misdeeds. There are separate toilets for
ladies and gents, and it has also been
possible to install what is a real rarity in the
world of micropubs: a disabled access WC.

Opening its doors in December 2014
with the threat of dry January coming up,
what could have been a risky enterprise
has been a success for Michael – there is no
drought at this watering hole. Michael used
to work in finance, and was disillusioned
with life when he decided to open his own
micropub. He was inspired by a family
visit to a micropub in Whitstable. Now he
says that he can't remember any other way
of life: he lives and breathes the micropub
ethic. Michael is so familiar with his new
station that we'd say he's returned home.

Ely, Cambridgeshire

ESSENTIAL INFORMATION
Forehill, Ely, Cambridgeshire, CB7 4AA
Telephone: 01353 662920
Email: ely.micropub@gmail.com
Website: www.draymans.co.uk
Facebook: www.facebook.com/
libertybellemicropub

Opening hours:
Monday-Wednesday 1700-1030
Thursday-Saturday 1100-2300
Sunday 1200-2230

Other reasons to go:
Ely Cathedral www.elycathedral.org;
Wicken Fen National Nature Reserve
www.nationaltrust.org.uk;
Oliver Cromwell's House
www.olivercromwellshouse.co.uk

This is slightly unusual because it occupies what was a mainstream pub, the Liberty Belle. A little of the old pub's atmosphere remains: the bell still stands at the top of the stairs, there are low stools and tables and a very official bar. However, much has been done to provide a fresh new atmosphere: an old motor bike stands by the stairs, old advertising signs decorate the walls and a pair of knitted dolls named Jo and Andy (after the landlady and her husband) stand on a shelf. It's not large, despite being on two levels, and the new conversion generally works well. It stands on a quiet, narrow road that's an extension of Ely's High Street.

Jo and Andy Pearson opened in 2013 after Jo decided that she wanted a complete change of career – she'd been a fundraising manager for Addenbrooke's Charitable Trust. Andy is a retired police officer and still works for Guide Dogs for the Blind - a 'collection dog' stands outside the door. She works full time behind the bar and he takes charge of keeping the beer and the cellar.

The name? Andy's father, a drayman at the local brewery, five doors away from the pub, died when Andy was eight months old – so it's a memorial to him.

They usually offer ten ales and if your'e not sure which one you want, just ask Jo or Andy or even a regular and they will be more than happy to give you advice. Two- and four-pint takeouts are available and there is a range of cider, local Ely gins, English whisky and vodka and soft drinks, including mocktails. Snacks include cheese and meat platters, pork pies and rolls.

A few of the beers they have offered include: Newby Wyke Brewery's Summer Session Bitter, a 3.8% ale brewed especially

for long, hot summer days (the pump clip shows a polar bear in the rain); Rother Valley Brewing Company's Black Ops, a 3.8% dark ale with a blend of hop and malt flavours; and Odyssey Brew Company's Cookie Monsters, a 6% chocolate, raisin and cinnamon flavoured oatmeal stout.

Disabled access ✓ to some areas
Child friendly ✓ until 2100
Dog friendly ✓

WHAT THE REGULARS SAY

'Simply the best pub in Ely. Done the way things should be. Especially keen on the pork pies and pickles, a perfect accompaniment to any one of the tremendous ales.'

'It's a really good place to have a drink with friends and it has a very good choice of real ales.'

'Excellent beers and service in a quirky but comfy bar. Makes you love living here.'

Faversham, Kent

ESSENTIAL INFORMATION
6a Preston Street, Faversham ME13 8NS
Telephone: 07747776200
Email: beer@furlongsalehouse.co.uk
Website: furlongsfaversham.wordpress.com
Facebook: www.facebook.com/
    FurlongsAleHouseFaversham

Opening hours:
Monday-Thursday 1600-2200
Friday 1500-2300
Saturday 1200-2300
Sunday 1200-2100

**Other reasons to go: Belmont House and
Gardens www.belmont-house.org;
Oare Marshes
www.kentwildlifetrust.org.uk;
Faversham Markets
www.favershammarket.org**

Andrew Sach (opposite, top right), who runs Furlongs with Martin Brenchley-Sayers, is insightful about the appeal of micropubs: "You end up talking to people because you're there with a common purpose. You're not there to watch football or television or to listen to the jukebox, you're there for the beer and the pleasant atmosphere."

Faversham is one of the brewing towns of England - Shepherd Neame, possibly the oldest brewer in the country, is based here. Furlongs, the 99th micropub to open in Britain, is the town's first micropub and religiously faithful to core micropub values, witness the innovative design of the seating. Most true micropubs have bar-height tables so that sitting or standing, drinkers can talk at eye level. Some offer tall stools as seating – OK but not relaxing - most people like to drink with their feet on terra firma. Some have raised wall-bench seating. Furlongs goes one further, providing church pews on plinths that allow your feet to rest firmly on the ground. The bar is unusual too: to save space, the handpumps are at the back rather than on the counter.

Everything is rooted in the locality: the pews are from the local church; paintings are from local artists; photographs are by

local photographer Phil. The premises used to be a fish shop but the name Furlongs is after Wally (Walter) Furlong who ran a barber's in this premises. The ales are mainly from Kent, though there is one from over the border in East Sussex. Andrew and Martin are real locals who love Faversham – "it's the only place I've ever lived in that feels like home" says Andrew, a former social worker.

On our visit we enjoyed The Wife of Bath's Ale from The Canterbury Ales, a 3.9% golden bitter with a spicy, citrus taste and a long, dry finish. Other supplies include Dark Star Brewing and Burning Sky in Sussex and Gadds' in Kent.

Disabled access ✓ **Child friendly** ✓ until 1900
Dog friendly ✓

WHAT THE REGULARS SAY

'Finally a place in Faversham with real atmosphere and real people.'

'Why travel to beer festivals when the beer can come to you?'

'What fantastic beer and such a warm welcome.'

Folkestone, Kent

ESSENTIAL INFORMATION
18 Cheriton Place, Folkestone, CT20 2AZ
Telephone: 07894 068432
Email: neil@firkinalehouse.co.uk
Website: www.firkinalehouse.co.uk
Twitter: @firkinalehouse

Opening hours:
Monday-Thursday 1200-2100
Friday-Saturday 1200-2200
Sunday 1200-1600

Other reasons to go:
Folkestone Creative Quarter
www.creativefoundation.org.uk;
Kent Battle of Britain Museum
www.kbobm.org;
Lower Leas Coastal Park
www.visitkent.co.uk

This guide doesn't want to be critical - the aim is to celebrate micropubs, but we couldn't make up our minds whether this place is so plain because the owner couldn't be bothered, or because he wanted its simplicity to be a virtue. The tiny former hairdressing salon has buff-coloured fake stone block material on the walls – which feels plastic to the touch. Decoration is minimal. The most striking element is the large sherry butt in the centre of the small room, which drinkers like to lean on in the absence of a bar.

In fact, owner Neil King has kept it simple deliberately. He wanted to make a gimmick-free environment, and to underline this offers a basic choice of ales - three Monday to Thursdays, and four Fridays to Sundays. Even the name is basic – the word firkin being used in at least three other micropub names as we went to press.

Neil used to work in the pub trade as a chef and as a pub manager, and as well as owning this place is a partner in The Smugglers, New Romney, page 212. He's usually here four days a week with two helpers covering other times.

It's not a bad place if you want to pop in for a quiet drink. The atmosphere is modestly cheery, and we guess it has a faithful following. On our visit we enjoyed Gadds' Green Top 4.8% - pale ale, crisp and resinous, with the malt taking a back seat. Keeping faith with core micropub rules, mobiles are banned – get a call and you're asked to put a fine in the charity box. The food is minimal – crisps, pickled eggs and onions when we visited. Take away ale can be bought in a variety of sizes including a mammoth 35 pints.

Folkestone, once a drab Channel port,

has had some regeneration in recent years, particularly near the harbour in the Old High Street area with its Creative Quarter of independent retailers and creative businesses. The Firkin Ale House is about a ten-minute walk from there.

Disabled access ⊗ **Child friendly** ✓
Dog friendly ✓

WHAT THE REGULARS SAY

'With a constantly changing selection of great ales you just can't go wrong.'

'It's a great little place, lovely decoration, nice atmosphere and friendly.'

'A quirky friendly place with friendly people.'

Gillingham, Kent

ESSENTIAL INFORMATION
2 Skinner Street, Gillingham, ME7 1HD
Telephone: 07725072293/ 07853312488
Website:
www.pastandpresentmicropub.co.uk
Facebook: www.facebook.com/Past-and-
  Present-micro-pub-269039096610948

Opening hours:
Monday-Tuesday 1200-1900
Wednesday 1200-1800
Thursday 1200-2100
Friday-Saturday 1200-2300
Sunday 1200-1800

Other reasons to go: Royal Engineers
Museum www.re-museum.co.uk;
Riverside Country Park;
The Strand Leisure Park
www.medway.gov.uk

Medway's first micropub blends in with its high street location with a bold red and mainly glass front. A white and black sign above proudly announces 'Past and Present' leaving you in no doubt that this is a place with a difference.

When a number of watering holes closed down in the area, two local couples took it upon themselves to open a new place where residents and visitors could enjoy a drink (or two) of good ales and ciders. Lorraine and David Hallowell, with the help of Sue and Colin Maskell, shut a door on the past and focused on the present in the pub scene.

Step in and you'll be greeted by a number of friendly faces from the corners of an L-shaped room. The place was once a square, second-hand record shop, but the addition of the air-conditioned beer room in one corner gave it its unusual shape.

The furniture is simple and cosy with wooden tables and high benches. A collection of photos of closed down Gillingham pubs, the 'past', and of new Kent micropubs, the 'present' decorate the walls. At the back is a narrow corridor that leads to the unisex toilet and then on to the decked garden area, reminiscent of a home backyard, which doubles as a smoking area.

There is no bar. To order a drink, ring the bell on your table to get the attention of the hosts. In the early days, these bells used to disappear all the time. The problem was solved by filling the whole place with them: on the tables and on the long shelves along the wall. Lorraine says that they still have to replace them at times, but at least they never run out.

A blackboard on the wall to the right of the entrance lists the ales and ciders, changed each week. A minimum of three

real ales – one from Kent – served from the cask and five still ciders from the chill room are on offer. The Past and Present was awarded CAMRA Medway joint winner Cider Pub of the Year 2015 and outright winner 2016. Their ciders come from all over the UK and there is always a wide selection. They also offer a few wines, soft and hot drinks, and the usual nibbles.

Locals come and go quickly. Someone enters to cries of "We didn't expect you here today!" His reply: "I'm not really here – just getting a half." Colin disapproves of dark beers and likes to pretend they don't exist. "What dark beers do you have?" asks a customer, "What *is* a dark beer?" comes the reply. The atmosphere is as friendly as it gets.

The Past and Present has been a huge success since opening – it gets so busy on Friday and Saturday nights that the doors close to new customers at 10.

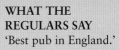

WHAT THE REGULARS SAY

'Best pub in England.'

'Excellent ales, excellent cider, always worth a visit.'

'A hidden gem.'

'Lived in Gillingham all my life, this has got to be the best pub I've ever been in. Staff are so friendly and helpful and I made some new friends.'

'I've been here once or twice I guess you could say!'

Disabled access ⊗ **Child friendly** ✓ until 1900
Dog friendly ✓

Gravesend, Kent

ESSENTIAL INFORMATION
7 Manor Road, Gravesend, DA12 1AA
Telephone: 07873918545
Facebook: www.facebook.com/
thecompassalehouse

Opening hours:
Monday Closed
Tuesday-Wednesday 1700-2100
Thursday 1200-1400, 17.00-2100
Friday 1200-1400, 1700-2200
Saturday 1200-2200
Sunday 1300-1600

**Other reasons to go: Shorne Wood Country
Park,** www.kent.gov.uk
Cyclopark, www.cyclopark.com,
New Tavern Fort, www.gravesham.gov.uk

Here are yet more people who decided to trade a stressful job, long hours and grinding responsibilities to open a pub. Charlie Venner hung up his white coat (at least part-time) in late 2014, to open The Compass in a disused estate agency's office joined by his other half Caroline Stroud. Both were NHS employees, as were their collaborators therapist John Warden and partner Rachel Roland. All four now spend more time among casks and pumps and less time in A&E.

Inside, The Compass is appropriately quirky and decorated with a nautical travel theme. Curtains with printed geographical maps hang over the shop window, old boat prints adorn the walls and even in the toilet you find seashells. Charlie explains that the name was inspired by the group's love of travelling and sailing. It also represents the four people that run it: each is a different cardinal point. While they still work for the NHS, the four owners hope one day to dedicate themselves solely to the beer trade.

The main room has high wooden benches and tables and plenty of sailing paraphernalia on shelves just below the ceiling. You can then pass through to a small room with no seating, a sort of a kitchen with counters and a sink, which leads to the unisex toilet, the air-conditioned cellar and the small rear garden. Charlie often hovers at the door between the main room and the kitchen, and at a customer's nod refills his glass with a favourite beer.

The ales and ciders on sale – you'll see are gleefully scribbled on blackboards; names from all over South-East England. Charlie admits to keeping a few malt whiskeys (a passion of his) and that this is

GOACHER'S BREWERY
telephone: 01622 682112
website: www.goachers.com

a minor infringement of micropub rules. His main interest, however, is ale: he likes to brew it at home as well as to sell it, and has collaborated with local breweries (such as Caveman) to produce beers especially for The Compass.

While we visited, one of the casks was finished and Charlie stood on a stool to delete the beer from the blackboard and add a new one – in seconds everyone was enjoying a fresh pint. No need to say that the beers are frequently changed.

By the door is a water bowl for thirsty four-legged friends, and children are welcome too with dandelion and burdock, cloudy lemonade and orange squash served for them – and for the drivers.

Kent's oldest microbrewery, based in the county town, brewing traditional real ales using traditional methods since 1983. Although the brewery moved to a new site in Tovil in the early 90s, the same wooden clad Mash Tun and steam fired Copper are still being used today. The range of beers are brewed exclusively using locally sourced Kentish hops, 100% Maris Otter barley and their own unique strain of yeast.

Disabled access ⊗ **Child friendly** ✓
Dog friendly ✓

WHAT THE REGULARS SAY
'Great pub and fantastic landlords.'

'A great atmosphere, we were made to feel very welcome.'

'Could have stayed all day, a great addition to Gravesend watering holes.'

Hartlepool, County Durham

ESSENTIAL INFORMATION
Hartlepool Railway Station, Station
Approach, Hartlepool, TS24 7ED
Telephone: 07903 479378
Website: www.ratracealehouse.co.uk
Facebook: www.facebook.com/Rat-Race-
 Ale-House-136050118266/?fref=ts
Twitter: @RatRaceAleHouse

Opening hours:
Monday Closed
Tuesday-Friday 1202-1415
then 1602-2015
Saturday 1202-2100
Sunday Closed

Other reasons to go: HMS Trincomalee
www.hms-trincomalee.co.uk;
Seaton Carew Beach
www.britishbeaches.info;
Hartlepool Maritime Experience
www.hartlepoolsmaritimeexperience.com

In 2009 Landlord Pete Morgan went to a talk given by Martyn Hillier at the CAMRA AGM. It was about setting up a micropub, and with redundancy a matter of weeks away the seed was planted for Pete's next career move. Six months later, after 25 years in IT, he seamlessly turned in to a micropub landlord, you would hardly have known he hadn't been serving beer and chatting to locals all his life.

The second ever micropub to open, The Rat Race Ale House is one hundred per cent faithful to the concept. The signs declaring this are hard to ignore: 'No Lager', 'No John Smiths', 'No ball games!', 'No Dogs', 'It's all about the Beer'. In a climate where around thirty conventional pubs are closing a week, Pete has managed to create a place where people want to come and drink and chat with no nonsense.

The Rat Race is in an old taxi office in Hartlepool station, and the location gives the pub an atmosphere that couldn't be contrived. Ceilings are high and the furnishings and decoration are charming, a mixture of ebay purchases and old train or bus seats providing an eclectic range of places to sit. There is no bar, instead a board on the wall provides a list of the beers on offer and you take your order to Pete. Another board keeps track of every barrel that has passed through, and the ceiling and walls show just how many different beers there have been: all the old pump clips have been kept. Elsewhere the walls are covered in knick-knacks that look as though they have been collected over many years.

The atmosphere on our visit was very friendly and all the locals were very happy to chat. Pete and his partner Kate also provide table service, so you don't need to

move if you're on to a good conversation. This is definitely a great place for banter.

There was a choice of four ales, a cider and a perry on offer when we visited. We chose a pint of Fell Yolo, 3.7% – it's true, you only live once. Others on offer were Moles' Dark Rat Dry Cider, 6%; and Stockmoor Farm Perry, 5.5%. Wine and soft drinks are also available as well as some excellent pork scratchings and crisps. If you don't fancy staying for a pint you can always order a take-out, available in three half pint bottles.

Disabled access ✓ **Child friendly** ⊗
Dog friendly ⊗

WHAT THE REGULARS SAY
'Cracking place, small but mighty.'

'Proper pub. Just perfect.'

'Top quality beer, great service and always good convo.'

'Always a crackin pint, there's always something new.'

CALAN'S MICROPUB

Hebden Bridge, West Yorkshire

ESSENTIAL INFORMATION
3 The Courtyard, Bridge Gate, Hebden
Bridge, HX7 8EX
Telephone: 07739 565983
Website: calansmicropub.com
Facebook: www.facebook.com/
  Calansmicropub

Opening hours:
Monday 1200-2000
Tuesday Closed
Wednesday-Thursday 1200-2100
Friday-Saturday 1200-2200
Sunday 1200-2000

Other reasons to go: Hardcastle Crags
www.nationaltrust.org.uk;
Gibson Mill www.nationaltrust.org.uk;
Specialist shops

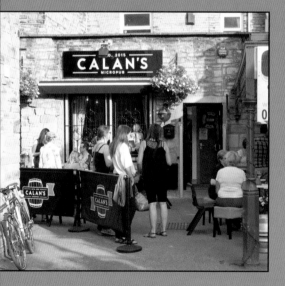

A kind-hearted micropub run by partners Alan and Alyson (opposite, top right). He worked in social services and she in HR management for a firm of solicitors in Bradford, so it's not surprising that they are both at ease with people. They did their research thoroughly, visiting micropubs north and south before opening in 2015: the place feels well thought out. We visited soon after they had suffered several months' closure following the flood of Boxing Day, 2015 - it was impossible to tell that the place had been under water.

The story behind the micropub's name is sad but touching: when Alyson's granddaughter Summer was small she called her step-grandfather Calan – short for Uncle Alan. She died from a childhood cancer.

The historic mill town of Hebden Bridge is built up the steep hillsides where the River Calder meets Hebden Water. There's not much flat land, but the pleasant pedestrian zone of Bridge Gate is an exception. Calan's is just off it, opposite the car park, in a courtyard, with its own enclosed outdoor drinking area which is the making of the place in warm weather. Before its rebirth as a micropub (the 123rd to open in Britain) this was a sweet shop, a tea shop and then a woollen clothes store.

The small interior is colourful and cluttered in a pleasant way, every inch of space put to good use. There's traditional chunky Kent micropub high tables at the front, plus low-level seating in a jolly snug corner at the back. Seating fabrics are attractive and homely. Behind the bar with its five handpumps is a glass screen showcasing the firkins. The front of the bar is covered in signatures of contented customers (opposite, top left). Unlike some

micropubs, mobiles aren't frowned on – they offer free wifi.

The ales, all cask conditioned, are constantly rotated, so you'll find something different each week. Alan ensures that all colours and styles are available - since opening they've served between 300 and 400 different ales. On our visit we drank and enjoyed a beer from Deeply Vale Brewery of Bury, a very dark, memorably smokey stout, 5%; and Vocation Brewery's Bread and Butter, an ultra-hoppy pale ale, 3.9% – customers are mortified when this one is off. It's a 'dry hopped' ale: after the main fermentation is complete, extra hops are added to deepen the flavour. They serve one cider, one bottled lager, a red and a white wine and simple bar snacks.

This is a family-oriented micropub, rather than a blokish watering hole. Says Alyson: "We're quite strict about closing time – we don't want last-minute drinkers or rowdy going-home scenes."

Disabled access ⊗ **Child friendly** ✓
Dog friendly ✓

WHAT THE REGULARS SAY
'Friendly and relaxed – what a pub should be like.'

'Exciting – new beer every time.'

FIRKIN FROG

Herne Bay, Kent

ESSENTIAL INFORMATION
157 Station Road, Herne Bay, CT6 5QA
Telephone: 07460 895527
Email: thefirkinfrog@hotmail.co.uk
Website: www.thefirkinfrog.com
Facebook: www.facebook.com/
  thefirkinfrog

Opening hours:
Monday 1700-2100
Tuesday-Saturday 1200-1500
then 1700-2100
Sunday Closed

Other reasons to go: Reculver Towers
www.english-heritage.org.uk;
Herne Bay coast and piers;
Beach Creative www.beachcreative.org

Close to Herne Bay's station, and to what remains of the pier, this former kitchen showroom was converted by landlord Steve Chandler (opposite, bottom left).

It's bigger than it seems. The smallish main room has a bar, with, at right angles to it, a glass partition through which you can see the beer room. The main room narrows to a corridor fitted with a shelf and bar stools. Off the corridor and behind the beer room is the snug room – a child friendly room with a collection of board games. Out at the back there's the small outdoor drinking and smoking area with benches and a jokey frog road sign. A variety of seating is on offer, with some areas furnished more like a small conventional pub than a micropub.

The decoration is military-patriotic with flags representing counties and the armed forces disguising the old showroom ceiling. The thoroughly British theme continues with portraits of Churchill, The Queen and Morecambe and Wise.

This place is football and rugby friendly: in the snug room a TV shows big games from time to time. Bit blokish? Not very micropub? Well, the TV is banished to the snug and does not cut across the true micropub atmosphere in the main room.

Moreover, in 2014 The Firkin Frog was voted Kent's best micropub for its appeal to a range of customers and to men and women alike. There's a quiz night every six weeks or so; from time to time a theme day remembering fallen armed forces heroes; and the occasional live music night.

Steve seeks out an equal mix of local Kentish beers and those from further afield. And he sells port by the glass – maybe the first micropub to do so. On our visit we

drank Gadds' No 7, a fresh, gluggable, amber-coloured 'session' ale. At 3.7% several pints will not stop you making a straight line home.

A firkin, by the way, contains 72 pints - too much for a frog at one sitting.

Disabled access ⊗ **Child friendly** ✓
Dog friendly ✓

WHAT THE REGULARS SAY
'Great pint. Proper real ale pub.'

'A great atmosphere and a really warm welcome from Steve.'

'Fantastic place for a pint and a pork pie.'

Herne Bay, Kent

ESSENTIAL INFORMATION
20 Bank Street, Herne Bay, Kent, CT6 5EA
Telephone: 07777 630685
Email: thebouncingbarrel@hotmail.co.uk
Website: www.micropubassociation.co.uk
Facebook:www.facebook.com/The-
   Bouncing-Barrel-487985854571936

Opening hours:
Monday 1700-2100
Tuesday-Friday 1200-
1430
then 1700-2100
Saturday 1200-
2300
Sunday 1200-1430

Other reasons to go: Reculver Towers
www.english-heritage.org.uk;
Herne Bay coast and piers;
Beach Creative www.beachcreative.org

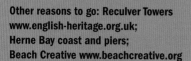

The Herne Bay area is the birthplace of the micropub revolution: the very first micropub, The Butchers Arms, page 140, was opened on Herne Street, Herne, by Martyn Hillier in 2005. In 2013 the Firkin Frog opened on Station Road, Herne Bay. The latest is the Bouncing Barrel, on a pedestrianized shopping street in the town centre, named after the Second World War bouncing bombs which were tested in the sea to the east of Herne Bay off Reculver. (If you're a tech-head in need of more information about this ingenious bomb, read the final paragraph of this review.)

As we went to press, Dover and Margate (four) and Southampton (five) had the largest number of micropubs, but Herne Bay with three and nearby Whitstable, also with three, were close behind. The population of Herne Bay is 38,000, and of Whitstable 30,000, so the density of micropubs per head of population is greater in Whitstable.

Trevor and Penny Wick's operation is a worthy addition, faithful to micropub core values. A sign that the owners take these values seriously is the mobile phone nailed to the wall: Trevor and Penny discourage phones in order to encourage conversation – "it should be about banter and chat, not people sitting in the corner tapping away." They've set up their large squarish room so people can talk to each other wherever they are sitting or standing, and as usual with a true

micropub, there's no music, no TV and no fruit machine.

The seating is the usual raised benches round the walls and two long, distinctive tables. At the rear is the large, temperature-controlled beer room with some space to the right for more seating. Decoration includes beer mats and a large chalk drawing on the blackboard of a bouncing bomb and bomber.

Trevor still works full time for BT, so Penny plus helpers are here most of the time. She wants women to feel comfortable, even if they come in alone and our reporters noticed 'the mixed community spirit. We chatted to young, old, men and women all enjoying the atmosphere and quality ales.'

Trevor buys from a mix of local and national brewers, and serves a few wines and local ciders. Old Dairy's hoppy Coppertop 3.4% is especially popular here.

'Dam buster' bouncing bomb memo: they looked like barrels, hence 'Bouncing Barrel' and were designed to bounce (like a skipping stone) across the surface of the water to by-pass mines and torpedo nets, then sink near the wall of a dam and explode underwater. They were dropped 60 feet above the surface, at 232 mph, and with backspin, for stability. They would bounce seven times and cover 800 yards before sinking. The underwater explosion was especially powerful and caused great damage to a key German Ruhr Valley dam in the famous Dam Buster Raid of 1943.

Disabled access ✓
Child friendly ✓ until 1900
Dog friendly ✓

WHAT THE REGULARS SAY
'A first class place to come and drink.'

'As a life long lager drinker, I have seen the light.'

'This place has made such a difference to Herne Bay.'

139

Herne, Kent

ESSENTIAL INFORMATION
29a Herne Street, Herne Bay, CT6 7HL
Telephone: 01227 371000
Email: thebutchersarms08@btconnect.com
Website: www.micropub.co.uk
Facebook: www.facebook.com/Micropub
Twitter: @RadiusArmsMicro

Opening hours:
Monday Closed
Tuesday-Saturday 1200-1330
then 1800-2100,
Sunday 1300-1500

Other reasons to go: Herne Mill
www.herne-mill.btik.com;
Whitstable Castle
www.whitstablecastle.co.uk;
Reculver Towers and Roman Fort
www.english-heritage.org.uk

The first micropub of all: the amazingly successful brainchild of Martyn Hillier (opposite, top), was opened in 2005, voted CAMRA branch Pub of the Year in 2008 and 2009, and has enjoyed local and national media attention, with good reason, ever since. From this one place in the heart of a Kent village, the micropub movement has grown to at least 200 throughout the country with new ones opening every week (see also Micropubs today, page 6, written by Martyn).

While selling take-away beer from the back of a florist, Martyn decided to turn this old Butchers shop into the first micropub.

Despite being surrounded by other pubs, The Butchers Arms is never short of customers looking for real ale and a chat. Martyn listens to what customers want and has created a space free of music, pool tables and mobiles. He has no desire to open a chain, believing that this would defeat the point of his micropub – a one-off place with a landlord whom people know.

The original butcher's chopping blocks have been retained as tables with high benches for seating, and Martyn has really gone to town with the decoration. Rubber meat and poultry hangs from the ceiling along with breweriana and several items donated by customers. It's a tiny place, with minimal floor space: 35 people is the maximum though a little like the London Underground at rush hour, 20 is rather more comfortable.

The outside has frosted glass displaying historic Kent breweries and the acronym NFL (no fizzy lager). A sign displays a portly butcher in an apron, further emphasising the no lager policy. Large writing also states that Chatham House rules apply. Here, then, is a

haven of conversation, inclusive debate and T.A.B. (Martyn's phrase – talking absolute balderdash).

Four beers are on offer at a time, with three regulars: Adnams' Broadside 4.7%; Dark Star's Hophead 3.8%; and Old Dairy's Copper Top 4.1%. Martyn offers two-pint pitchers – apparently his own preference - as well as take away beer. White wine, free lemonade for drivers, crisps and pickled eggs are also available.

You're a 10-minute drive from the sea here, so it's perfect to combine with a walk.

Disabled access ⊗ **Child friendly** ⊗
Dog friendly ✓

WHAT THE REGULARS SAY
'The original micropub!'

'A gorgeous, eccentric little pub.'

'The best beer in a unique setting.'

WHO BREWS THE BEER?

GADDS' THE RAMSGATE BREWERY
telephone: 01843 868453
website: www.ramsgatebrewery.co.uk

GADDS' ales have been served in the Butchers Arms since 2008.

HIGHLIGHT BEERS:

GADDS' Number 5 Best Bitter Ale 4.4%
A traditional Kentish Best Bitter – the aroma is toffee, malt and fresh green hops, the flavour is malt, hops and red berries, with a full body and lingering bitter finish. Yeh.

ELBOW ROOM

Hinckley, Leicestershire

ESSENTIAL INFORMATION
26 Station Road, Hinckley, LE10 1AW
Telephone: 07900 191388
Email: elbowroomalehouse@icloud.com
Facebook: www.facebook.com/
elbowroomalehouse
Twitter: @elbowroomales

Opening hours:
Monday Closed
Tuesday-Thursday 1400-2300
Friday-Saturday 1200-2330
Sunday 1200-1900

Other reasons to go: Hinckley Golf Course
www.hinckleygolfclub.co.uk;
Twycross Zoo www.twycrosszoo.org;
Bosworth Battlefield Heritage Centre
bosworthbattlefield.org.uk

This is the second micropub in Hinckley. The Pestle and Mortar (page 144), is just a five-minute walk away on Castle Street, and both seem to be thriving. Like most micropub landlords Tim Arnold (opposite, bottom, far right) had had a lifelong passion for real ale which he finally turned into a living. He still works as a commercial manager in the IT division of a large outsourcing company, dividing his time between it and the new venture. He opened in late 2015, and is helped out by his wife Wendy and two sons.

So far this place has not repeated a single ale, which has been achieved by buying from breweries that either have a large range of ales or who are constantly changing their brews. These include Abbeydale, Cloudwater and Pig and Porter. A maximum of eight ales are on offer at a time with six being the usual weekend offering and no fewer than four during the week. There are also eight real ciders.

The exterior is modern and minimalist, located not in an old derelict shop, but in a new-build cinema complex. What it lacks in exterior character is made up for inside. The ceiling has exposed pipes, warehouse style; large metal lamp shades; the bar is covered with white tiles and the furniture is a mix of high and low wooden benches and tables with casks underneath. The walls are decorated with black-and-white photos of well-known faces such as Winston Churchill and Marilyn Monroe. Pump clips surround the bar area but don't dominate. There's a glass-fronted cold room behind the bar where the ale is served straight from the cask.

On our visit we enjoyed Dow Bridge Brewery's Ratae'd, a 4.3% light session

amber ale with a strong hop flavour and a bittersweet finish; Abbeydale Brewery's Birdhouse Tea Beer, a 4.2% ale brewed (if you can believe it) with green tea, jasmine, hibiscus, rose petals and summer fruits; and The Bees Knees from Bartrams Brewery, a 4.2% amber ale brewed with honey and with a crisp, bitter finish.

Tim is a big fan of the English alternative rock band Elbow. This, and the small amount of room available in his premises typical of micropubs, combined wittily.

Every other Wednesday they have an open mic night or a local artist playing.

Disabled access ✓
Child friendly ✓ until 2000
Dog friendly ✓

WHAT THE REGULARS SAY
'Love it in here. Nice place, nice atmosphere, nice people.'

'Great place to visit, just what Hinckley needs. Some real nice ale.'

'Brilliant place with delicious beer and great owners. New favourite place to drink! And they do a two pint takeaway!'

'So excited about this place. Great drinks, friendly, relaxed atmosphere and dog biscuits on the bar.'

Hinckley, Leicestershire

ESSENTIAL INFORMATION
81 Castle Street, Hinckley, LE10 1DA
Telephone: 07715 106876
Facebook: www.facebook.com/The-Pestle-Mortar-496499697194324
Twitter: @PandMPub

Opening hours:
Monday-Thursday 1400-2300
Friday-Saturday 1200-2330
Sunday 1200-2230

Other reasons to go: Concordia Theatre www.concordiatheatre.co.uk;
Grange Farm www.grangefarmcopston.co.uk;
Hinckley & District Museum www.hinckleydistrictmuseum.org.uk

Occupying the premises of the former Halsteads Chemists Ltd, demonstrated by the name of this place, The Pestle and Mortar officially opened in 2015.

Landlady Sue Williams had previously gained 30 years mainstream pub trade experience, eight of which was as the landlady of Hinckley's Greyhound Pub, before she decided to run a freehouse on her own terms.

The interior is set out in rich plum and warm cream tones, with a smart modern layout dominated by wood and laminate. The front is decorated with photographs and paintings while the back is more sparse.

A generous serving counter means there is ample room at the bar and to the right of that are stools, tall seats and wall-fixed table tops. There's also a small snug with a sofa, padded chairs and an electric fire enclosed by two fitted bookshelves. Hanging on the wall is an attractive apothecary mirror, obviously a reference to the former business (further notes of which can be found in the frames here and there about the pub).

At the back, a white wooden panelled section contains three tables and assorted wooden chairs along with a table football game, for those so inclined.

The gent's urinals are made from recycled metal casks and the sink is a reclaimed metal bucket.

The bar area is a sight to behold, with crazy boxed shelving on the back wall and cabinet storage space for the cider boxes. There's a lot of stock on show but it's displayed in a tidy manner. Ceramic tiles numbered from one to nine indicate the cask beers available (usually six on at a time) and the beers are poured using

handpumps a bit further along the bar. The range changes constantly and can come from as far afield as Devon but Sue always has at least one local ale. The house beer is Ale-Chemist – a 4.2% ABV session ale brewed specially for the micropub by Hinckley based microbrewery Elliswood Brewery. Around 12 ciders are available and are again sourced from all over the country. Sue also sells meads, wines by the bottle or glass, teas and coffee. Pub snacks include pickled eggs, crisps, nuts and cold cobs at the weekend.

Local Branch Cider Pub of The Year 2016 and East Midlands Cider Pub of The Year 2016, this is yet another success story in the micropub trade and certainly a firm favourite with local residents.

Disabled access ⊗ **Child friendly** ✓
Dog friendly ✓

WHAT THE REGULARS SAY
'Nice relaxed environment and no loud music so you can have a chat.'

'Fantastic pub with a great atmosphere! Sue the landlady always offers a warm welcome, a great place to catch up with friends and enjoy a beer or two!'

'Best pub in Hinckley by far. Friendly owners and staff, great atmosphere and always a warm welcome.'

The Pestle & Mortar

ABV4.2%

ALE-CHEMIST

THE WATCHMAKER'S ARMS

Hove, East Sussex

ESSENTIAL INFORMATION
84 Goldstone Villas, Hove, East Sussex,
BN3 3RU
Telephone: 01273 776307
Email: info@thewatchmakersarms.co.uk or
   thewatchmakersarms@gmail.com
Website: www.thewatchmakersarms.co.uk
Facebook: www.facebook.com/
   thewatchmakersarms
Twitter: @WatchmakersArms

Opening hours:
Monday Closed
Tuesday-Thursday 1200-1400 then 1700-
2100 Friday 1200-1400 then 1700-2300
Saturday 1200-2300 Sunday 1200-1500

Other reasons to go: Brighton Toy Museum
www.brightontoymuseum.co.uk;
The Royal Pavilion
brightonmuseums.org.uk;
North Laine www.northlaine.co.uk.

Just outside Hove station, this attractive and modern-looking micropub was the dream venture for two couples, Dave and Ali White, and Rick and Ruth Evans. With backgrounds in teaching and IT, their more recent lessons in ale-keeping and running a successful micropub seem to be paying off. Having opened in May 2015, The Watchmaker's Arms is already established in the real ale world: it was given a double-page spread in local publication *The Argus*, and was listed as one of the top ten places to visit in *The Cheeky Guide to Brighton*.

After a bit of research at The Keep records office it was discovered that back in the 19th-century the site was a clock and watch repair shop. In 2013 the couples visited The Tankerton Arms in Whitstable and fell in love with the micropub concept. When they opened their own two years later, the Whites and Evans' decided on naming it The Watchmaker's Arms to honour the premise's original business.

The sign uses a simple font against a smart dark grey background. The part-frosted glass displays the micropub's watch dial logo and celebrates The Watchmaker's as Brighton and Hove's first micropub.

Inside is spacious, and decoration follows a horological theme: the art or science of measuring time. Clocks and watches are displayed about the pub and there is a charming border of timepieces across one of the walls. The place is painted in warm tones which sit nicely with the wooden furniture and panelling. The woodwork is all very attractive, with a variety of grains and stains. Some of the original wallpaper has been left on parts of the panelling. Old and new are seamlessly married together, respecting the building's

history and embracing the micropub ethic of recycling and renewal.

The seating follows the standard micropub model of high benches, seats and stools. It is roomy, especially for a micropub, and fits around 30 people comfortably. The lighting is very simple but effective – long cords and bulb sockets encased in preserve jars. There are enough to light the pub perfectly.

The beer choice is typically five casks that are tapped, with a dark beer, a best bitter, a pale (IPA, traditional Pale or American Pale), and either a golden or red/ruby ale. The casks are kept in a chilled stillage room with auto-tilt. The stock is rotated and predominantly local, but they also source outside the area via wholesalers.

Whilst there I tried Downlands Brewery's Oatmeal Stout, a 4.9% dark and creamy stout with a liquorice aftertaste, as well as Top-Notch Brewing Company's Royal Fanfare, a 4.6% premium bitter, gently spiced with a lovely floral hop flavour. Wines (red and white) are provided by local wine merchant Quaff, and the food – pork scratchings, porkpies and sausage rolls – are provided by McStrongs who also sell at Brighton's Open Market on Saturdays.

WHAT THE REGULARS SAY
'I am a big fan. I have followed micropubs for a while now.'

'I had heard about this one opening and like the fact that it supports the local area.'

'Small pub atmosphere, a great community spirit.'

Hythe, Kent

ESSENTIAL INFORMATION
160A High Street, Hythe, Kent
Telephone: 07780877226
Facebook: www.facebook.com/
    pottingshedhythe
Twitter: @shed_potting

Opening hours:
Monday Closed
Tuesday 1200-1800
Wednesday-Thursday 1200-1900
Friday-Saturday 1200-2100
Sunday 1200-1600

Other reasons to go: Chartwell
www.nationaltrust.org.uk;
Kent Battle of Britain Museum
www.kbobm.org;
Brockhill Country Park www.kent.gov.uk;
Etchinghill Golf Course
www.etchinghillgolf.co.uk

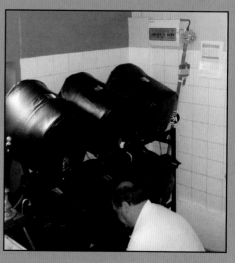

Our reporter Richard Reeve says this place is somewhat more micro than most micropubs. He arrived at the end of a lunchtime session on a Sunday and found it was standing room only. He describes it as a 'no-nonsense, no-frills little boozer where drinking beer is the main, if not the only task in hand.' It's on the quiet 'ye olde worlde' High Street in the centre of Hythe, in an old stone building (Grade II listed) with a modern shop front grafted on. You may not notice it at first – the name is not announced in large lettering, but etched into the glass window. A high counter, we guess from its previous life as a café, is still in place and acts as the bar.

You get a warm welcome from landlord Peter Dorman who is chatty but not intrusive. He runs three ales at a time from jacket-cooled casks behind the bar plus one from a handpump and a selection of ciders. Peter and his wife Belinda take trouble making single women and couples feel at home and are helped in this by their useful

choice of wines. Before launching The Potting Shed in 2014 they operated several mainstream pubs in the area.

The interior is plain and unpretentious, a blend of pale green paint and floral wallpaper which reminded our reporter of the 1960s.

On our visit we drank local brewer (based in West Hythe) Hop Fuzz's 3.7% Yellow Zinger session IPA. This is possibly one of the most refreshing 'summer pints' we've drunk and dangerously moreish.

It's easy to reach this micropub by bus: at least five services including the useful No. 16 connect Hythe with local towns and villages and towns such as Ashford and Folkestone. Hythe is a pleasant place to visit – one of the historic Cinque Ports and now a quiet market town on the edge of Romney Marsh. Hythe is an Old English word meaning haven, harbour or landing place.

There are restaurants and mainstream pubs all over the country called The Potting Shed, but this is probably the only one which really is what it says on the label – and proves that you don't need a theme or a gimmick to be popular.

Disabled access ⊗ **Child friendly** ⊗
Dog friendly ✓

WHAT THE REGULARS SAY

'The best pub in Hythe, no music, just good old conversation or the paper. Plus a super selection of beers.'

'Fantastic micro pub with a fine selection of real ale.'

'I especially enjoy the atmosphere and the Wise Owl cider – dry and very smooth.'

The Potting Shed
Real aleCider
160a
Hythe High Street

RUTHERFORD'S

Kelso, Scottish Borders

ESSENTIAL INFORMATION
38 The Square, Kelso, TD5 7HL
Telephone: 07803 208460
Website: www.rutherfordsmicropub.co.uk
Facebook: www.facebook.com/
   Rutherfordsmicropub.co.uk
Twitter: @R_fordsMicropub

Opening hours:
Monday-Thursday 1200-2100
Friday-Saturday 1200-2200
Sunday 1200-2100

Other reasons to go: Kelso Abbey
www.kelso.bordernet.co.uk;
Floors Castle www.roxburghe.net;
Kelso Racecourse www.kelso-races.co.uk

As we went to press Rutherford's was the first and only micropub in Scotland. It opened in 2015 in Scotland's largest town square, in the middle of Kelso, the Borders market town which boasts an abbey dating from 1128.

Owner Simon Rutherford formerly a graphic desinger and period property renovator, learnt about micropubs from his father, who worked in brewing and distilling. After visiting The Curfew in nearby Berwick (page 36), he couldn't think of a reason not to open his own.

His wife Debbie helped him look for the site – ideally, they wanted a run-down retail outlet that, after conversion, would breathe new life into its surroundings.

The result, in the context of staid Kelso, is eye catching. The exterior looks like a smart London bar, with its black and white shop front and awning. Inside, it's unique, especially the bar, designed by a friend. This runs all the way down one side providing a welcome leaning post, while on the other side is a row of tables and benches.

The decoration follows a scientific theme: samples of all the beers are displayed in test tubes (opposite, bottom left) and the single handpump on the bar – filled with gin – is an old microscope (opposite top right). There's a stethoscope on the wall. It's painted bright red and an assortment of pictures decorate the walls along with a penny farthing. A standard lamp stands in one corner with a leopard print shade and a string of bare light bulbs hang from the ceiling: quirky is the best description.

All the firkins are kept behind the bar, with four ales on offer, one which is pale. If Simon finds any of his ales in a

supermarket, he stops selling them.

On our visit we enjoyed: Fyne Ales'
Highlander, a 4.8% strong ale with a
citrus aroma; Knops Brewing Company's
Musselburgh Broke, a 4.5% chestnut
coloured ale with caramel, toffee and cocoa
flavours; and Stewart Brewing Company's
Hollyrood, a 5% pale ale with a grapefruit
flavour.

Disabled access ✓ not to WC
Child friendly ✓ until 1500
Dog friendly ✓

WHAT THE REGULARS SAY
'A breath of fresh air - good beers and
wines. Lovely staff and ambience.'

'A bit quirky in a good way with an
excellent range of drinks.'

Kidderminster, Worcestershire

ESSENTIAL INFORMATION
98 Comberton Hill, Kidderminster,
DY10 1QH
Telephone: 01562229413
Facebook: www.facebook.com/
    theweaversrealale/?fref=ts

Opening hours:
Monday-Wednesday 1400-2330
Thursday-Saturday 1200-2330
Sunday 1200-2230

Other reasons to go:
Carpet museum www.museumofcarpet.org;
Hartlebury Castle
www.hartleburycastletrust.org;
West Midland Safari Park
www.wmsp.co.uk;
Harvington Hall www.harvingtonhall.com

The name 'The Weavers Real Ale House' is a direct reflection of Kidderminster's heritage as a carpet making town. The town developed from being a small market town to becoming the centre for factories of carpet in the 1700s. It remained the heart of carpet making in Britain until the 1960s and The Weavers Ale House name brings a nice historical touch to this micropub.

It was opened by Richard and Adele in June 2013 and was such a huge success that Richard opened a sister pub in Park Lane, also called The Weaver, so check you are visiting the right one.

Richard previously worked delivering lease cars but his real passion lies in maintaining this micropub, free of technology and full of real ale and real conversation. He hopes that by creating more micropubs there will be a halt in the decline of pubs that has taken place over the last ten years. His certainly seems to be doing well.

Placed in an old Polish restaurant with the Polish supermarket still in residence next door, it is minutes away from Kidderminster station and a short walk from the centre of town. Don't be put off by the outside appearance, on the inside this micropub is well decorated and cosy. The walls are covered from ceiling to floor in old beer clips and there is a mixture of wooden tables and chairs and leather arm chairs to relax in.

The bar has a black board above it spanning the entire width detailing everything there is on offer. This varies from nine handpumps: six for ale and three for cider, to specialist whiskeys and gins, cobs, pork pies and scotch eggs. There is no lager, no TV and no music. A few

WHAT THE REGULARS SAY

beers they have offered include: Bewdley Brewery's Worcestershire Sway, a 5% pale golden beer, sweet and full bodied; Fownes Brewing Company's Frost Hammer, a 4.6% pale ale which was dry and bitter with a taste of grapefruit; and Wye Valley Brewery's Butty Bach, a 4.5% gold, full bodied ale (Butty Bach means little friend).

'Visited for the first time last week, very friendly people and great selection of real ales, will definitely be back.'

'Love it here, fab cider and ale, proper pub, no music, no hassle, no rowdy idiots, perfect for a nice evening! Oh and the pork pies are lovely too.'

Disabled access ✓ **Child friendly** ✓
Dog friendly ✓

'Popped in on Sunday for a couple... It's like walking into a nice old pub.'

Leighton Buzzard, Bedfordshire

ESSENTIAL INFORMATION
6 Hockliffe Street, Leighton Buzzard,
LU7 1JH
Telephone: 07581 146491/07717 22064
Website: www.baldbuzzard.co.uk
Facebook: www.facebook.com/
    pages/The-Bald-Buzzard-Alehouse-
    Leighton-Buzzards-First-
    Micropub/494069230762487
Twitter: @Baldbuzzard4u

Opening hours:
Monday Closed
Tuesday-Thursday
1200-2100
Friday-Saturday 1200-2200
Sunday Closed

Other reasons to go: Leighton Buzzard
Railway www.buzzrail.co.uk;
Bletchley Park www.bletchleypark.org.uk;
Waddesdon House and Gardens
www.waddesdon.org.uk

This charming little place, previously a chocolate shop, has been a great success from the start. It officially opened on Saturday 4th of July 2015, coinciding with Leighton Buzzard's 'Independent's Day' – part of a national campaign to promote local, independent shops, market traders and local producers. The Bald Buzzard has certainly put another local business on the map, and is proving that micropubs can be beneficial to the communities they serve – it helped fundraise for the Leighton Buzzard Narrow Gauge Railway, with a 'Buzzrail Ale Trail'. It is such a popular spot that their first Friends and Family Night ended with – as the owners put it – 'half of Leighton Buzzard turning up'.

Proprietor Philip Thompson (opposite) opened the Bald Buzzard with his wife Alison. After 20 years working for Mercedes Benz, Philip decided a change was long overdue. He watched a television programme on micropubs, and after doing some research online, he became hooked on the idea of owning a micropub with Alison. The micropub's name honours Philip, who makes a friendly host and is the 'bald, old coot' of the title. Alison came up with the name. She wanted something that captured the essence of their personalities as well as the local area. They put a strong emphasis on community links and tradition.

Philip and Alison are very accommodating, and nothing seems to be too much trouble. Philip carefully attends to the ale stock while Alison produces good food – homemade scotch eggs (made from duck eggs), ploughman's lunches, traditional pork pies and the Bald Buzzard speciality – a Bedfordshire clanger made with pulled pork and apple.

The decoration is smart but simple.

Most of the pictures and signs on the walls follow a railway theme – the owners have a fondness for trains. The lighting is quirky – lamps are made from recycled bits of plumbing tubes. The main serving area has a bar counter and behind it a glass-fronted, chilled stillage room.

The inside seats around 18 people on two tables. There is also a pretty outdoor courtyard with seating, which feeds out into Peacock Parade – a small alley with several attractive, little shops. No slot machines here – but there is a selection of board games to while away the hours in this lovely alehouse.

Four (or more) beers are usually served during the week, and five at the weekend. The choice always features a pale ale, an IPA and a dark beer. During my visit I sampled Hornes Brewery Triple Goat IPA, a 5.0% ale with a pleasant floral and citrus taste. There are also two ciders from Berkshire's Tutts Clump family brewery. Also on offer are a small selection of wines, soft drinks and Alison's speciality alcohol-free 'Mocktails'.

Disabled access ✓ **Child friendly** ⊗
Dog friendly ✓

WHAT THE REGULARS SAY
'The clientele is different and I love homemade beers and quality ciders.'

'Micropubs care about real ale.'

WHO BREWS THE BEER?

LEIGHTON BUZZARD
BREWING CO.
═══ CRAFT BEER ═══

LEIGHTON BUZZARD BREWING COMPANY
telephone: 07538 903753
website: www.leightonbuzzardbrewing.co.uk

Opening in July 2014 this brewery has rapidly built a reputation for consistently high quality and tasty beer with an emphasis on bold use of malt and hops. There is a beer for everyone in the core range of five beers.

HIGHLIGHT BEERS:

Narrow Gauge 3.9%
Brewed with 100% Marris Otter Pale Malt this golden ale delivers a strong citrus finish and long dry bitter aftertaste thanks to the use of Sorachi Ace, Cascade and First Gold hops.

Restoration Ale 4.6%
A chestnut coloured beer with a fruity hop character provided by the large additions of Cascade hop at the end of the boil. Often available at the Bald Buzzard from one of the brewery's wooden casks.

Black Buzzard 5.8%
A crazy marriage of six malts delivers a rich, complex and refreshing porter.

Leyland, Lancashire

ESSENTIAL INFORMATION
33 Hough Lane, Leyland, PR25 2SB
Telephone: 01772 623363
Website: www.themarketalehouse.co.uk
Email: Facebook: www.facebook.com/
themarketalehouse
Twitter: @leylandalehouse

Opening hours:
Monday Closed
Tuesday-Thursday 1400–2200
Friday-Saturday 1200-2300
Sunday 1400–2000

Other reasons to go:
The Old Corn Mill (antiques market)
www.oldcornmill.co.uk;
British Commercial Vehicle Museum
www.britishcommercialvehiclemuseum.
com; Hoghton Tower
www.hoghtontower.co.uk

The Market Ale House is next door to Leyland Market, which has a firm place in the town's history. Industrialised in the early 1800s, Leyland later became famous for car manufacture. The market occupies the site once used by Leyland Motors.

Alison and Danny opened their micropub in 2013 - the first in the area, with an excellent location in a former travel agent on the high street. Having read about micropubs in a trade magazine, they visited several in Kent for inspiration before taking the plunge. They also run The Railway pub in Leyland, starting this new venture because they wanted somewhere to cater to a new audience. They have certainly achieved that. While The Railway is entertainment and sport based, The Market Ale House, true to micropub core values, has no music, no TV, no mobile phones and no lager.

The interior is modern but homely, with dark wooden flooring and bar-height tables and chairs. The walls are decorated with black and white photos of market scenes. Including the seating area at the front, the whole place can fit 35 people seated, so this is by no means a small micropub. Still, it has the genuine micropub atmosphere, with good conversation and great beer.

The bar has seven handpumps, six for ales and one for cider, although the full line up is only used at weekends. If you want to taste a selection, they serve three one third pints. There is also wine, Prosecco and a selection of malt whiskies. For the peckish, there are pork pies and Lancashire cheese.

If you visit after 5.30pm on a Friday you can enter the Friday Meat Raffle, with prizes ranging from legs of lamb, beef, pork or poultry and variety packs

from Whittakers Butchers. At £1 a ticket, you could get a bargain. They put on occasional live music nights: check The Market Ale House Facebook page for dates.

We drank Crown Best Bitter 4.2% from Stockport Brewing Co which was excellent, with a toffee apple flavour and a bitter finish; Bishop's Crook Tanked Up 4.3%; and Lytham Brewery's Berry Blonde - as good as it sounds.

Disabled access ✓ **Child friendly** ⊗
Dog friendly ✓

WHAT THE REGULARS SAY
'Highly rate this little ale house. Continental feel to the place and great beer. Excellent.'

'Fantastic fun and friendly. Real ale served how it should be - no frills no fuss.'

'Cracking little micropub next to Leyland market.'

'Had a great pint of Blackedge Black Port, went down a treat.'

Lincoln, Lincolnshire

ESSENTIAL INFORMATION
417 High Street, Lincoln, LN5 8HX
Telephone: 07514916172
Facebook: www.facebook.com/
   Barleylincoln
Twitter: @HopMicro

Opening hours:
Monday-Wednesday 1600-2300
Thursday 1400-2300
Friday-Saturday 1200-2300
Sunday 1200-2200

Other reasons to go: Lincoln Castle
www.lincolncastle.com;
Lincoln Cathedral
www.lincolncathedral.com;
Museum of RAF Firefighting
www.firemuseum.uk

This micropub is the only one within a 20-mile radius – a major incentive when Steve and Sammi Marston opened it in Lincoln in 2016. It serves the lower end of the high street, providing a community hub for people outside the city centre. They felt Lincoln needed something new, and as the owners of Cathedral Heights Brewery they knew a thing or two about looking after real ale.

On a four-lane main road, it's not the most obvious place for a drink but once inside it's all conversation and enthusiasm. It occupies a single room with only enough space for 20 people, and was formerly a hairdressing salon.

The furniture is mainstream pub - classic low round tables and chairs, but the bar is modern, and brings some character to the room. Along it are high chairs. There are four handpumps with the casks visible behind them. Jam jars display samples. Steve emphasises that this place is not an extension of his brewery: they offer Cathedral Heights beers sometimes, but the focus is on constantly changing ales from all over the country.

Painted a deep blue, the room is fairly dark, perhaps a little too dark. There is little decoration, with old pump clips being the main theme. Blackboards cover the left wall displaying quotes as well as the beers on offer. In contrast to the main room, the bathroom is plastered in X Men comics providing some light relief.

On our visit we enjoyed Flipside Brewery's Hangman's Purse, a 3.8% mildly hopped beer with caramel malt and berry flavours; Leatherbritches Brewery's Scoundrel, a 4.1% full-bodied dark porter with a chocolate malt and roast barley

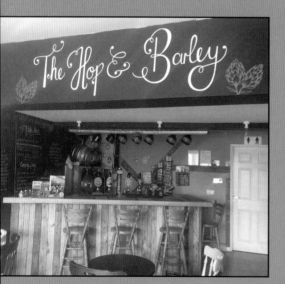

flavour; and Steep Hill Bitter Copper Ale from Cathedral Heights, a 4.3% ale with malty tones and a fruity finish.

Besides real ale there's cider, one craft keg beer (any more and this place would have to be in the back section), vodka and gin. Snacks include Pipers crisps and nuts.

Disabled access ⊗ **Child friendly** ✓
Dog friendly ✓

WHAT THE REGULARS SAY

'This is Lincoln's first micropub. Yes, it is small but has a great big heart.'

'Something different on the street from the usual public house. Gives people a chance to sample ales that will never make it into the High Street chain.'

'Nothing pretentious, good honest beer served very well. Not sure what you want? Try their third of a pint glasses to have a go at three of their selection.'

THE WHIPPET INN

Lichfield, Staffordshire

ESSENTIAL INFORMATION
21 Tamworth Street, Lichfield, Staffordshire
WS13 6JP
Telephone: 07858 753653
Email: whippetinn.micro@gmail.com
Website: whippetinnmicro.co.uk
Facebook: www.facebook.
com/The-Whippet-Inn-
Micropub-612889978772943

Opening hours:
Monday-Tuesday Closed
Wednesday-Thursday 1200-1430
then 1630-2200
Friday-Saturday 1200-2200
Sunday 1200-1700

Other reasons to go: Lichfield Cathedral,
www.lichfield-cathedral.org
The Samuel Johnson Birth Place,
www.samueljohnsonbirthplace.org.uk
Erasmus Darwin House,
www.erasmusdarwin.org

This cheekily named micropub in the otherwise well-behaved cathedral city of Lichfield seems to be one of two in the UK with the same name – the other is in Kensal Rise, London. The owners got the name from the pub that featured in one of the innuendo-laden Carry On films, *Carry on at Your Convenience* (1971).

Our reporter writes wittily that he only had time for a quickie while at The Whippet Inn. A sign at the bar invited him to Whippet Out, but this referred just to their take-away beer service.

Opened in April 2014 by Paul Hudson and Debbie Henderson, this is in the centre of Lichfield, on a narrow cobbled street in a corner site that used to be a dress shop. Next door is a disused cinema – or was as we went to press. The frontage is elegant, with a cleverly done whippet logo, well-designed graphics and Victorian-style frosted glass decorations.

Inside, the drinking area is quite small and narrow, which perhaps feels like you're drinking in a corridor, not that there's anything wrong with that. There's seating for about 25 people, and the total capacity is 40 or so. The decoration is basic and traditional, with pew seating and small round tables with iron legs.

Across the right hand side is a traditional bar equipped with handpumps. If you walk past the bar on the way to the toilets you'll see the casks stored vertically in an air-conditioned and space-efficient cupboard. On our visit there were four real ales on the bar, with the idea of moving to five if demand allows. Paul and Debbie like to showcase both local and more far-flung ales, with a definite focus on the more interesting end of the market.

None of the beers have rude-sounding names, so our reporter settled for a pint of Milk Race Stout from Fixed Wheel Brewery, Blackheath, West Midlands, an interesting 4.5% milk stout made with the addition of lactose for sweetness – it's dark and flavourful, with no bitterness.

As well as the cask ales, ciders and fruit wines are on sale. This is a 100 per cent genuine micropub, with no key kegs.

Before starting this venture Debbie worked for a family plastics business and Paul on a country estate, spending more than 20 years outdoors. The micropub's website describes Debbie as an 'advisor and motivator' – not much innuendo here, because Paul has no problem saying that that's exactly what she does – they're clearly a good team.

Disabled access ✓ **Child friendly** ✓
Dog friendly ✓

WHAT THE REGULARS SAY

'Superb back to basics pub, small, friendly and great beer.'

'Popped in this afternoon for a quick drink with the family, kids and dog, the atmosphere could not have been nicer. Great beer and a really welcoming place, perfect.'

'The best pub for miles! Forget all those generic pubs and out of touch breweries, head down to The Whippet for proper ales and a great atmosphere.'

'Friendly couple and great atmosphere.'

ARVON ALE HOUSE

Llandrindod Wells, Powys

ESSENTIAL INFORMATION
Arvon House, Temple Street, Wales
Llandrindod Wells, LD1 5DL
Telephone: 07477 627267
Email: arvonales@gmail.com
Facebook: www.facebook.com/
arvonalehouse
Twitter: @arvonalehouse

Opening hours:
Monday-Tuesday Closed
Wednesday-Thursday 1600-2200
Friday-Saturday 1600-2300
Sunday 1600-2200

Other reasons to go: The Hall at Abbey
Cwm Hir, www.abbeycwmhir.com
National Cycle Museum,
www.cyclemuseum.org.uk
Llandrindod Wells Golf Club,
www.lwgc.co.uk

John Buckley and his wife Laura (opposite, bottom right) relocated to Wales from London when Laura got a job there. John continued his London work from home. Later they felt they needed a change and decided to start their own business. They'd seen a few articles on micropubs, and knew they could be successful even if started on a shoestring.

Opening in 2015 they were keen from the start to be a destination, not just a village pub. In order to make themselves unique in the area they offer, on top of real ale, Irish whisky, speciality gins, eight artisan (mostly local) ciders and perries, plus a range of snacks and wines. Customers are surprised at how much good stuff they have managed to squeeze in.

John agrees that the name is unimaginative. The building is called Arvon House, which was painted above the door before they converted the place, so Arvon Ale House was the line of least resistance.

One of their aims has been never to sell a sub-standard pint and they are pleased by how easy this has been to achieve. They buy from a wide range of breweries and dispense from five handpumps on the bar. A

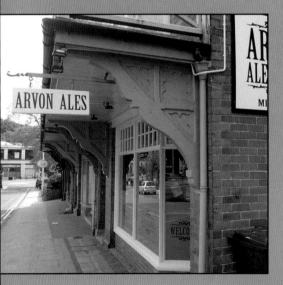

WHAT THE REGULARS SAY

'Always a pleasure and an education. Best drinks in town with an abundance of great conversation.'

'Fantastic little pub in the centre of town, really nice friendly folk, very good beer and cider, good craic and dog friendly. Love it.'

'A proper comfy, homely, community pub with an atmosphere to match.'

'The best pub in Wales.'

bookshelf behind displays spirits. Artwork decorates the walls and the furniture consists of low tables, chairs and benches. Framed blackboards also have coat hooks in order to reduce clutter at the tables.

On our visit we enjoyed Ma Pardoes' Old Swan Entire, a 4.4% sweet, copper-coloured ale; Fownes Firebeard's Old Favourite No. 5, a 5% ruby-coloured mild ale with malt and fruit flavours; and Alright, Treacle? From The Waen Brewery, a 4.2% dark stout.

On the third Sunday of every month they hold acoustic, blues and folk sessions.

Disabled access ✓ not to WC
Child friendly ✓
Dog friendly ✓

ARVON
ALE HOUSE
MICROPUB

Long Eaton

ESSENTIAL INFORMATION
40 Market Place, Long Eaton, Derbyshire,
NG10 1LT
Telephone: 0115 946 0999
Email: theyorkchambers@gmail.com
Website: www.yorkchambersmicropub.co.uk
Facebook: www.facebook.com/pg/
   YorkChambersMicroPub
Twitter: @yorkchambersmi1

Opening hours:
Monday 1600-2200
Tuesday-Thursday 1300-2200
Friday-Saturday 1100-2300
Sunday 1200-2200

Other reasons to go:
Trent Lock Golf and Country Club
www.trentlock.co.uk;
Wollaton Hall www.wollatonhall.org.uk;
Attnborough Nature Reserve
www.attenboroughnaturecentre.co.uk

MONDAY
TUESDAY
WEDNESDAY
CAMRA
MEMBERS
25p OFF
A PINT

Housed in a handsome reddish stone detached building, it looks solid and upmarket on the outside. The premises were built as York Chambers in 1903 to provide accommodation on the upper floors and on the ground floor a suitable location for a bank. A couple of banks occupied the site in the early 1900s followed for about 70 years by a popular café. This new incarnation is a genuine one-room micropub with a cold room that serves real ales straight from the cask, plus ciders, wines, limited spirits and minimal bar snacks. Reinforcing the message is a prominent sign in a corner by the blackboards spelling out 'Lager isn't sold here' (opposite, bottom left).

Joint owners Bert Sanderson (who also owns The Chequered Flag in Castle Donington, page 72) with Bev and Andy Goring had some complications with planning permission, at first being allowed restricted hours but which have now been extended. The owners stay in the background while John Van Helden and Lee Clayton capably manage it full time with four part-time helpers.

Inside, the solid, respectable feel of the Grade II building is preserved by dark wooden wall panelling, wooden pew seating and an eye catching Art Nouveau stained glass panel above the door. It's a traditional dark wood ambience, but not posh or formal: the clientele are regular folk, typically CAMRA members midweek and out-of-town visitors at weekends, encouraged by the micropub's location 100 yards from the excellent Derby-Nottingham bus service stop.

Prices are fair – £3.25 a pint – though we've seen cheaper.

Thursday night is Ladies Night, when girls get a free glass of Prosecco if with a paying customer between 6 and 9 pm.

On our visit we enjoyed Falstaff's 4.5% amber-coloured A Fistful of Hops, smelling powerfully of hops and with a mouth-filling flavour plus citrus aftertaste.

The owners also run Bennetts Bar, Restaurant and Hotel, which has nine rooms within walking distance of the micropub.

Disabled access ✓ **Child friendly** ⊗
Dog friendly ✓

WHAT THE REGULARS SAY

'Superb micropub, with great selection of beers and friendly staff. Keep up the good work.'

'This is a great addition to the Long Eaton drinking scene.'

NEEDLE AND PIN

Loughborough, Leicestershire

ESSENTIAL INFORMATION
The Rushes, Loughborough, LE11 5BE
Telephone: 07973754236
Facebook: www.facebook.com/
    LoughboroughMicropub
Twitter: @Needle_Pin_Pub

Opening hours:
Monday Closed
Tuesday-Thursday 1700-2300
Friday 1530-2300
Saturday 1200-2300
Sunday 1200-2200

Other reasons to go:
Bradgate Park www.bradgatepark.org;
Charnwood Museum
www.charnwood.gov.uk

Sean O'Neill, who runs several local businesses, including serviced offices and a microbrewery, saw the growing demand for micropubs and decided that Loughborough could support one. The Chip and Pin (page 188); The Cask and Pottle (page 62); and Just Beer (page 202) gave him inspiration for the new venture, and when he and his wife found a ramshackle, disused electronics shop for sale they knew they had to buy it. It needed major renovation, but in December 2015 they opened for business.

Needle and Pin? Mainly because of the vinyl collection and record player that Chris keeps upstairs. Customers are encouraged to chose a vinyl to play as they enjoy a drink - that's the needle. Pin is a term for half a barrel of beer. On the wall there's a framed copy, naturally, of *Needles and Pins* (1977) by The Searchers and Smokie. Finally, Loughborough has had a long association with the textile industry. There

'A refreshing break from the norm. Great drinks selection veering from the usual suspects.'

'Best pub in Loughborough. Super knowledgeable and friendly with an unmatched beer selection and atmosphere.'

'An amazing place to learn about amazing beers. If you're unsure what the difference is between porter and stout, ale or beer, these guys provide an unintimidating and comfortable, friendly place to learn.'

was once a local needle factory.

The place is on two levels: downstairs is the main drinking area, upstairs is for music and board games. Both these small spaces have a real buzz and are usually full. Outside, the place looks something like an old-fashioned sweet shop, but inside it's modern and immaculately done: cream walls; a wooden floor upstairs and a tiled one downstairs; high padded benches and wooden tables; plus a clock face with bottle tops for numbers. It's minimalist, modern and hugely inviting.

During renovation Sean did some market research on Facebook. The responses convinced him he should put in a cellar, with ales served via handpumps; that he should offer a range of bottled craft beers; run regular tasting evenings; and organise a craft beer club.

A few of the changing beers and ales they have offered include: North Riding Brewery's Rum and Raisin Dark Mild, 4.3%; Salopian Brewery's Lemon Dream, a 4.5% pale ale brewed with lemons; and Tollgate Brewery's Billy's Best Bitter, a fruity, heavily hopped 4.6% amber ale.

A friend owns a pizzeria round the corner and will deliver sourdough pizza in ten minutes.

Disabled access ✓ ramp available
Child friendly ✓
Dog friendly ✓

THE GASLAMP LOUNGE

Louth, Lincolnshire

ESSENTIAL INFORMATION
Unit 13 Thames Street, Louth, LN11 7AD
Telephone: 01507 607661
Facebook: www.facebook.com/The-Gas-
    Lamp-132075890197979

Opening hours:
Monday-Friday 1700-2300
Saturday-Sunday 1200-2300

Other reasons to go: Louth Museum
www.louthmuseum.org.uk;
Old Maltings Antique Centre
www.antiquecentrelouth.co.uk;
Rushmoor Country Park
www.rushmoorpark.co.uk

Close to the Louth Canal and occupying the former office of Louth Gas Light Company, this is one of only 22 pubs in the United Kingdom that are still lit by gas.

Phil Ellis of Fulstow Brewery had already established a microbrewery on the premises before deciding to open a micropub - the brewery tap that would be mainly a showcase for Fulstow's beers. It's now owned by Jason and Louise who have renamed the brewery Firehouse Brewery.

However, it follows genuine micropub principles, offering guest ales regularly. The Firehouse Brewery can claim to be the first in Louth in more than 100 years. The micropub opened in December 2010 and is possibly the first new pub in Louth for some 40 years. In other words, a useful extra step in regenerating Louth's canal side.

Initially you could think you had walked into a traditional pub - it more or less follows the typical layout of a public house: bar area, tables and seating are conventional. There are three long wall benches, one further small bench and around 12 wooden-backed cushioned chairs. Several pictures adorn the walls showing transport or scenes from years long past and there are display cases with diecast models of vintage vans and carts.

At the opposite end to the bar there's a log fire, cosy in winter, and together with the gas lamps conjures up the atmosphere of the old alehouses. There is bench seating outside, pleasant in warm weather.

Four regular cask conditioned beers are served, with one guest ale. There is a selection of spirits and soft drinks and a small selection of wines along with the usual basic pub snacks. On our visit we enjoyed Pride of Fulstow Premium English Pale Ale,

a 4.5% ABV full bodied malty ale with a dry finish and a hint of blackcurrant.

A lovely place in which to relax before or after a walk along the canal.

Disabled access ⊗ **Child friendly** ✓
Dog friendly ✓

WHAT THE REGULARS SAY
'Olde worldy type of pub, a hidden treasure.'

'Lovely atmosphere and great choice of beers, ciders and wines. The bar staff and locals are always friendly and dogs are more than welcome.'

'Everyone needs to enjoy a beer in the sun at the Gas Lamp Lounge at least once in their life!'

Maidstone, Kent

ESSENTIAL INFORMATION
The Old Brewery, Buckland Road,
   Maidstone, ME16 0DZ
Telephone: 01622 761045
Email: thecellarsalehouse@gmail.com
Website: thecellarsalehouse.co.uk
Facebook: www.facebook.com/
   thecellarsalehouse
Twitter: @cellarsalehouse

Opening hours:
Monday Closed
Tuesday-Wednesday 1630-2100
Thursday 1630-2300
Friday-Saturday 1200-2300
Sunday 1200-1800

Other reasons to go:
Leeds Castle www.leeds-castle.com;
Kent Life www.kentlife.org.uk;
Archbishop's Palace
www.akentishceremony.com

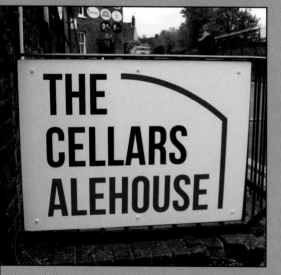

This micropub has a great location in one of the cellars of the former Medway Brewery, built in 1806 and more or less completely demolished in 1975. All but a small part remains, now known as The Old Brewery, and below it, reached by steps, is The Cellars. It's Maidstone's first micropub, run by owner Duncan Spencer and his son David (opposite, top middle). There's something special and authentic about drinking beer in this underground space with its long association with brewing. In the old days the cellars were used for maturing barley wine in wooden casks, a process taking several months, after which the casks were winched up the steep steps by a derrick and on to the brewery drays.

Duncan liked brewing his own beer at home. "I wanted to do something I enjoyed, something I could involve my son in – and something that combined good beer and good banter."

Part of his job satisfaction is dealing with the local and national microbrewers who supply The Cellars. He also serves gin from an on-site gin distillery; gluten-free bottled beers; wine, Prosecco and soft drinks. There are also crisps, pork scratchings and peanuts

The Cellars attracts a happy, mixed crowd – big groups, cider drinkers, singles and couples. A young couple playing draughts told us they came regularly and praised the friendly staff and quality ales. Disabled may not find it appealing because of the steep steps and the uneven floor.

On our visit we drank Old Dairy Summer Top 3.6%, brewed with smooth Maris Otter malt for a light, refreshing citrus taste; and Titanic Iceberg 4.1% – which was going down a storm with many of the customers that day.

Every two weeks on Tuesday there's a quiz night. There's also a gin evening where you can tour the distillery and a Meet The Brewer evening where a local brewer talks about his craft.

This is one of the largest, buzziest micropubs in the guide and if its popularity grows at the present rate it could end up expanding into an empty cellar next door.

Disabled access ⊗ **Child friendly** ⊗
Dog friendly ✓

WHAT THE REGULARS SAY

'Can't believe we have only just found this place. Great atmosphere and set up, can't wait to return.'

'Very unique place with great ciders. Had a good time.'

FARMER'S YARD

Maldon, Essex

ESSENTIAL INFORMATION
140 High Street, Maldon, CM9 5BX
Telephone: 01621 854 202
Email: info@maldonbrewing.co.uk
Website: www.maldonbrewing.co.uk
Facebook: www.facebook.com/
    farmersyard1
Twitter: @FarmersYard

Opening hours:
Monday- Friday 1100-1400
then 1700-2100
Saturday 1100-2100
Sunday 1200-2100

Other reasons to go:
Maeldune Heritage Centre
www.maelduneheritagecentre.co.uk;
Promenade Park www.visitmaldon.co.uk;
Stow Maries WW1 Aerodrome
www.stowmaries.org.uk

This charming micropub and bottle shop, an outlet of the Maldon Brewing Company, mainly serve their own stock and occasionally feature guest ales: four during the week and five on a Friday.

Nigel Farmer began brewing professionally in 2001 having been a nuclear power plant engineer, an avid home-brewer, and an anecdotalist. The name Farmer's Yard comes from the Yard of Ale glass that has pride of place above the display shelving – perhaps a personal comment on Nigel's drinking style? The beer is good and there is plenty of it, represented by the complete range of Farmer's Ales, bottled beers and a complement of selected guest ales.

Farmer's Yard itself came about after a family holiday spent enjoying the delights of The Just Reproach micropub (page 98). It set Nigel thinking about opening his own as an extension to the microbrewery. Opening in September 2015 with Annie Janes-Fraser as manager, it has attracted great local interest as well as from further afield, thanks to the visitors from the narrow boats, local camping grounds and hotels.

Outside, the simple green-on-white sign gives it a passing resemblance to a village shop or a local butcher's. That said, with a quick look through the window you know exactly what you're getting. The premises are Grade II-listed, dating back to around 400 years and are truly micro. There's seating for about 12 and a similar number standing. With a surprisingly down-to-earth atmosphere, it is snug but not confined.

True to the micropub model, the furniture is made and supplied by a local fitter. Two high legged tables and high-backed wall mounted benches are surprisingly comfortable. Not much

decorates the walls other than a couple of pictures alluding to the benefits of beer and a few local newspaper articles. The electrical wiring, incorporated into copper plumbing pipes, blends nicely with the overhead beams - one of which may be original.

From The Maldon Brewing Company range, I enjoyed a pint of Rudolph's Red 4.3% ABV Traditional Ruby Ale, a rich red ale with a nicely hopped finish; Essex Strong Pale Ale 5.3% ABV, a robust crisp ale bursting with El Dorado hop flavour.

Also on offer are two or three real ciders, sourced from across the UK, a delightful range of meads, wines, Prosecco and soft drinks. There are four varieties of tea - including Alishan High Mountain Oolong. Standard pub snacks are available.

Disabled access ⊗ **Child friendly** ✓
Dog friendly ✓

WHAT THE REGULARS SAY
'The atmosphere is great. I'm a teetotaller but was surprised by the lovely atmosphere.'

'A nice selection of bottled beers. If I found a place like this in Norwich I would use it.'

'I'd been to a couple of micropubs six years back but didn't like them. I really like this set up though.'

WHO BREWS THE BEER?

THE MALDON BREWING COMPANY
telephone: 01621 851000
website: www.maldonbrewing.co.uk
facebook: facebook.com/farmersales
twitter: @farmers_ales

HIGHLIGHT BEERS:

Puck's Folly 4.2%
A golden ale using East Kent Goldings to give the beer a spicy character.

Farmer's Golden Boar 5%
A much awarded amber beer, refreshing and crisp with a little sweetness to balance the lashings of Cascade hops.

THE MIGHTY OAK TAPROOM

Maldon, Essex

ESSENTIAL INFORMATION
10 High Street, Maldon, Essex, CM9 5PJ
Telephone: 01621 843 713
Website: www.micropubmaldon.uk
Facebook: www.facebook.com/
 mightyoaktaproom
Twitter: @MightyOakBrew

Opening hours:
Monday Closed
Tuesday-Sunday 1200-2200

Other reasons to go:
Combined Military Services Museum,
www.cmsm.co.uk
Promenade Park,
www.itsaboutmaldon.co.uk
Heybridge Basin, www.visitmaldon.co.uk
Stow Maries Great War Aerodrome,
www.stowmaries.org.uk

The Mighty Oak Tap Room stands proudly on Maldon's high street and, less than a year after opening, is already an institution. It is housed in a historic building (up to five hundred years old) with a cheerful blue exterior and a painting of the brewery's logo: impossible to miss.

Stepping into the pub you have to watch your head – the main room has a low roof and exposed beams. There is high seating on both sides, with the bar at the end of the room. Behind it stands one of the Tap Room's unique features: the wall of beer. Large, round holes have been bored into the wall, through which the front and taps of the casks fit perfectly. It looks good and it's also practical, as the beers enjoy the conditioned temperature of the cellar room on the other side of the wall while being easy to pour from behind the bar. Next to each cask is a small container showing the beer's colour.

John Boyce, owner of the brewery and tap room, built the wall himself – he was employed by a brewery as an engineer, and old habits die hard. He started working in the industry in 1976, and 20 years later he opened The Mighty Oak Brewing Company. The Tap Room is the latest development of this enterprise.

There is a fireplace on the left, now filled with books and board games, and above is the blackboard with the menu. There are permanent beers from The Mighty Oak, specials, wines, ciders and just one spirit, a 40% malt tipple called the Wilde Spirit which you're unlikely to find elsewhere. They also serve cheese and paté boards, traditional pub snacks, tea and coffee.

Upstairs is a snug room with comfortable armchairs and sofas, perfect for reading or

enjoying a peaceful pint. Don't rush down the stairs, but stop to take in what's hanging on the wall. The Mighty Oak has been producing a different 'monthly special' for 15 years, and here (also downstairs) you can see the quirky artwork they created for each beer. Each year has a different theme, from *Sgt. Pepper's Lonely Hearts Club Band* to motorcycles. The first monthly special ever produced was Space Oddity.

To finish off your visit, admire The Mighty Oak's timeline: a journey back to 1999 featuring all the award-winning beers they produced, from Oscar Wilde (Supreme Champion Beer of Britain 2011) to Maldon Gold (Champion Golden Ale of Britain 2007).

The Mighty Oak Tap Room is almost a museum for the beer lover, and the cosy and friendly atmosphere ensures that even hardened teetotallers will not be bored.

They organise the occasional folk music live event (Music on tap): check the website to see all the dates.

Disabled access ✓ not to WC
Child friendly ✓
Dog friendly ✓

WHAT THE REGULARS SAY

'There is a good selection of Mighty Oak beers, my favourite is Oscar Wilde Mild.'

'Great choice of beer, trouble is you could easily drop in for one and end up staying the evening.'

BEER SHACK

Mansfield, Nottinghamshire

ESSENTIAL INFORMATION
46 White Hart Street, Mansfield,
Nottinghamshire, NG18 1DG
Telephone: 07484 878401
Website: www.langwithbrewing.co.uk
Facebook: www.facebook.com/pg/Beer-
   Shack-Mansfield-306874849467176

Opening hours:
Monday-Tuesday Closed
Wednesday-Thursday 1500-2230
Friday-Saturday 1200-2230
Sunday 1300-1700

Other reasons to go: Sherwood Forest;
Newstead Abbey
www.newsteadabbey.org.uk;
Creswell Crags www.creswell-crags.org.uk

There's evidence of a settlement in Mansfield dating as far back as the Romans – a villa was found between Mansfield Woodhouse and Pleasley in 1787 and Roman coins were discovered near King's Mill in 1849. Following this, Mercian kings often visited to enjoy the hunting in nearby Sherwood Forest and English kings from Edward the Confessor to Henry VIII had a royal manor here. The town is mentioned several times in the Domesday book, each time with a different spelling and until the 1990s Mansfield thrived on the local coal and textile industries. Since then, however, the population has been in decline – as have job prospects.

The Beer Shack is therefore a much-needed community hub for this historic town. It was originally opened as part of a chain, and was not a true micropub. Later it was bought by Langwith, a small six-barrel brewery. They closed it to refurbish and reopened the current micropub in November 2016.

It's located on White Hart Street, directly below the viaduct that runs impressively through the town, and whose imposing archways give character to an otherwise small street. The micropub is on two levels: downstairs is the bar, upstairs is a snug decked out with comfortable tub chairs, cushions and rugs. Candles sit on small round tables and the walls are painted brick, making it feel something like a medieval tower room. Downstairs the decoration is modern and fresh. A large mirror on one wall makes the tiny space appear larger than it is while bare light bulbs hang artistically from the ceiling. A shelf with tall chairs runs along the wall underneath the stairs, while the bar is along the other.

On our visit we enjoyed: Shardlow Brewery's Cavendish Gold, a 4.5% gold bitter with a malty, earthy flavour; and Langwith Brewery's own Scuba Mozz, a 5.2% amber ale with fruit flavours.

Despite the abandoned look of White Hart Street, this place is well worth a visit and is only a four-minute walk from the station.

Disabled access ✓ small step to enter
Child friendly ⊗
Dog friendly ✓

WHAT THE REGULARS SAY
'Only popped in for a couple but great to see Beer Shack back – plus I'm liking the Langwith Brewery beers.'

FEZ

Margate, Kent

ESSENTIAL INFORMATION
40 High Street, Margate, CT9 1DS
Facebook: www.facebook.com/pages/Fez-
    Margate/1004144649627700

Opening hours:
Monday-Saturday 1200-2230
Sunday 1200-2200

Other reasons to go: Turner Contemporary
www.turnercontemporary.org;
Shell Grotto www.shellgrotto.co.uk;
Margate Tudor House
www.margatemuseum.wordpress.com

Margate gets asylum seekers and immigrants, legal and illegal, from across the Channel, and has experienced the resulting tensions: facts which played a part in Phil Evans's (opposite, bottom) choice of name for his micropub. He's a former sculpture teacher at the University of Creative Arts (UCA), Canterbury, with a liberal outlook: "xenophile, not xenophobe." The fez, the cylindrical felt hat characteristic of the Ottoman Empire and Eastern Europe, including the Balkans, in the 19thC, was adopted by British and North American men in the early 1900s as a sign of their openness to other cultures, often as part of luxury smoking outfits. All nationalities are welcome here, and he intends the name to sum that up.

We keep seeing micropubs decorated with an eclectic assembly of retro items, often from junk shops or even skips, but this one takes retro and eclectic to new lengths. It's stuffed with eye-catching, artfully arranged curiosities from every decade of the 20th century, including amusement arcade paraphernalia; a huge 'Cunarder' sign; and two 1950s professional 'beehive' driers used in hairdressers to set perms, and now contributing a slightly surreal effect. The atmosphere is cluttered and lived in: you might not want to eat your crisps direct from the fabric of the settee in the window.

Before Phil took over, this was a small greetings card shop towards the quiet lower end of Margate's High Street. At maximum capacity it fits around 55 drinkers shoulder to shoulder so table service is not an option.

Besides at least four real ales, all gravity fed, from the cold room at the back, Phil

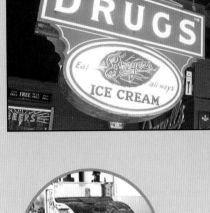

sells ciders, wine, soft drinks, tea and coffee. To the simple bar snacks already available he plans to add a wider variety of vegan and regular snacks home made by a local. On Saturday and Sunday mornings he puts cloths on the tables and serves tea and cakes. Another twist to the formula is his ukulele classes on Tuesdays.

On our visit we enjoyed Oddly VIPA 5%, an unfined, ie cloudy bitter with a full-on fruity taste. Oddly is a very small new Yorkshire brewer who delivers firkins from the back of his car. Most of Phil's ales are, however, from Kent brewers.

Don't miss out on its near neighbour, The Two Halves (page 182).

Disabled access ✓ not to WC
Child friendly ✓
Dog friendly ✓

WHAT THE REGULARS SAY

'What other pub has seating choices comprising ex cinema seats and a waltzer car?'

'Great little bar in Margate with plenty of different beers and ciders to try. The décor is jaw droppingly amazing too.'

Margate, Kent

ESSENTIAL INFORMATION
Units 7-8, Margate Harbour Arm, The
Stone Pier, Margate, CT9 1JD
Telephone: 07776 183273
Website:
www.harbourarmsmargate.co.uk
Facebook: www.facebook.com/
harbourarms.margate
Twitter: @Harbourarmsmarg

Opening hours:
Monday Closed
Tuesday-Thursday 1600-2130
Friday-Saturday 1200-2230
Sunday 1200-1700

Other reasons to go:
Shell Grotto
www.shellgrotto.co.uk;
Margate Museum
www.margatemuseum.wordpress.com;
The Old Kent Market
www.theoldkentmarket.com

As mentioned elsewhere in this guide, micropubs should have names that connect them with their locality. This one is literally and wittily connected: it stands half way along Margate Harbour Arm, the broad, solidly Victorian stone jetty that curves out from the east end of town, sheltering both the town's beach and sea front houses from the north and the east. There's pay and display parking on the inner half of the Arm, only a few paces away from The Harbour Arms itself. A stroll out along the Arm, starting where it joins the land near Turner Contemporary, is a pleasure not to be missed.

Outside the micropub you'll find tables and chairs giving the best view of the comings and goings of small craft moored near the Arm, and of Margate's sweep of beach and sea front houses, reminding you of the town's former status as a major Victorian and Edwardian seaside resort. In other words, this is a dream location for a micropub, one of the best in the guide, especially if you like a marine atmosphere and the smell of the sea – without getting cold or windswept.

Inside the micropub is informal, cosy and friendly with standard micropub high tables and seating. As you would expect from yet another micropub inspired by The Butcher's Arms, page 140, the only beers on offer are cask-conditioned, gravity-fed, real ales from the cold room. There are plenty of ciders, including one with a salted caramel flavour; they also sell sloe gin, Prosecco, and dark rum.

We didn't meet the owners Carol and Richard when we visited, but got the impression that they form a close team

with friendly Tony Tooke (above, centre), who was manning the bar. Before opening this place, Carol and Richard worked at the Lighthouse Bar, the conventional pub at the end of the Arm.

There's a quiz night once a month with especially hard questions set by Laura, Tony's partner, a teacher. Monday night is jamming night.

On our visit we tried Headland Red 4.3% from Yorkshire brewer Woldtop: a traditional red, malty Yorkshire bitter with a lingering finish.

Other attractions close to The Harbour Arms include Michael Richardson Fine Art, next door; and next along, for lunch or supper after a few pints, BeBeached, a terrific US West Coast-style café with an imaginative menu including good home-made food and original cocktails (www. bebeached.co.uk).

Disabled access ✓ **Child friendly** ✓
Dog friendly ✓

WHAT THE REGULARS SAY
'Superb pub with lovely friendly people. Very welcoming.'

'A brilliant find. Fabulous ales and my first pickled egg. All experiences I'll be repeating very soon.'

Margate, Kent

ESSENTIAL INFORMATION
Marwell House, 2-3 Marine Drive, Margate,
CT9 1DJ
Facebook: www.facebook.com/The-Two-
    Halves-480809142083462
Twitter: @TheTwoHalvesAle

Opening hours:
Monday-Thursday 1215-2230
Friday-Sunday 1200-2230

Other reasons to go: Shell Grotto
www.shellgrotto.co.uk;
Turner Contemporary
www.turnercontemporary.org;
Powell Cotton Museum
www.quexpark.co.uk;
Spitfire and Hurricane Memorial Museum
www.spitfiremuseum.org.uk

If you happen to visit the Fez, page 178, don't miss out on this one, just around the corner. You turn left out of the Fez, left at the bottom of Margate's High Street into Marine Drive and in a few yards you find a place that's as different to the Fez as you could imagine.

Shaun Smethers' place, which opened in July 2015, is neat, fresh, light and minimally decorated with framed pictures and prints, one of them by none other than local Turner Prize winning artist Tracy Emin. As Shaun rightly says, there's no need, and it would be silly for the interior design to try to compete with the view out of the front windows, which could claim to be the most impressive of any micropub in the country: a 180-degree panorama of the Thames Estuary where it flows into the North Sea. On warm days the large, picture windows framing the view can be folded right back leaving drinkers to enjoy the scene virtually in the fresh air.

The relatively small interior space is carefully organized with a mixture of raised and conventional height tables, chairs and stools. The bar is at the back with the temperature- controlled beer room behind it, visible through a glass pane. Many micropubs are blokish, but this one is deliberately unisex – Shaun wants women to feel at home here – which they do thanks to the neutral design. Both sexes will enjoy the collection of naughty seaside post cards in the toilet.

Shaun, who spent his working life as a ceramic tiler, has been a beer enthusiast all his life – at home he has a bar with handpumps. The Two Halves is a 100% authentic micropub: cask-conditioned real ales at £3 a pint are what Shaun is

all about, but he also serves 12 ciders, one speciality bottled lager, 8 wines and one gluten-free beer. On our visit we enjoyed Westerham Brewery's Tackle, a 4% quaffable ale made with English barley and English hops.

This is a carefully thought out, practical operation, run by a practical man with a sense of humour. Why is it called The Two Halves? One of Shaun's favourite jokes, which he delivers every time he orders a beer, goes like this: "I'd like two halves please." "In separate glasses?" "No, one on top of the other." This gag actually derives from a Laurel and Hardy sketch, but Shaun has made it is his own. Shaun's other party piece doesn't need words: he's a walking Harry Redknapp lookalike (see photo above).

Disabled access ⊗
Child friendly ✓ until 1900
Dog friendly ✓

WHAT THE REGULARS SAY
'Lovely family run bar offering good selection of ales in a perfect location with fantastic views of Margate beach.'

'What a lovely place! And a beautiful view.'

'Great bar, great beer, great atmosphere, great owner.'

BEERHOUSE

Market Harborough, Leicestershire

ESSENTIAL INFORMATION
76 St Mary's Road, Market Harborough,
   LE16 7DX
Telephone: 07738 086194
Facebook: www.facebook.com/
   beerhouseuk
Twitter: @beerhouses

Opening hours:
Monday 1800-2300
Thursday-Saturday 1200-2100
Sunday 1200-2200

Other reasons to go:
Harborough Museum www.leics.gov.uk;
The BoilerHouse www.fipt.org.uk;
West Lodge Rural Centre
www.westlodgeruralcentre.co.uk.

Just a five-minute stroll from the station, Market Barnorough's first micropub is perfectly positioned if you are at a loose end. It won't be long before you find yourself spoilt for choice with the wide range of beers on offer at Beerhouse.

Somewhat stretching the definition of micropub in terms of size, Beerhouse occupies the airy space of a converted furniture shop. There are also regular comedy and live music nights, lagers are features in the beer menus, and kegs are regularly used – this pub certainly doesn't follow the micropub philosophy as strictly as some. But it is comfortable and friendly, and with civilised opening hours and no gaming machines, loud music or hot food – that's good enough for us.

Jon Pollard and Ivan Sheldrake co-founded Beerhouse, which opened in December 2014. Jon used to be an off-licence manager, so is not a complete stranger to the industry. They have now employed a former regular, Ben Marlowe-Booth, as barman, who makes a new addition to the business.

Seating thirty-five or so inside and perhaps an additional twenty on benches outdoors, Beerhouse is at the upper size limit of a micropub. There is also a small stage area for the live entertainment. Jon and Ivan had originally hoped to buy a smaller venue in the centre of town but it fell through – and they have certainly made the most of their second choice. The back room serves as an impromptu office, keg and cask storage room, and even a meeting space for the local Geocache society – every square inch is used. Seating varies from hard wooden benches to upholstered stools and chairs, plus one

comfy sofa. Aside from the pump clips on the ceiling beams and the pub's name and tagline 'Putting the public back into public houses' dominating the back wall, the decoration is pretty Spartan.

The serving area has coolers stocked full of bottled beers, wines and soft drinks. The casks are well kept – they are water cooled, wrapped in insulating jackets, and sit on self-tilting stillages. Typically on offer are nine bottled beers, five keg beers and up to 12 real ales on cask. There are also boxed ciders and a selection of wines, as well as the usual micropub snacks.

During my visit I sampled the Indian Brewery Indian Summer, a 3.8% lightly-hopped Golden Ale with a spicy aftertaste, and North Brink's Black Dog, a 3.6% traditional English Mild which was smooth, light and gently malty.

Disabled access ✓ **Child friendly** ⊗
Dog friendly ✓

WHAT THE REGULARS SAY

'It's an eye-opener really. Micropub owners go back to basics and serve their beer properly. They talk to people and engage in banter.'

'It is sociable, the atmosphere and the beer is good. There's no fuss.'

Matlock, Derbyshire

You'll deserve your pint once you've made it to this place. Perched half way up a steep hill on Matlock's High Street, it has great views, despite the former factory directly opposite – it's pretty much in your face, with a tall chimney, so you can't miss the micropub's location.

Husband and wife team Michael and Michalene McMaster also own the Bumpmill Brewery in Belper. One of its beers is always on offer – look for the vinyl pump clip. On display behind the bar are a number of other old pump clips from their brewery, all named after a song, including, *Lightning Bolt* (2012) by Jake Bugg and *Moonraker* (1979) sung by Shirley Bassey.

Michael used to be a kitchen fitter and brewed his own beer as a hobby, which triggered the idea to open his own micropub. He still brews much of the beer – hence the restricted opening times. This doesn't deter customers; we visited a few minutes after opening time and the place was already half full.

The premises used to be a café, so it has a great layout on two mini levels, with the bar on the lower level. The furniture consists of low tables with stools and chairs and a few church pews. There is room for around 40 people.

The decoration matches the pump clips and is musically themed with a vinyl clock, an accordion, a guitar and a zither on the walls. The Beatles feature heavily in the pictures and there are even musical cushions. A corner of the room is dedicated to board games such as Jenga, Four in a

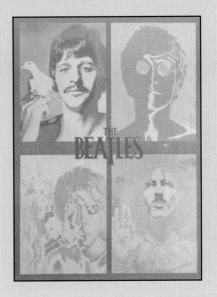

Row and Backgammon.

They put on some live music events, but mainly this place is about good beer and good chat. There are no kegs, lager or TV. The bar has five handpumps serving real ale and two ciders.

The place is named after Michael's father Stanley, as was one of the beers on offer while we were there. Other beers served on out visit were Cotleigh Brewery's Osprey, a 5% strong ale with a well hopped bitterness and Raw Brewing Company's Nid Welsh 4.5%. They also offer soft drinks, wine and Prosecco.

As we went to press Michael and Michalene had just sold the place. The new owners didn't get back to us about changes they plan to make, so readers' feedback would be welcome.

Disabled access ⊗
Child friendly ✓ until 2000
Dog friendly ✓

WHAT THE REGULARS SAY

'A brilliant addition to the Matlock scene.'

'Friendly atmosphere, great beer and fantastic view.'

'Treated like we'd been coming here for years. The hill is a bit of a climb, but well worth it.'

Melbourne, Derbyshire

ESSENTIAL INFORMATION
8-10 High Street, Melbourne, Derbyshire, DE73 8GJ
Telephone: 07957 806454
Email: info@chipandpinpub.com
Website: www.chipandpinpub.com
Facebook: www.facebook.com/
    chipandpinpub
Twitter: @chipandpinpub

Opening hours:
Monday Closed
Tuesday-Thursday 1630-2130
Friday-Saturday 1200-2130
Sunday & Bank Holidays 1200-1430

Other reasons to go: Melbourne Hall and Gardens melbournehallgardens.com;
Ashby de la Zouch Castle,
www.english-heritage.org.uk;
Calke Abbey www.nationaltrust.org.uk

This proves that former bank premises can make great micropubs. David (opposite, top) and Elaine Carpenter (opposite, middle) converted this characterful building into a meeting place for the local community and people from further afield.

They drew on the nearby Cask and Pottle (page 62) for design inspiration, so, unusually for the Midlands, it has much in common with a Kent-style micropub. High tables and benches are arranged round the walls, with standing room in the middle. Ales are served straight from the cask in an air-conditioned stillage room, and there's no bar. However, the furniture and decor is less 'rustic' and more 'polished' than in a Kent micropub. The high arched windows, as well as adding character, provide more of a feeling of privacy than the plate glass shop windows of many micropubs.

In common with some other micropubs they had a roughish ride during the licensing and planning process: some residents objected to the mayhem that might follow the opening of a new drinking place. Fortunately, as often seems to be the case, these fears have turned out to be unfounded, and instead Chip and Pin has created a new sense of community.

Banks have to have a manager's office. The Bankers Draft (page 28) uses the manager's office as the stillage room; the Chip & Pin, in contrast, uses the office as a private room for meetings or private functions. It seats up to ten people and has separate serving facilities.

A large number of the beers come from within a 20-mile radius but, there are plenty from further afield, including Dorset. They try hard to offer unique or unusual brews.

On our visit we enjoyed Falstaff's Moon Landing, a 4.3% dark brown, mild ale with chocolate aromas and a toffee and chocolate flavour; and Towcester Mill Brewery's Mill race, a 3.9% pale blond ale with a grapefruit and herb finish. David and Elaine also offer locally sourced snacks such as pork pies and scotch eggs.

Disabled access ⊗ **Child friendly** ⊗
Dog friendly ✓

WHAT THE REGULARS SAY

'The Chip and Pin was just great. Very friendly staff and great choice of ales. Cheese board was lovely.'

'Fantastic, quaint and small place with a great ambiance. There's lovely warmth from the owners who make you feel so welcome.'

DR PHIL'S REAL ALEHOUSE

Middlesbrough, North Yorkshire

ESSENTIAL INFORMATION
10 Pilkington Buildings, Roman Road,
Linthorpe, Middlesbrough, TS5 6DY
Telephone: 01642 941516
Email: drphilsrealalehouse@gmail.com
Website: drphilsrealalehouse.co.uk
Facebook: www.facebook.com/Dr-Phils-
    Real-Ale-House-530590170346131

Opening hours:
Monday Closed
Tuesday-Friday 1500-2130
Saturday 1300-2200
Sunday Closed

Other reasons to go:
Middlesbrough Institute of Modern Art
www.visitmima.com;
The Dorman Museum
www.dormanmuseum.co.uk;
Stewart Park visitmiddlesbrough.com

Middlesbrough might have a cluster of micropubs in the city centre near the train station, but Dr Phil's Real Alehouse, about a mile further out in the Linthorpe area, is well worth travelling to. It opened in August 2013 as Middlesbrough's first micropub – a one-man operation run by real ale lover and father-of-two Dr Phil Thompson. Phil spent 14 years in the civil service and completed a PhD in local government research before becoming one of the country's most educated pub landlords. Phil comes from nearby Hartlepool, home to the Rat Race Ale House micropub (see page 132) where he was once a regular. He liked the concept so much that he took the step to open his own.

As I have travelled further north, more micropubs have started to resemble scaled-down versions of regular pubs with conventional bars and handpumps. Dr Phil's is a refreshing change, and it sticks closely to the original micropub ideals. It's small – 14 feet squared – and is nestled in between a tattoo parlour and a curry house in a former lettings office. There is no bar as such, but a small serving hatch through to the beer room serves as a counter, and behind it you can see the jacket-cooled casks. I visited just before the beer room was due a refit – Phil was having air conditioning installed – for the beer rather than for the punters.

The interior is plainly furnished with wooden flooring, benches, tables and bookshelves. Decoration is simple and stripped back, with blackboards, beermats and a peculiar 'tactical nuclear penguin' clock on the wall. Phil's focus is on good beer and conversation, but there are also several board games. When I visited the pub

was packed with friendly, chatty regulars who were keen to hear all about my travels.

Phil's alehouse has around four ales on offer at any one time, as well as draft ciders, perry and bottled beer. Drinks are priced by ABV (alcohol by volume). During my visit I had a pint of Wall's Alvertune, which was a snip at £2.80. Their ales are sourced from a wide variety of breweries across the UK – you can find a map of these on Dr Phil's Real Alehouse's (very informative) website. They also sell wine, soft drinks and pub snacks (crisps, nuts, pork scratchings). Dr Phil's is an excellent example of a classic micropub.

As we went to press we were unable to contact the new owners, so readers' feedback would be welcome.

Disabled access ✓
Child friendly ✓ until 1800
Dog friendly ⊗

WHAT THE REGULARS SAY
'There's just a great atmosphere – everyone is friendly.'

Middlesbrough, North Yorkshire

ESSENTIAL INFORMATION
7 Baker Street, Middlesbrough, TS1 2LF
Telephone: 07789 277364
Email:
sherlocksatmiddlesbrough@outlook.com
Facebook: www.facebook.com/
   Sherlocks-726694120714076
Twitter: @sherlocksbaker

Opening hours:
Monday-Saturday 1100-2300
Sunday 1200-2300

Other reasons to go:
Wild Animal Adventures
wildanimaladventures.co.uk;
Newham Grange Country Farm
www.middlesbrough.gov.uk;
RSPB Saltholme www.rspb.org.uk

Several micropubs have sprung up in Middlesbrough over the last few years, but no prizes for guessing where this one on Baker Street gets its name.

Sherlock's opened in June 2014, and is owned by Shaun Crake and his business partner Robert Robinson. Shaun, an experienced publican, already owned three pubs nearby – The Star, O'Connells and the Dubliners – while Robert, a mental health nurse, has continued his work alongside running Sherlock's. Unfortunately, neither was in during my visit, but I enjoyed chatting to the barman Nick, and a couple of Sherlock's regulars.

This is a smart-looking micropub, and it was hard to imagine that it had only been open for a few months when I visited. The exterior is sleek, painted in black with yellow-gold writing. The interior is vintage themed – dark and atmospheric with flock wallpaper and wood paneling reclaimed from a school in South Shields. The bar is also reclaimed, and comes from Wales. There is a variety of handsome furniture, including comfy benches and drinking shelves with barstools, and a wood burner with patterned tiles behind it adds to the cosy atmosphere. There's also a small outside space at the back – perfect for a quiet drink and a chat.

At first glance Sherlock's may seem to be breaking some important micropub rules – there is a TV here and a lager on offer – but both might be forgiven. The TV is a concession to Middlesbrough's countless football fans, and only plays sports with the sound off, while the lager, Sharp's Cornish Pilsner, is described by Sherlock's as 'the world's best lager'. Sherlock's gives its customers what they want, and also

gets involved in the local community – the weekend after my visit a charity dragon-boat race was scheduled to take place between three micropubs (Sherlock's, The Twisted Lip, The Golden Smog) and a pub called The Storytellers.

Sherlock's serves a range of real ales, Belgian beers, wines and spirits. On the bar are three hand pumps for casks ales. I chose a pint of Saltaire Triple Chocoholic Stout, which contained actual chocolate as well as a chocolate malt – a bit too chocolatey for me, but definitely a novelty.

Disabled access ✓   **Child friendly** ✓
Dog friendly ✓

WHAT THE REGULARS SAY

'Like the staff, like the drink selection. Yet to have a bad night there.'

'Brilliant cosy little retreat with a friendly atmosphere. Best pub in town for me.'

Middlesbrough, North Yorkshire

ESSENTIAL INFORMATION
84 Grange Road, Middlesbrough, TS1 2LS
Telephone: 07828 039434
Facebook: www.facebook.com/
 TheInfantHercules

Opening hours:
Monday-Sunday 1300-1100

Other reasons to go:
Ormesby Hall www.nationaltrust.org.uk;
Saltholme Nature Reserve
www.rspb.org.uk;
Hatlepool Maritime Experience
www.hartlepoolsmaritimeexperience.com;
Wynyard Golf Club
www.wynyardgolfclub.co.uk;
Wynyard Hall Gardens
www.wynyardhall.co.uk

As we went to press, Middlesborough had six micropubs, The Infant Hercules being the newest. It was opened in March 2015 by Mick Hill, Chris Moloney and Neil Hodds, who were already pros at the business, having worked in pubs and clubs.

Slightly away from the other high street shops, this place is a five minute walk from the station and two minutes from the grand Victorian Town Hall adjoining a square of fountains and green space. Being on a main road, it's not ideally placed, however the atmosphere and locally sourced ale more than makes up for this.

Previously The Olde Young Tea House (which has now moved to a larger premises next door), The premises didn't need much conversion. The long narrow space has been used well: a conventional bar with four hand pumps occupies most of the back wall with a snug seating area to the side. The rest of the space has wooden tables and comfy chairs providing a somewhat 1960s feel.

Many of the walls are decorated with quotes encouraging the appreciation of the small things in life. Photographs depicting Middlesborough's industrial heritage cover the remaining space, notably the Transporter Bridge, and one wall depicts William Gladstone's famous quote (1862): "This remarkable place, the youngest child of England's enterprise, is an infant, but if an infant, an infant Hercules."

One of their best-selling ales is Sharp's Cornish Pilsner 5.2%, a pale beer with a lemony aroma and dry finish. We drank Copper Dragon Brewery's Golden Pippin 3.9%, a blonde ale with a citrus flavour; and Titanic Brewery's Cherry Dark 4.4%, which had a good balance of sweetness and bitterness with an almond and cherry taste.

For CAMRA members there is a 20p per pint discount and most ales served are local to the North East.

This place offers a 'try before you buy' system, so it's hard to go wrong. A typical offering includes a golden, bitter, pale and a stout. Spirits and soft drinks are also available along with pickled eggs, olives and nuts. This place can get very busy but you're sure to make friends quickly.

Disabled access ✓ **Child friendly** ⊗
Dog friendly ⊗

WHAT THE REGULARS SAY
'Lovely staff, friendly atmosphere, a must visit!'

'Nice friendly atmosphere and a great pint, what more do you need.'

'Nice little bar.'

Minster, Kent

ESSENTIAL INFORMATION
73 High Street, Minster, CT12 4AB
Telephone: 07885 362326
Email: gary@securatel.co.uk
Website:
www.hairofthedogpub.co.uk
Facebook: www.facebook.
   com/hairofthedogminster
Twitter: @HairOfTheDogPub

Opening hours:
Monday-Thursday 1200–2200
Friday-Saturday 1200–2300
Sunday 1200–1500

Other reasons to go: Minster Abbey,
www.minsterabbeynuns.org
Spitfire and Hurricane Memorial Museum,
www.spitfiremuseum.org.uk
Manston Golf Centre, www.
manstongolfcentre.co.uk

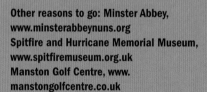

Minster's full name is Minster-in-Thanet and it's the old capital of the Island of Thanet. This is essentially the extreme north-east bit of Kent which until around the mid 1600s was separated from the mainland by the Wantsum Channel running from the Thames Estuary to the English Channel near Sandwich. The Wantsum silted up progressively until by the 1700s it was impassable by ships; later it turned into flat, marshy land and the island was no more.

Minster derives from the Latin word for monastery and as you might expect there has been either a monastery or priory here from the earliest Christian times.

In among this history is Hair of the Dog, a pure Kent micropub that benefits from the coach loads of tourists visiting the town. Sometimes owner Gary Hake puts on an ale at 1 which is gone by 6. He's an electrician, who runs his business alongside the micropub, helped by his daughter Chloe Beaney and his wife Julie who once worked in the local hop fields. Completing the copper-bottomed authenticity are no phones, no music, no TV and of course no food, but you may bring in fish and chips from over the road.

There's raised seating, a stillage room and a cellar. Three real ales change daily. They've made an informative and decorative feature of the blackboard announcing the current ales. Gary reckons his formula is about right and has no plans to change it unless his customers make noises.

They don't do themed nights, but they do have birthday gatherings for which Julie will bake a cake. They decorate the pub for Valentine's Day and St George's Day, when there's often a visit from Morris dancers.

On our visit we enjoyed Salopian Brewery's Treasure Trove, a 4% blond ale with a tropical fruit taste and citrus finish; Arundel Brewery's Black Stallion, a 3.7% dark ale with chocolate and roast flavour with minimal hops to make it relatively sweet; and Green Jack Brewery's 4.6% Trawler Boys, full-bodied, copper-coloured, rich and malty.

The premises used to be a hairdresser, so Hair of the Dog, meaning an alcoholic drink that will cure a hangover, is not a bad choice of name.

It's minutes on foot from Minster train station and Kent Airport is nearby.

Disabled access ✓   **Child friendly** ✓
Dog friendly ✓

WHAT THE REGULARS SAY
'There is always a lively and friendly atmosphere.'

'Best place ever. Always meet brill people and the owners are a lovely pair.'

'I love this place. My second home in Minster!'

THE HERITAGE

Minster on Sea, Kent

ESSENTIAL INFORMATION
17-19 Minster Road, Minster on Sea,
Sheerness ME12 3JE
Telephone: 07984167216
Facebook: www.facebook.com/
theheritagemicropub
Twitter: @Heritagemicropb

Opening hours:
Monday Closed
Tuesday 1630-2100
Wednesday-Thursday 1200-
1400 then 1630-2100
Friday 1200-1400 then
1630-2300
Saturday 1200-2300
Sunday 1200-2000

Other reasons to go:
Elmley National Nature Reserve
www.elmleynaturereserve.co.uk;
Flynns Bee Farm www.flynnsbeefarm.co.uk;
Blue Town Heritage Centre
www.thecriterionbluetown.co.uk

The Isle of Sheppey on the Thames Estuary is a unique place with its own ambience, arising perhaps from being narrowly separated from, yet part of, mainland Kent. It got its first and so far only micropub when The Heritage opened in 2014. The glass double-frontage is – for a micropub - expansive and makes a prominent feature in Minster's main street. The pavement outside is wide enough for a few tables and chairs, so on a fine day the party is already in progress before you walk through the door. It's taken over an old post office and has brought a much needed drinking place to the area. It has become a regular haunt of Swale Cyclists Touring Club.

Owners Melvin and Margaret (opposite, top right) Hopper serve their drinks over a small bar in the corner, the ale having been poured directly from casks in a stillage room behind, kept cold with cooling jackets. Margaret was a teacher and, even before opening, a real ale enthusiast. Melvin was a London police officer and loves motor bikes. He once owned a Harley Davidson Heritage – which explains the name of this micropub.

The interior is full of motor bike and brewery memorabilia, and the atmosphere is friendly and hospitable. It's a split level room with the bar and seating up a few steps on the left and more seating on the right. The furniture is a mixture of low tables and stools near the bar and high benches and tables the other side. Sometimes there's live music - Wednesday is jam night, while Tuesday is quiz night. Every year they hold a beer festival.

On our visit five ales were on offer, plus two unusual items - spiced cider and mead.

We drank G2 Vela 4.2%, a refreshingly crisp blond ale; Canterbury Ales' Wench's Charrington Heritage (Margaret has links with the Charrington brewing family); and the excellent Merchant's Ale 4%, also by Canterbury Ales, a smooth stout with a fruity finish.

The Heritage, like all true micropubs, makes a contribution to its community economically (it mainly buys from Kent microbrewers) and socially, bringing people together often from the same street who have never previously spoken. In 2015 it won a local business award for contribution to the community.

Disabled access ✓ no ramp
Child friendly ✓
Dog friendly ✓

WHO BREWS THE BEER?

GADDS' THE RAMSGATE BREWERY
telephone: 01843 868453
website: www.ramsgatebrewery.co.uk

The Heritage and its customers are a firm favourite with the GADDS' crew.

HIGHLIGHT BEERS:

GADDS' Seasider Amber Ale 4.3%
A mellow, easy drinking ale brewed with a little crystal malt and a lot of East Kent Golding hops. Nothing flash, just a very decent malty body and a balancing hop flavour.

WHAT THE REGULARS SAY
'Amazing place with brain teaser quizzes.'

'A bright and friendly place.'

'Fantastic ales, welcoming staff and lovely atmosphere.'

'Mad Dog beer was excellent.'

Mold, Flintshire

ESSENTIAL INFORMATION
Unit 2, Earl Chambers, Earl Road, Mold,
CH7 1AL
Telephone: 01352 218188
Email: enquiries@moldalehouse.co.uk
Website: www.moldalehouse.co.uk
Facebook: www.facebook.com/pg/
    MoldAlehouse/about
Twitter: @MoldAleHouse

Opening hours:
Monday-Tuesday Closed
Wednesday 1400-2200
Thursday-Friday 1600-2200
Saturday 1400-2200
Sunday 1600-2100

Other reasons to go:
Moel Famau;
Theatr Clwyd theatrclwyd.com;
Mold Street Market

This place does what it says on the tin – it's an ale house and it's in Mold, North Wales. Keeping it simple is what micropubs are all about and this is very much what they do here.

Landlord Gareth Jones worked for Royal Mail for 21 years as a postman and then a manager before deciding he needed a change of scene. His wife Rebecca still works full time as an office manager for a local cleaning company, but helps out behind the bar and even more behind the scenes. After much research and persuasion Gareth convinced Rebecca that micropubs were the way to go: low start-up and running costs coupled with his passion for real ale were irresistable.

Located in a rather imposing Grade II listed red-brick building, this is not your typical abandoned high street shop premises. There is a keystone arched entrance and arched windows. Instead of a name sign, there are banners in English and Welsh announcing Mold Alehouse – Tafarndy yr Wyddgrug. There's no decoration: the walls are a cool olive colour and all the furniture is dark wood, modern in style, with benches and tables attached to the walls and supported by scaffolding poles (opposite, bottom left). Around the edge of the room are narrow shelves with high chairs. It has the look of an independent London café. The room is an odd shape - a pillar stands in the middle virtually dividing the place in to two rooms. A long granite-topped bar at the back has six handpumps.

On a normal day four cask ales and four real ciders are offered but when they hold a 'meet the brewer' event there are six cask ales on the bar. Wooden tasting trays

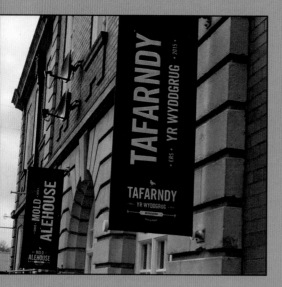

holding three beers at a time are popular with customers and there is a two-pint take-out option (below middle, opposite top).

On our visit we enjoyed Haford H.E. 4.3%, a light and fruity pale ale with a vanilla taste and a clean finish; Spitting Feathers' Thirst Quencher, a 3.9% refreshing pale hoppy bitter; and Lymestone Brewery's Lymestone Cowboy, a 4.2% pale red beer with a caramel and nut flavour.

Disabled access ⊗
Child friendly ⊗
Dog friendly ✓

WHAT THE REGULARS SAY

'A tremendous place to go for a drink or two in Mold. Great staff and great drinks.'

'The place in Mold for a great relaxing and enjoyable experience.'

'Superb place for an adult drink with none of the usual nonsense, great beer and an atmosphere where you can talk to people without having to shout to be heard.'

Newark-on-Trent, Nottinghamshire

ESSENTIAL INFORMATION
32A Castle Gate, Newark-on-Trent,
Nottingham, NG24 1BG
Telephone: 01636 312047
Email: pub@justbeermicropub.biz
Website: www.justbeermicropub.biz
Facebook: www.facebook.com/
    justbeermicro
Twitter: @justbeermicro

Opening hours:
Monday-Thursday 1300-2300
Friday-Saturday 1200-0000
Sunday 1200-2200

Other reasons to go: Newark Air Museum
www.newarkairmuseum.org;
The Workhouse Southwell www.
nationaltrust.org.uk; Newark Castle
www.newark-sherwooddc.gov.uk

Tucked away from the main street reached through an arch, this place is an escape from the everyday bustle of Newark. It's small and cosy and feels as if someone's front room has been converted into a bar. Dunc, Merf, Phil and Stu (above) run the place together and have created a unique and welcoming atmosphere.

They offer their customers beers from a wide range of microbreweries around the country, and keep it in top condition. During the week there are four and at weekends five or six, served by handpump. A fun feature is the blackboard above the bar which keeps tabs on the number of casks and different beers sold over time. Silence falls when the number is about to be changed and there's a sense of community spirit among those who have helped to maintain the record. One ale is always local, coming from within a 20 mile radius.

The drinking area is long and thin. The right wall is exposed brick while the left is covered in wall paper depicting old match books. Low benches line the walls and round tables and stools fill the rest of the space. Lantern-style lamps line the right

wall, adding to the character. Above the bar is a selection of stash including T-shirts and polo shirts with the JB (Just Beer) logo. A yard glass hangs from an exposed beam in the middle of the room and the walls are packed with old pictures, beer trays and awards. There are plenty of games to be played here: a darts board hangs next to the door and cribbage is popular among regulars. There's also a book exchange.

On our visit we enjoyed King Clipstone Brewery's Amazing Gazing, a 4% red coloured beer with a floral aroma; and House on the Hill from Duckeries, a 4.1% session ale with a caramel, nutty, dry finish.

Disabled access ✓ **Child friendly** ⊗
Dog friendly ✓

WHAT THE REGULARS SAY

'Even amongst the wide choice of pubs in Newark this is well worth a stop. Lovely welcome, quaint but most importantly bloody good beer.'

'Ace beer choices and a great cheese platter.'

'Does exactly what it says on the tin and does it well.'

Newbury, Berkshire

ESSENTIAL INFORMATION
1 Inches Yard, Market Street, Newbury,
Berkshire, RG14 5DP
Telephone: 07517658071
Email: ianbatho@gmail.com
Website: www.cowandcask.co.uk
Facebook: www.facebook.com/cowandcask

Opening hours:
Monday Closed
Tuesday–Wednesday 1700-2100
Thursday 1200-1400 then 1700-2100
Friday 1200-1400 then 1700-2200
Saturday 1200-2100
Sunday Closed

Other reasons to go: Highclere Castle
www.highclerecastle.co.uk;
Shaw House
www.westberkshireheritage.org;
Bucklebury Farm Park
www.buckleburyfarmpark.co.uk

Tucked back from the main road, among a cluster of cafés and shops, this micropub is rather hard to find. You're unlikely to stumble upon it by accident, but word of mouth means that it's regularly packed with chatting locals.

Owner Ian Batho previously had a tenancy at the Woodpecker in Wash Water, but decided to free himself from commitment and to spend more time with his wife. His new venture opened in 2014 and is very much a one man band. There are no staff - Karen provides support, but from the other side of the bar. Ian's aim – keep it plain, keep it simple – is demonstrated by the small floor area (25 m2) and the casks on view behind the bar.

True micropub values have been religiously applied, including zero electronic entertainment. This place really is a hub for conversation and despite most of the locals knowing each other, on our visit it wasn't hard to initiate a chat.

As you walk in, the bar is in the far corner. Ales are served from jacket-cooled casks sitting in a stillage. There are two tables with wooden chairs, a long pew and some bar high stools: there's seating for around 20 people.

Be prepared for a burst of colour as you enter: the walls are bright red and the floor is multi-coloured lino. Somehow they work, creating a busy atmosphere and certainly providing a different feeling from a traditional pub. Every inch of wall space is used - a blackboard covers one wall and the remaining space is taken up with pump clips, where you can see for yourself whether the beer really is local – and it is.

In common with most micropubs, the name of this place is locally inspired – there

was originally a cattle market nearby, which closed in 1969. Take a look at the amusing artwork on the sign as you enter.

There are several board games you can play, most notably crib – Ian has a team that plays in the local league. Don't worry, most of the games are not that competitive.

There were three real ales on sale when we visited, and several draught ciders. We tried Milestone Brewery's Cathedral Gold, a 3.6% golden ale; Animal Brewery's Newt, a 4.6% pale ale made with Columbus hops; and Indigenous Brewery's Moonstruck, a 4.8% full bodied, malty, dark porter.

Disabled access ⊗ **Child friendly** ✓
Dog friendly ✓

WHAT THE REGULARS SAY
'A cracking little pub'

'A wonderful place to meet'

'Superb beer and a fantastic atmosphere, what a great addition to the Newbury scene.'

BRIDGE STREET ALEHOUSE

Newcastle-under-Lyme, Staffordshire

ESSENTIAL INFORMATION
Holburn Court, Froghall, Newcastle,
ST5 2RY
Telephone: 01782 499394
Email: ferret@bridgestreetalehouse.co.uk
Website: www.bridgestreetalehouse.co.uk
Facebook: www.facebook.com/
    BridgeStreetAleHouse

Opening hours:
Monday-Thursday 1300-2200
Friday-Saturday 1200-2200
Sunday 1200-2100

Other reasons to go:
Moorcroft Pottery www.moorcroft.com;
Central Forest Park www.visitstoke.co.uk;
Wolstanton Golf Course
www.wolstantongolfclub.co.uk

One hundred per cent genuine and full of character, starting with the landlord, Graham Newbury, known as Grum to his mates, whose email address, ferret@ferretales.co.uk gives a clue to his approach to life. Ferret? Well, there is a stuffed ferret that sits on the fire alarm. This accompanied him on an epic micropub crawl that he and Tansy, his collaborator in the Ale House start-up days, made around Kent in order to 'research' their new venture. Still not got it? Tansy is the name of a flower fairy. Fairy tales sounds like ferret-ales.

If you think this is a bit bananas, don't be fooled. Graham's operation, though original in some ways, is commercially down to earth. Despite the presence of a bottle shop and a mainstream pub in the same street, his place is thriving.

Unusually, Graham keeps his cellar, complete with cooling unit, in the front window, which means easy access to the firkins when they need changing. Outside, the front is painted bright red; inside, the walls are a deep red. Among other decorations, Graham's favourite Superhero and Batman posters compete for attention with a mural-collage made up of photos of 40 of his regulars. There are three connecting drinking areas: the front with high tables and benches; the snug with wing-back chairs and the back room with conventional seating for 12-18 people.

Like many micropub landlords he deliberately keeps away from mainline beer, trying to offer the new and the rare. Besides three or four rotating real ales he also now offers rum. On our visit we enjoyed Urban Huntsman's 6% Mutiny very hoppy IPA – which Graham describes as a "proper"

IPA – "IPA should be 6%". Another unusual offering is Tank Driver's Tipple, a 5% golden ale named after Graham's grandfather, a tank driver at the Second World War Battle of Alamein who died recently. The beer is a replica of the old man's favourite home-brew recipe – an old school best bitter. As we went to press there was a plan to mount his walking sticks on to the wall.

Graham runs a regular event which he calls the Battle of the Brewers. Each night he puts on ales from a couple of brewers identified only by numbers. Whichever sells most in the evening goes through to the next round. The knock-out continues for up to three months and the winner gets a small trophy plus the chance to get trollied with Graham.

This place is housed in a building that's stood here for more than 350 years and in recent times was a school and jeweller. Graham does bar service when it's busy, and table service during quieter times.

Disabled access ✓
Child friendly ⊗
Dog friendly ✓

WHAT THE REGULARS SAY

'Like a pub, only better. What a pub should be. Dogs actively welcomed.'

'My weekend local beer is always spot on and there's always someone to natter to.'

'Excellent selection of ales and ciders. A warm welcome awaits you all the time. With a great atmosphere, you will want to visit again, and again.'

THE SPLIT CHIMP

Newcastle Upon Tyne, Tyne and Wear

ESSENTIAL INFORMATION
Arch 7, Westgate Rd, Newcastle upon Tyne,
NE1 1SA
Email: mark@splitchimp.pub
Website: www.splitchimp.pub
Facebook: www.facebook.com/splitchimp
Twitter: @SplitChimp

Opening hours:
Monday 1500-
2000
Tuesday-Thursday
1500-2200
Friday-Saturday 1300-2300
Sunday 1500-2000

Other reasons to go: Laing Art
Gallery laingartgallery.org.uk;
Life Centre www.life.org.uk;
Great North Museum: Hancock
greatnorthmuseum.org.uk;
Hatton Gallery
www.hattongallery.org.uk

This is the only Micropub in Newcastle city centre, five minutes on foot from Central Station and Grey Street, located in a railway arch. Owner Mark used to be an Ambulance Paramedic and an NHS troubleshooter until he decided on this new career after hearing a radio interview about micropubs with Martyn Hillier (see pages 6-10 for Micropubs Today).

The Split Chimp, named after the wedge of wood used to tilt a cask, originally opened in May 2015 in an arch just around the corner from the present site. The new site, a former tattoo parlour, allows a cool room behind the bar and plenty of room for both standing and sitting. The furniture includes beer barrels as tables, church pews, Chesterfield sofas and low stools. It's an eclectic mixture of old and new that gives the place an individual feel. In the corner is a guitar, rescued in perfect working order from a skip, and on one wall is a piano which anyone may play.

Upstairs is a skittle alley – the only one in the North East – the pub serves pork pies, pickled eggs and basic snacks.

True to core micropub values, the seating is laid out to encourage strangers to talk and Mark is good at introducing people. "The other day I had a Micropub owner and a Microbrewer in here and they'd never met, so I got them talking to one another." This place attracts mature drinkers - which

doesn't mean old people, rather, people who know a great deal about beer and who aren't there just to get drunk. It also attracts beer enthusiasts who tour pubs only drinking beers they have never had before.

There's background music, though quiet, there's wifi and Mark doesn't mind people using their phones. "If they're tweeting about having a drink in here, I'm not complaining", he says. However, the essential focus here is on real ale and purists will be relieved that there are no slot machines or TVs.

The bar has six hand-pulls, serving a permanent house beer, and five rotating beers. A number of breweries were approached to create a house beer: the winner was Errant Brewery's Clever Chimp 4%. Also on offer on our visit were: Fell Brewery's Tinderbox 6.3%; Left Handed Giant's Pale 4.1%; and Cairngorm's Black Gold 4.4%.

Disabled access ✓ **Child friendly** ✓
Dog friendly ✓

WHAT THE REGULARS SAY
'Lovely little chilled out place.'

'Canny bar and canny pint.'

'Mark is welcoming and very knowledgeable about his beers.'

COBBLERS

Newent, Gloucestershire

ESSENTIAL INFORMATION
7 Church Street, Newent, Gloucestershire,
GL18 1PU
Telephone: 07990 992545
Email: cobblersmicropub@gmail.com
Facebook: www.facebook.com/
    Cobblers-538864509491965
Twitter: @TheFirkinpub

Opening hours:
Monday-Thursday 1700-2100
Friday-Saturday 1700-2200
Sunday 1700-2100

Other reasons to go:
International Centre for Birds of Prey,
www.icbp.org/index
Eastnor Castle, www.eastnorcastle.com
Westbury Court Garden, www.nationaltrust.
org.uk/westbury-court-garden

A sign on the wall says 'We don't need firkin wifi – we talk to each other' – a neat way of announcing that this is a no-compromises micropub. The ales are gravity poured from jacket-cooled casks sitting at the side of the small bar – of course, no lager or key keg, but owner Ian Jones (above) does sell cider.

Other signs on the bar such as 'Nobody notices what I do until I don't do it' and 'Did I just roll my eyes out loud?' contribute to the friendly, homely atmosphere that is Cobblers' trademark – our reporter says the place (formerly a shoe repair shop) could make you feel as if drinking in your living room. Ian has worked tactfully since opening in early 2013 (he thinks he might have been the 13th to open nationwide) to make it a place where people can enjoy themselves unselfishly. Another sign that occasionally appears says 'This pub is so small we don't have room for swearing.' His regulars are a pleasant crowd.

Newent is a small town, but the high street could be in a village, with Tudor-style and red brick houses and shops. Inside it's bigger than the exterior might suggest,

with two floor levels. Chairs and tables are conventional, the ceiling beamed. Blue is the dominant colour – blue carpet, blue bar and some blue paint on the walls.

On our visit we tried Lancer from local brewer Goff's of Winchcombe: a refreshing, citrus 3.8% pale ale. Ian has worked out that for his size of customer base, four regularly changing ales (he used to keep six) allows him to keep the beer in good condition and offer maximum variety. Food is simple – crisps, nuts and pork scratchings. There's no music.

Ian, who once ran tied pubs, used to own three micropubs in the area, all called Cobblers: this one, one at Coleford and one at Cinderford. He sold the last two, which have both been renamed The Dog House, one of which is in the guide – see page 86.

He charges a very fair price for his beer - £2.50 a pint, and still makes a margin.

Disabled access ⊗ **Child friendly** ⊗
Dog friendly ✓

WHAT THE REGULARS SAY

'Firkin good beer, Firkin nice people. You don't need to go in a group, I often go in on my own and join in with a conversation.'

'What a great little gem of a pub. Quirky and very friendly, with really good real ale at very reasonable prices.'

'Warm welcome and great 'old style pub' atmosphere. Beer 10 out of 10.'

SMUGGLERS' ALEHOUSE

New Romney, Kent

ESSENTIAL INFORMATION
10 St Lawrence Court, High Street,
New Romney, TN28 8BU
Telephone: 07712 354733
Email: beer@smugglersalehouse.co.uk
Website: www.smugglersalehouse.co.uk
Facebook:
www.facebook.com/smugglersAH
Twitter: @smugglersAH

Opening hours:
Monday-Thursday 1200-2100
Friday-Saturday 1200-2200
Sunday 1200-1800

Other reasons to go:
The Romney Marsh Wartime Collection
www.rmwcollection.co.uk;
Littlestone Golf Club
www.littlestonegolfclub.org.uk;
Romney Marsh www.theromneymarsh.net

In the Middle Ages New Romney was a port on the River Rother before it silted up, with plenty of smuggled contraband passing through. Today it's a mile from the sea on the edge of Romney Marsh, an area of rich agricultural land created by the same silting process. It was one of the original Cinque Ports, an association of medieval ports that provided shipping services to the Crown and is regarded by some as the cradle of the Royal Navy. It gets plenty of visitors, not least because it's a stop on the Romney, Hythe and Dymchurch miniature railway. This history, and the passing trade, make it a canny location for a micropub.

Co-owners Lance Grist and Neil King (who owns The Firkin Alehouse, page 126) have created a functional but pleasant drinking place in keeping with New Romney's small-town character. The front (below left) is simple but pleasant with its three slender glassed-in arches; inside, the same grey-green is repeated on the walls. Antique muskets hang on the walls, and as we went to press the blackboards had been upgraded into an attractive feature.

The customers on weekdays are mainly local, and the place keeps faith with local brewers. Even at weekends, when the passing trade picks up, there are three local beers and one guest beer on offer, mainly served from the cold room, but there is a bar in a corner as you enter where you can also collect a drink. As well as the real ales they do five ciders, three wines, three spirits and soft drinks.

On our visit we drank the hugely popular Amber Ale from Romney Ales, a 4.0% light-coloured, slightly bitter hoppy pale ale.

Lance moved to New Romney in 2013.

He'd been a postman for 20 years, running as a hobby a private ale house in a shed at the bottom of his garden. Then he saw The Firkin Alehouse in Folkestone, met Neil King, and persuaded him to join him in this new venture. These days Lance is a railway signaller – the shiftwork allows him to put in time at the Smugglers' alongside his day job, but he and Neil also rely on two helpers, Julie and Dave who are trained and knowledgeable about real ales.

The Smugglers' leaflet makes clear that 'unruly children' are not welcome, and if you get a call on your mobile you'll be asked politely but firmly to take it outside.

Disabled access ⊗ **Child friendly** ⊗
Dog friendly ✓

WHAT THE REGULARS SAY
'Perfect micropub. Great beers, great service. Cosy, clean and welcoming.'

'Lovely smuggler themed micropub with real ales. Superb friendly atmosphere. Definitely worth a visit.'

'This place is dangerous. Phenomenal beer, friendly folk. Will my marriage survive it?'

Nottingham, Nottinghamshire

ESSENTIAL INFORMATION
78 Derby Road, Nottingham, NG1 5FD
Telephone: 07780 662244
Email: steve@scribblers-ales.co.uk
Website: www.aroomwithabrew.pub
Facebook: www.facebook.com/
    aroomwithabrew
Twitter: @aroomwithabrew

Opening hours:
Monday Closed
Tuesday 1700-2200
Wednesday-Thursday 1200-2200
Friday-Saturday 1200-2300
Sunday 1400-2100

Other reasons to go: Galleries of Justice of
Museum www.galleriesofjustice.org.uk;
City of Caves www.cityofcaves.com;
Nottingham Castle
www.nottinghamcastle.org.uk

Nottingham's Derby Road was a classic declining high street, with one in six retail sites boarded up, and this was one of them until Stephen Mayes, Richard Nettleton and Roger Frost transformed it. Rich and Rog ran a microbrewery 20 minutes away for a couple of years and before that they were serious home brewers. Wanting to sell their beer to the public as opposed to only retailers they asked Steve, who sold software to the television industry, to bring his sales expertise to the partnership. It was Steve's idea to open a micropub and they sold their first ales in early 2016.

Rich is an author – he published The Great Book Swindle in 2012 - and consequently named his microbrewery Scribbler's Ales. The literary theme led them to call the micropub A Room with a Brew, which is a reference to E. M. Forster's novel A Room with a View, 1908. Other beery, literary puns are on display all over the interior, such as Beerfest at Tiffany's, Masher in the Rye, and One Brew over the Cuckoo's Nest. They do at least three handpump options at any time, plus five guest beers.

A huge mirror covers the wall behind the bar. There's an eclectic mix of benches, high tables, stools and arm chairs. Literary posters cover the walls.

They organise Spoken Word open mic nights once a month where anyone can read up to 1,200 words of their work, and quiz nights every Wednesday. Snacks include cheese platters, pork pies and sausage rolls.

This place was one of two micropubs in Nottingham city centre as we went to press.

On our visit we enjoyed Scribblers' Beyond Reasonable Stout 6% (bottom

middle), more of a porter than a stout. They couldn't resist the name: the test version was so strong that it stained the glass. The regular version is not so potent. We also tried Tollgate's Kalika, a 4.5% IPA made with two English hops and two New World hops "for a lift on the finish"; and Nethergate's GB, a 3.9% amber coloured bitter, with a hint of spice and a hoppy finish.

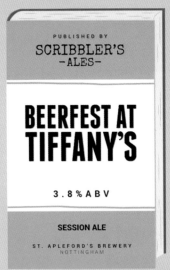

PUBLISHED BY
SCRIBBLER'S
—ALES—

BEERFEST AT TIFFANY'S

3.8% ABV

SESSION ALE

ST. APLEFORD'S BREWERY
NOTTINGHAM

Disabled access ✓   Child friendly ⊗
Dog friendly ✓

WHAT THE REGULARS SAY
'One of my favourite spots to sit for a pint or two and chat to random folk.'

'Totally awesome place, love the vintage style lightbulbs especially the two large squirrel cage bulbs in the windows.'

PUBLISHED BY
SCRIBBLER'S
—ALES—

HOPPY POTTER & THE GOBLET OF ALE

4.2% ABV

HOPPY BEER

ST. APLEFORD'S BREWERY
NOTTINGHAM

PUBLISHED BY
SCRIBBLER'S
—ALES—

BEYOND REASONABLE STOUT

6.0% ABV

PORTER

ST. APLEFORD'S BREWERY
NOTTINGHAM

Nottingham, Nottinghamshire

ESSENTIAL INFORMATION
7 Hurts Yard, Nottingham, NG1 6JD
Telephone: 0115 9243018/07896 820585
Facebook: www.facebook.com/The-Barrel-
   Drop-758853557509255
Twitter: @Thebarreldrop

Opening hours:
Monday-Saturday 1200-2200
Sunday 1200-1800

Other reasons to go: Lee Rosy's Tea Shop
www.lee-rosy.co.uk;
Nottingham Castle Museum & Art Gallery
www.nottinghamcastle.org.uk;
Nottingham Playhouse
www.nottinghamplayhouse.co.uk.

Disabled access ✓   Child friendly ✓
Dog friendly ✓

This secluded micropub is found at the very top of Hurts Yard – the narrow thoroughfare connecting Angel Row and Upper Parliament Street in the heart of Nottingham's city centre. It can be tricky to locate if you're new here, but it's worth the effort and perseverance.

Owner Chris Farnham named his micropub after the habits of a local 19thC landlord, John (or perhaps Charles — accounts differ) Hurt. Hurt had pubs on both Upper Parliament Street and Angel Row, and used the alley — or 'twitchell' (the local term) — to roll barrels and casks between them. Thus the alley became known as Hurts Yard, and more recently Chris' micropub became The Barrel Drop.

At first glance, the lighting, the filigree wallpaper and the wallpaper with a book-spine pattern — creating the impression of shelves full of books – give the place a conventional pub feel. Indeed, Chris comes from a mainstream management background, having worked for The Spirit Pub Company before their takeover by Greene King. But, with a longstanding love of great beer and a desire for career independence, he left to open The Barrel Drop — and it is certainly a true micropub. Chris' personal touch is evident throughout, whilst his knowledge, expertise and enthusiasm have seen his pub quickly gain a solid reputation for delivering consistent service and a variety of quality ales. It is no wonder so many real ale fans flock here.

The seating is comfortable and ranges from benches and padded stools to cushioned chairs with backs. There are eight different-sized tables, as well as an area by the bay window where you can sit and rest your pint on the sill.

The panelling and wooden floor boards are attractively stained, but the bar area with cask racking (opposite left) is the real highlight of this pub. A hand-built labour of love, it makes a striking showpiece. The racking accommodates nine ales mid-week and around 11 at the weekend.

The team at The Barrel Drop try to balance supplies from local and national sources, and include a range of Ruby, Dark, Golden/Pale and India Pale Ales and beers. The ABV percentage varies but they try to stay under 6.5%, and Chris looks for unusual beers that can't be found elsewhere in Nottingham. With 42 breweries within a 20-mile radius, they're not short of local, quality produce, and it is no surprise that they are approved by CAMRA LocAle. I sampled Glamorgan Brewing Company's West Coast Red 4.8% ABV Ruby Ale — richly hopped and deliciously malty, and Pheasantry Brewery's Artisan Stout 4.8% ABV — dark and robust, with hints of chocolate and coffee, and a nice dry finish.

There's also a selection of soft drinks, and between nine and 12 traditional ciders. They have no license to sell wines, but they have a bring your own bottle policy. Snacks include a range of nuts and crisps, and an excellent selection of chocolate confectionary provided by Mary Berry Truffles. I personally recommend the cracked black pepper and dark chocolate.

WHAT THE REGULARS SAY

'They sell decent beers. I come whenever I'm in Nottingham.'

'I'm for the micropub philosophy.'

'This place is not full of idiots.'

Nottingham, Nottinghamshire

ESSENTIAL INFORMATION
351 Mansfield Road, Nottingham, NG5 2DA
Telephone: 0115 960 7985
Email: info@doctorsordersmicropub.co.uk
Website: www.doctorsordersmicropub.co.uk
Facebook: www.facebook.com/domicropub
Twitter: @Domicropub

Opening hours:
Monday-Sunday 1200-2230

Other reasons to go: Galleries of Justice
www.galleriesofjustice.org.uk;
City of Caves www.cityofcaves.com;
Wollaton Hall www.wollatonhall.org.uk

Magpie Brewery in Nottingham, a six-barrel microbrewery that uses only British hops and prides itself on being as environmentally friendly as possible, has two sales outlets – Crafty Cow, a mainstream pub, and Doctor's Orders, a true micropub. The brewery was started in 2006 after three friends, Ken, Bob and Nick, realised that an early retirement and playing golf wasn't quite satisfying enough. They were all keen home brewers so went in search of a premises for a microbrewery. It now brews 299,520 pints every year according to their website.

They opened Doctor's Orders in 2012 with Dan Hancocks as landlord. Dan had been a general manager at Nottingham Contemporary, a modern art museum, but gave up to pursue his passion for real ale.

The interior has been refurbished to look like a chemist shop – it was formerly a pharmacy. Shelves of corked bottles, old-fashioned scales and pot plants cover one wall while another is exposed brick covered in blackboards. The furniture is low tables and chairs and there's a small bar at the back with five handpumps – however, they do table service here. A window into the cooling room reveals the casks and above it hangs a sign reading prescriptions. There's a large choice of craft bottle beers on sale and if you want to take some beer home there are four pint beer carriers. There's an outside drinking area with a couple of tables, but the four-lane road is noisy.

There's always one ale on sale from Magpie Brewery, while the rest are from all over the country. On our visit we enjoyed Magpie's Hoppily Ever After, a 3.8% single hopped blonde beer; Full

Mash Brewery's Red Dog, a 3.8% amber ale with a slightly malty flavour and a smooth, bitter finish; and Crouch Vale's Brewers 4% Gold, a Supreme Champion Beer of Britain at the Great British Beer Festival in 2006. It is pale, and very hoppy with a tropical fruit flavour.

There's no food, just simple bar snacks.

Disabled access ✓ **Child friendly** ✓
Dog friendly ✓

WHAT THE REGULARS SAY
'Awesome little pub, great for a couple of pints and a pork pie on an afternoon. Nice laid back atmosphere and fantastic changing selection of beers.'

'Wonderful little boozer with a marvellous set up and sweet design.'

LORD HOP

Nuneaton, Warwickshire

ESSENTIAL INFORMATION
38 Queens Road, Nuneaton, CV11 5JX
Telephone: 024 7798 1869
Email: lord_hop@hotmail.com
Facebook: www.facebook.com/pg/Lord-
 Hop-Micropub-880505602026925

Opening hours:
Monday-Sunday 1200-2200

Other reasons to go:
Nuneaton Museum and Art Gallery
 www.nuneatonandbedworth.gov.uk;
Hawkwise Falconry
www.hawkwise-falconry.co.uk;
Nuneaton Heritage Centre
www.nuneatonheritagecentre.org.uk

Nuneaton is the largest town in Warwickshire with a sizeable professional commuter population, typically travelling to and from Birmingham or Coventry each day, some of whom are regulars at Lord Hop. George Eliot, the 19th century author, spent much of her early life here. Her real name was Mary Ann Evans - she used the pen name George Eliot because she wanted to avoid the widespread prejudice in those days against women writers.

Another very different local character, before George Eliot's time, was bad-guy local landowner Edward Stratford, who made himself unpopular by enclosing common land. A serious drinker, he was known as Lord Hop, and one day his house burnt down while he was getting aggressively drunk at a pub near the site of this micropub. Rushing home, he fell off his horse, and died of his injuries. His ghost is said to have haunted the locality ever since, so Lord Hop is a fair-enough name for this micropub, the only one in town.

There's a small downstairs drinking area with a welcoming log-burning stove. It holds perhaps 25 people while a larger room upstairs fits as many as 45. 'Pure' micropubs have just one room, but in all other ways this is genuine, offering only cask-conditioned real ales from the cold room, plus a couple of ciders. Food is limited to pork pies and crisps. Tables and chairs are low – mainstream pub style, decoration plain. Customers are all ages from 20 to 70 or more (under 18s not allowed). Single women can feel comfortable here – the atmosphere is peaceful and relaxed. Landlords Garry and Barry Thomas (not related), known to their

mates as Baz and Gaz, were firemen before they started this venture.

On our visit we enjoyed Nene Valley's 4.5% End of Days, an intensely flavoured dry-hopped light to mid brown ale.

It's five minutes' walk from the railway station.

Disabled access ✓ **Child friendly** ⊗
Dog friendly ✓

WHAT THE REGULARS SAY
'No lager, no music, no fruit machines etc. If you just want exceptionally well kept real ale & a pleasant environment to drink this is the place to be.'

'What a great pub - my colleagues and I cannot get enough of the place.'

'It's the best pub in Nuneaton.
I've been in all of them and it's certainly the best.'

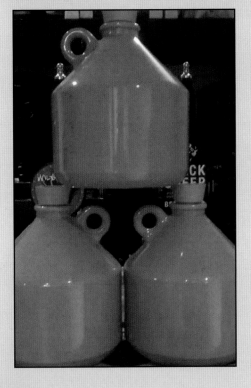

ONE INN THE WOOD

Petts Wood, Bromley, Kent

ESSENTIAL INFORMATION
209 Petts Wood Road, Orpington, BR5 1LA
Telephone: 07799 535982
Email: Barry@oneinnthewood.co.uk
Website: www.oneinnthewood.co.uk
Facebook: www.facebook.com/
   Oneinnthewoodmicropub
Twitter: @oneinnthewood

Opening hours:
Monday Closed
Tuesday-Thursday 1200-1430
then 1700-2130
Friday 1200-1430 then 1700-2300
Saturday 1130-2300
Sunday 1200-2000

Other reasons to go: Hall Place and
Gardens www.bexleyheritagetrust.org.uk;
Chislehurst Caves
www.chislehurst-caves.co.uk;
Eltham Place and Gardens,
www.english-heritage.org.uk

Barry Bridge (top, opposite, left) opened this place with his wife Sarah in 2014, determined to be the first in the area. After working for 27 years as a money broker, he'd been offered voluntary redundancy at the perfect moment. He wasn't entirely new to the world of pubs: his grandparents had owned one, and he'd grown up learning the tricks of the trade. Following their footsteps seemed natural, but, "it could have been a bit of a mid life crisis too?"

The name? The expression 'put one in the wood' often used in his grandparents' pub, means paying for a pint before the customer wants it, and for some reason it stuck in Barry's head. The punning double 'n' neatly fits with the micropub's location in Petts Wood.

One Inn the Wood can claim to be a local social hub with a large and friendly group of regulars who make a point of welcoming newcomers. It won the CAMRA local pub of the year award two years running, plus the Greater London title in 2015.

True to Kent micropub style, the tables and chairs are high and set around the edge of the room. Blackboards cover most walls showing all there is on offer from beer to cheese boards; a country landscape picture covers another wall. There's a small, L-shaped brick bar at the back, with a glass door behind allowing a peek into the cold room. Outside at the front there's more seating - fluorescent chairs and colourful casks. The exterior is clean and modern with an entirely glass front – it could be a central London café.

They stock five ever-changing real ales and a sixth at weekends to keep things interesting. Everything is kept as local as possible: the wine, the cider and the crisps are all made nearby.

Beers they have offered include: Brightside's The Optimist, a 3.8% session pale ale with a citrus aroma and flavour; and Mauldon's Black Adder, a 5.3% dark bitter stout with nut aromas. They often serve Burning Sky's Plateau, a 3.5% pale ale with a crisp malt flavour.

Disabled access ✓ not to WC
Child friendly ✓ **Dog friendly** ✓

WHAT THE REGULARS SAY
'A brilliant community micropub.'

'Best place for a drink and a chat in Petts Wood; good gluten-free beers and a great atmosphere for striking up an interesting conversation with random people!'

WHO BREWS THE BEER?

KENT BREWERY

KENT BREWERY
telephone: 01634 780 037
website: www.kentbrewery.com

HIGHLIGHT BEERS:

Prohibition 4.8%
A highly hopped American Pale Ale which has become a firm favourite of Barry the landlord.

OLD DAIRY BREWERY
telephone: 01580 763867
website: www.olddairybrewery.com

The Old Dairy Brewery is nestled deep in the 'Garden of England', just moments from Tenterden's picturesque High Street. With glorious views over rolling countryside, the brewery is housed in two old WW II Nissen buildings next to the Kent & East Sussex Railway. One has been converted into a 30 barrel brewery, complete with shop with brewery tours available.

Red Top: a 3.8% 'Classic' best bitter.

Gold Top: a 4.3% Golden pale ale.

Blue Top: a 4.8% India pale ale.

Pewsey, Wiltshire

ESSENTIAL INFORMATION
20 North Steet, Pewsey, Wiltshire, SN9 5EX
Telephone: 07769 812643
Email: shedalehouse@gmail.com
Website: www.theshedalehouse.com
Facebook: www.facebook.com/The-Shed-
   Alehouse-Pewsey-1414498185534575
Twitter: @ShedAlehouse

Opening hours:
Monday-Tuesday Closed
Wednesday-Thursday 1700-2130
Friday 1600-2200
Saturday 1400-2200
Sunday 1300-1700

Other reasons to go:
Pewsey Heritage Centre
www.pewsey-heritage-centre.org.uk;
Avebury Stone Circle
www.nationaltrust.org.uk;
The Kennet and Avon Canel

Pewsey is a large village in north Wiltshire near Devizes, with a population (in 2011) of 3,634. Then, it had no less than six pubs plus a curry house, a Chinese takeaway and a kebab shop - so the locals clearly enjoy a drink and a snack after work. However, since 2011 at least one of the six pubs has closed, and The Shed opened, in July 2015. The success of the extremely simple Shed against this competition says much about the strength of the micropub concept, and about the way people are turning away from unimaginative, formulaic drinking places and favouring ones which make them feel like individuals, not consumers.

From the outside it's a functional brick-built add-on (formerly a tiny beauty salon) to a house in Pewsey's main street. Stepping inside, you might mildly feel as if you were entering Dr Who's Tardis because suddenly you find yourself in a garden shed. The walls are lined with sawn pine planks; the ceiling is timber and chipboard, the floor is wooden. Even by micropub standards, the interior is tiny: 3.5 yards wide and 7 yards long, with the bar at the far end. There's room for 25 people.

A sign on the wall announces 'What happens in my shed stays in my shed' – amusingly to the point. The intimate, relaxed atmosphere means that people talk: as one drinker put it when we visited, "You can't hide secrets in here."

Owner Gordon Edwards (once a production co-ordinator at Honda) and his wife Samantha (opposite, top) named their venture after the garden shed where alongside his day job Gordon ran a modest microbrewery – Shed Ales - selling to a few local customers.

The Shed offers five constantly rotating ales with only a handful of repeats – more than 300 had been through in just over a year since opening. The firkins are stored in a temperature-controlled space and he has a system which allows the ale to be drawn via handpump from the top rather than the bottom. This means fresher beer – what's exposed to the air is used first.

Gordon is a relaxed, friendly host around whom the atmosphere is easygoing and matey, helped by the pleasantly uncluttered, light ambience created by the pale wooden walls and simple decoration. Besides five real ales he sells one hand crafted pilsner, four still real ciders, Prosecco, red, white and rosé wine and soft drinks plus bar snacks.

On our visit we tried Castle Hill 4.2%, a full-flavoured bitter from Dukeries Brewery. Gordon finds that bitter is less popular than pale ales.

Disabled access ⊗ **Child friendly** ✓ until 1900
Dog friendly ⊗

WHAT THE REGULARS SAY
'One of Pewsey's social assets.'

'People come here all the way from Reading.'

'Breath of fresh air.'

Prudhoe, Northumberland

ESSENTIAL INFORMATION
10 Front street, Prudhoe, Northumberland,
NE42 5HJ
Telephone: 01661598150
Email: worlocalmiropub@hotmail.com
Facebook: www.facebook.com/Wor-Local-
    Micropub-Prudhoe-457275207789136

Opening hours:
Monday-Wednesday 1600-2100
Thursday-Friday 1500-2230
Saturday-Sunday 1400-2230

Other reasons to go: Prudhoe Castle
 www.english-heritage.org.uk;
Aydon Castle www.english-heritage.org.uk;
Langley Castle www.langleycastle.com

Disabled access ✓
Child friendly ✓ until 2100
Dog friendly ✓

A few miles west of Newcastle lies the historic town of Prudhoe. A town that was built as a series of castles just after the Norman conquest and whose castle was the only one in Northumberland to successfully resist the Scots. It's also home to one of the North East's few micropubs.

Alison Thear and her husband Terry originally wanted to open an all cider pub after visiting several in Somerset, but they decided that it wouldn't be so popular in the North East. They soon discovered micropubs along with numerous microbreweries in the local area and loved the idea of combining real ale with cider as well as making their place as local as possible. The friendliness and lack of technology were also a huge appeal - there's not a TV or jukebox in sight.

They opened in early 2016, and have stuck to their wish of serving as much as possible from other local businesses; their name reflects this - Wor Local is Geordie for Our Local. They've created a place where you can come for a quiet drink while reading the paper, or chat with friends over a game of dominoes or one of the other numerous games they have on offer.

The premises used to be a computer games shop and the once garishly bright pink and fluorescent green walls are now a calm turquoise. The furniture was saved from Felling Social Club - a working man's club. The bar and carpet also came from the club and the pinballs and skittles came from a local charity shop. The decoration was a family affair with Alison and Terry's children helping to paint the place and it now has a cosy and welcoming feel to it. The walls are decorated with black and white photos of Prudhoe through the years.

The bar serves four real ales from

The Prudhoe Micro Pub

handpumps, all from local microbreweries. The cider is from Devon as there isn't a cider maker near who can provide cider year round.

They sell a few spirits – again all local. The Gin and Vodka come from Durham and The One whisky comes from the Lake District. There are also soft drinks available. Snacks come in the shape of pork pies, cheese platters and crisps and nuts.

A few beers they have had on offer are Sonnet 43 Brew House's The Raven, a 4.3% bitter porter with chocolate and bourbon; Olde Potting Shed's Cheeky Beaky 4.3%; and Alnwick Brewery's Alnwick Gold, a 4.2% golden ale with a strong hop flavour and a hint of honey.

WHAT THE REGULARS SAY
'Just what Prudhoe needed.'

'A friendly and relaxed place with puzzles on all the tables.'

'A propa mint place.'

DOGS WELCOME PEOPLE TOLERATED

Rainham, Kent

ESSENTIAL INFORMATION
121 High Street, Rainham, Medway, Kent,
ME8 8AN
Telephone: 07982 756412
Email: info@princeofales.co.uk
Website: www.princeofales.co.uk
Facebook: www.facebook.com/
    theprinceofales

Opening hours:
Monday-Thursday 1730-2130
Friday-Saturday 1200-2200
Sunday 1200-1500

Other reasons to go:
Berengrave Nature Reserve
www.thisismedway.com;
Rochester Castle
www.english-heritage.org.uk;
Blue Bell Hill

Medway already had three micropubs when this place opened, but it was Rainham's first (this Rainham is not to be confused with the suburban town in east London). Chris Strachan and Karl Martin knew that in Kent, the micropub home county, you could never have too many, and they were right. The Prince of Ales is always full despite being opposite a mainstream pub.

Both were CAMRA members and real ale enthusiasts who got fed up of not having pubs nearby that they liked. They opened the Prince of Ales in 2016, choosing the name as a pun on the overused name of so many mainstream pubs.

It's a safe and comfortable haven from the busy narrow road outside: the exterior doesn't give much away and doesn't do the cosy interior justice. The premises was a post office and convenience store, and it's still painted a royal purple, but with a scruffy corner shop look. Inside though, it's modern, slick and immaculately done up. With a wooden floor, half-panelled walls and high benches and tables, the layout is typical Kent micropub. On one side the tables and benches adjoin to encourage conversation with strangers. On the other, there are low partition walls creating space for those who want to enjoy a drink just with friends. There's no bar, and the casks can be seen through a large window at the back. Decoration is sparse but arranged well and a few barrels serve as extra resting places for glasses. A substantial garden at the back is a suntrap and provides plenty of extra seating in warm weather.

There are six members of staff including the two landlords, an unusually large number for a micropub, but they all have

day jobs as well. They are proud of the fact that they have stuck to the fundamentals of a micropub and haven't swayed from the ethos to raise profits, determined to remain an ale house rather than broadening the choice with spirits or food. They offer between three and six ales at a time.

On our visit we enjoyed Goacher's Fine Light Ale, a 3.7% pale amber bitter with a floral hop character; Tripple fff Brewery's Pressed Rat and Warthog, a 3.8% dark mild ale with coffee and chocolate elements and tasting of dried fruit and sour cherry, suitable both for those who love a mild and a bitter; and Stairway to Heaven from Burton Bridge Brewery, a 5% ale with a hoppy aroma. Beware, it drinks as easily as a 4.2%.

Disabled access ⊗ Family friendly ⊗
Dog friendly ⊗

WHAT THE REGULARS SAY

'Well done on bringing an establishment like this to Rainham, long may you continue.'

'Great little watering hole. Always pop in when I get the chance. Lovely atmosphere and always a good and different range of beers.'

'Fantastic little drinking hole.'

Ramsgate, Kent

ESSENTIAL INFORMATION
4C Grange Road, Ramsgate, Kent,
CT11 9LR
Telephone: 07890 203282
Email: landlord@conqueror-alehouse.co.uk
Website: www.conqueror-alehouse.co.uk
Blog: conqueror-alehouse.blogspot.co.uk
Facebook: www.facebook.com/
conqueroralehouse

Opening hours:
Monday Closed
Tuesday-Saturday 1130-1430
then 1730-2130
Sunday-1200-1500

Other reasons to go: Ramsgate Tunnels
www.ramsgatetunnels.org;
The Micro Museum www.visitkent.co.uk;
The Grange www.visitthanet.co.uk

This is about ten minutes on foot from Ramsgate Harbour on Grange Road which leads north, away from the sea, from the junction of Royal Esplanade and St Augustine's Road. The location is nothing special and the place itself is small and simple – a pure micropub. Landlord Colin Aris (above) is very much part of the furniture and he's been around, in micropub terms, a respectable length of time – it opened in November 2010. Since then it's won three CAMRA awards.

The premises were a florist for many years. Like many others, Colin was inspired to open a micropub by Martyn Hillier of The Butcher's Arms (page 140) and by working on the organizing committee of the Thanet Beer Festival. "If you can keep 2,000 people happy with 160 beers, then it must be possible to keep 15 happy with three" was his logic.

The name Conqueror is a nod to Colin's grandfather who was captain of Paddlesteamer Conqueror, a characterful 131-foot iron ship that worked as a tug in winter between Kent ports and in summer

taking people on cross-Channel trips. In the First World War she served as HMS Bustler. The walls are decorated with photographs of Colin's grandfather, the boat and the crew. These plus other local pictures and photographs define the ambience of the place and tell you plainly what it is – honest and local.

Colin does real ale properly by offering just three (plus two ciders and a perry from the barrel) served straight from a cool room out at the back.

Colin is a very genuine sort of landlord – "People should go to micropubs as much for the landlord as the pub" - who works at keeping customers happy but doesn't put up with nonsense. His regulars are locals rather than passing trade and include single women, couples and all ages except children. Swearing is discouraged. Before setting up here he worked most of his life in IT for a local hovercraft operator.

On our visit we drank Portobello Brewing's West Way, a golden pale ale that is much more full bodied than its 4% alcohol content suggests.

If you want to come by bus, the Conqueror is two minutes on foot from the Thanet Loop stop outside Grange Road Coop, which also stops at Ramsgate's railway station.

This is one of two micropubs in Ramsgate as we went to press – the other is The Hovelling Boat Inn, page 232.

Disabled access ⊗ but will help
Child friendly ⊗
Dog friendly ✓

WHAT THE REGULARS SAY

'Exceptional drinking experience for all, come for the friendly atmosphere, the best quality ales and ciders, and if you get stuck with your crossword Colin the friendly landlord is always on hand with the correct answer.'

'Welcoming atmosphere, knowledgeable and friendly owner, with a good selection of ales and ciders. Well worth a visit.'

'A genuinely superb example of a micropub. Colin, an avuncular advocate of good beer, sells three different beers, straight from the cask, along with real cider and wine. Don't expect to get lager here. It's as welcoming as any bar I know.'

Ramsgate, Kent

ESSENTIAL INFORMATION
12 York Street, Ramsgate CT11 9DS
Telephone: 07974 613030
Email: hello@hovellingboatinn.co.uk
Website: www.hovellingboatinn.co.uk
Facebook: www.facebook.com/
  hovellingboatinn.ramsgate
Twitter: @hovellingboat

Opening hours:
Monday-Thursday 1130-2130
Friday-Saturday 1130-2300
Sunday 1200-1600

Other reasons to go:
Ramsgate Maritime Museum
www.ramsgatemaritimemuseum.org;
Sea Searcher Boat Trips
www.ramsgatetown.org;
UpDown Gallery www.updowngallery.co.uk

A hoveller was a dock worker, or stevedore, who loaded or unloaded ships. A hovelling boat was a small boat that bought cargo for unloading ashore from large ships unable to come alongside the quay. They were also used for salvage work and fishing. In Ramsgate's harbour there used to be plenty of hovelling boats and the pub named The Hovelling Boat Inn that stood here until 1909 was a local landmark, a few steps inshore from the harbour – or these days the yacht marina. The pub closed in 1909 and became The Perseverance Dining Rooms until the 1980s, when the premises fell into disrepair. Now the old pub has a new lease of life under the care of Paul Spickett and his family. Paul was a carpenter-builder who wanted a change, thought about opening a mainstream pub but opted for the micropub formula for all the usual reasons. He likes to wear loud shirts.

The old-fashioned exterior has been preserved and is a little deceptive because inside it's relatively bright and contemporary. The seating, some of which is church pews, and the tables are all low because there are a significant number of regular older drinkers. All ages feel comfortable here, though.

The set-up is more conventional mainstream pub than pure Kent micropub. There is plenty of exposed brick and the busy blackboards announcing the beers and other drinks are a major feature. The place stands out for its calm, relaxing atmosphere, helped by the natural materials: a good place to wind down.

There is outdoor seating at the back in a courtyard – a pleasant place for an outdoor drink, or a game of petanque, says our

reporter. There is also a gallery space for local artists.

This is a genuine micropub with no bar, no key keg and three or four cask-conditioned real ales served direct from the cold room, seen through a window. Come at the right time and you can try a seasonal Ramsgate ale. Paul also sells tea, coffee, wine, bottled craft ales from Northern France and Belgium, bottled lager and some ciders, including a raspberry cider from Canterbury. Food is limited to cold bar snacks.

On our visit we tried Loddon Brewery's Potus Ale, an American-style 4.7% intensely hoppy pale ale. Potus stands for President of the United States. As we were there in the final days of 2016 presidential election campaign it was enjoyable to drink something that made us forget Trump and Clinton for a while.

Disabled access ✓ **Child friendly** ✓
Dog friendly ✓

WHAT THE REGULARS SAY

'A small venue with a very big heart.'

'Really good pub, everyone talks to anyone, the staff are all lovely, would recommend this to anyone, lovely place to visit.'

'The variety of ales and ciders is jaw dropping.'

Retford, Nottinghamshire

ESSENTIAL INFORMATION
3 Town Hall Yard, Retford, DN22 6DU
Telephone: 01777949631
Email: retford@beerheadz.biz
Website: www.beerheadz.biz/beerheadz-retford
Facebook: www.facebook.com/BHZretford
Twitter: @BHZretford

Opening hours:
Monday -Thursday 1300-2300
Friday-Saturday 1200-0000
Sunday 1200-2200

Other reasons to go:
Idle Valley Nature Reserve
www.nottinghamshirewildlife.org;
Bassetlaw Museum
www.bassetlawmuseum.org.uk;
Mattersey Priory
www.english-heritage.org.uk

In the centre of Retford, just off the market square, behind the town hall with its ornate clock tower (whose very audible chimes remind you just how many hours you've been sitting here drinking beer) is this little micropub.

Phil Ayling (opposite, second left) was a draughtsman for 30 years until redundancy sparked him into opening Just Beer, Newark (page 202). It was a success, so BeerHeadZ was the obvious next step. He wanted to bring to the town beers that were unavailable elsewhere, and to discover new breweries. The formula has worked well enough in Newark for him to have opened a second BeerHeadZ in Grantham (page 322) and he plans to open others as well. This original BeerHeadZ is sufficiently one-off to deserve a place in this guide but if it becomes part of a chain, losing its owner-managed feel, we might have to reconsider.

Phil wanted a name that sounded catchy and summed up the business. It certainly does sound 'street', and their website warns you to 'expect different'. Inside it's fairly traditional however, with low benches and stools and round tables. One wall is plastered with newspaper and magazine articles while the others are painted orange and blue. The wall behind the bar is covered in old pump clips and the bar is at an angle in one corner, painted bright blue. A blackboard spans the length of the bar above it advertising what's currently on offer as well as BeerHeadZ stash you can buy – t-shirts, baseball hats and polo shirts.

Our visit on a Sunday meant that we could sample a free selection of cheese and biscuits - a nice touch. There were five cask ales and three ciders all served by handpump at the bar. The temperature

controlled beer room is next door and visible through a small window. There's also a large fridge behind the bar with a selection of international bottled beers and soft drinks. We tried Knops' East Coast Pale, a 3.8% light aromatic beer with a biscuit and fruit taste; and Swannay Brewery's Island Hopping, a 3.9% golden ale with a fruity aroma and dry finish. Both were excellent and good value.

Disabled access ✓ **Child friendly** ⊗
Dog friendly ✓

WHAT THE REGULARS SAY
'Real ale lovers paradise, best pub in the area, friendly staff, always new and exciting beers to try. A must visit. Love Sundays cheese board.'

'Cosy, friendly, great ales - pop in and enjoy!'

Rochester, Kent

ESSENTIAL INFORMATION
378 High Street, Rochester, ME1 1DJ
Email: thenorthernseaman@gmail.com
Website: www.thenorthernseaman.
wordpress.com
Facebook: www.facebook.com/
thenorthernseaman
Twitter: @thenorthernseaman

Opening hours:
Monday-Thursday 1600-2300
Friday-Sunday 1200-2300

Other reasons to go: Rochester Castle
www.english-heritage.org.uk;
Rochester Cathedral
www.rochestercathedral.org;
Upnor Castle www.english-heritage.org.uk

M ax Heywood, Tim Dwyer and Sam Holmes, who describe themselves as 'mavericks with a vision', formed their partnership in 2016 with the aim of supporting local businesses and promoting social diversity in the quiet end of Rochester High Street. The result was this micropub, as we went to press one of the newest in the guide. They wanted to put the customer at the centre of the venture and be able to act on any feedback given, setting themselves apart from mainstream pubs.

Their ales and wines are bought from local brewers and vineyards and they hope to create a community of real ale enthusiasts in a relaxed environment where the focus is great beer and good conversation.

Max balances his job in further education with working at the micropub; Tim works there full time and Sam, a musician and choral scholar at Rochester Cathedral, also balances two jobs.

The site needed work done to it before the trio could move in. Full of rubbish and in a rather dilapidated state, architects, plumbers and technicians were called in. On cleaning the shop front, leaded windows were revealed which now add

character to the place.

The name refers to the fact that two of the three are northerners, who have come to live down south in a distinctly maritime environment. Close by are the Chatham dockyard and Medway towns. Hence the anchor on the outside window and the life belt and captain's hat behind the bar.

The L-shaped wooden bar looks like a very tidy log pile. The rest of the furniture is low tables and benches, with plenty of room left for standing.

Range Ales Brewery in Hythe have created, with Sam, a unique ale for The Northern Seaman, CQB 4%. On our visit we also enjoyed The Canterbury Ales' The Pardoners Ale, a 3.8% light golden ale with a grapefruit flavour; and Vale Of Glamorgan Brewery's Dark Matter, a 4.4% porter with liquorice, coffee and blackcurrant flavours. The Northern Seaman offers a large range of vegan ales.

Disabled access ✓ **Child friendly** ✓ until 1900
Dog friendly ✓

WHAT THE REGULARS SAY
'It's cosy, the ale is varied, interesting and delicious.'

'If you want to spend quality time with friends and family with good old-fashioned conversation where you actually talk face-to-face then get yourselves down here.'

'A real hidden gem, and a wonderful place to meet new people, enjoy a drink and be looked after by lovely people.'

Rugby, Warwickshire

ESSENTIAL INFORMATION
3-4 St. Matthews Street, Rugby,
Warwickshire
Telephone: 01788 576767
Email: sales@rugbytap.co.uk
Website: www.rugbytap.co.uk
Facebook: www.facebook.com/RugbyTap
Twitter: @RugbyTap

Opening hours:
Monday-Thursday 1000-1800
Friday-Saturday 1000-2100
Sunday 1200-1500

Other reasons to go:
Webb Ellis Rugby Football Museum
www.enjoyrugby.co.uk;
Rugby Art Gallery and Museum
www.ragm.org.uk;
Draycote Water
www.stwater.co.uk/draycote

This two-part micropub stands in a great location opposite imposing Rugby School. One part is a real ale off-licence for bottled beer or take-away ale poured from firkins. The other part is the micropub. The off-licence came first and when next door became available, expanding seemed the obvious thing to do.

Colin Arthur has lived in Rugby for more than 20 years working in the hotel, catering, wine merchant and mainstream pub trades. It was a bold move to open the off-licence while business was still flat in 2012, but he planned it in great detail, knew his target market and had a clear business plan. To keep the rent down he avoided a high-street location. He was realistic, even pessimistic with his sales estimate which he believes was a good discipline, encouraging him to watch costs.

An assortment of chairs, tables and benches fill the place, none matching. Some are low, some are bar stools and there's a table made from a pile of crates. Old pub signs decorate the walls. To create the space, two rooms were knocked into one, which is obvious from the change in the floor. There's no bar and Colin claims to provide

the fastest table service in town.

Despite being on a busy road there's outdoor seating, but this place is all about the indoor area: there are regular live music nights and plenty of games and books.

The ale comes mainly from a 30-mile radius. Colin also sells wines, spirits, meads, sloe gin, elderflower gin and malt whiskies. The bottled beers come from around the world including Belgium, the USA and Germany.

On our visit we enjoyed Byatt's Urban Red, a 4.5% ruby red ale with a floral aroma and fruit and spice flavours; Oakham Ales Oblivion, a strong 5.7% amber ale; and Crouch Vale's Essex Boys Best Bitter, a 3.8% session beer made with 100 per cent English barley malt.

Disabled access ⊗ **Child friendly** ✓
Dog friendly ✓

WHAT THE REGULARS SAY
'Nice vibe and great staff, all two of them. Makes a great change from a 'pub'.'

'Best pub in Rugby by far. Great beer selection.'

'Great afternoon in the Rugby Tap. Lovely atmosphere, great beer and friendly people. So much more relaxed than many of the pubs around.'

'Great beer, very quirky, a fabulous new venture.'

THE GROCERS

Salford, Greater Manchester

ESSENTIAL INFORMATION
152A Liverpool Road, Manchester,
M44 5DD
Telephone: 07950 522468
Facebook: www.facebook.com/The-
    Grocers-Micro-Pub-514698971966253

Opening hours:
Monday Closed
Tuesday-Thursday 1700-2200
Friday 1700-2230
Saturday 1400-2200
Sunday 1400-2100

Other reasons to go:
The Lowry www.thelowry.com;
Ordsall Hall www.visitsalford.info;
Salford Museum and Art Gallery
www.salfordcommunityleisure.co.uk;
Salford Cathedral www.salforddiocese.net

No prizes for guessing what used to occupy this site. On Liverpool Road, opposite Cadishead Park, it's next door to a mainstream pub, The Plough, but this doesn't seem to bother the owner, Martin Shallcross (opposite, bottom).

He has created an entirely different atmosphere to any mainstream pub, combined with an always-changing array of ales. Martin likes the back-to-basics nature of micropubs and the fact that he's pioneering a new form of drinking place in this part of Manchester.

Unusually for a North-West micropub, it has no bar and the ales are served straight from the cask. The casks are kept in a cool room, leaving the rest of this small space for a maximum of 20 seated customers and a few more standing in a kind of corridor.

The furniture is low wooden tables and chairs and the place has a clean and modern look. Framed blackboards on the walls display the choice of drinks along with a few old signs. Bare lightbulbs encased in jars hanging from the ceiling add a quirky touch. The exterior, with its large windows, has been spruced up with new paint. At the back is a small yard with extra seating for warm days.

Besides the ales Martin offers cider, soft drinks and some crisps.

A couple of Martin's favourite beers have included: Track Brewing Company's Sonoma, a 3.8% session pale ale; Dunham Massey's Milk Stout, a 4% full bodied ale, brewed with lactose for sweetness and with a roasted malt character; and Seven Brothers' citrus-flavoured IPA 5% with grapefruit added for bitterness.

On quiz nights the place gets rammed.

Disabled access ✓ **Child friendly** ✓
Dog friendly ✓

WHAT THE REGULARS SAY

'Martin has turned this empty building into a fab drinking place that's friendly. You can chat to people even if you don't know them.'

'A destination pub. Martin runs an excellent house, this place must be on any ale fan's itinerary.'

'What a lovely little place. Actually talked to the other customers, what a novel idea!'

Sandgate, Kent

ESSENTIAL INFORMATION
96 Sandgate High Street, Sandgate,
Folkestone, CT20 3BY
Telephone: 07944 958118/ 07958474473
E-mail: inndoorsmicropub@outlook.com
Website: www.inndoorsmicropub.co.uk
Facebook: www.facebook.com/Inndoors
Twitter: @InnDoors

Opening hours:
Monday-Thursday 1700-2200
Friday-Saturday 1230-2300
Sunday 1230-1700

Other reasons to go:
Kent Battle of Britain Museum
www.kbobm.org;
Westenhanger Castle,
www.westenhangercastle.co.uk;
Kent Downs

Gary Edwards (opposite, bottom right) and his partner Jane Sharpe know east Kent's Thanet District micropub scene well having worked at Bake & Alehouse (page 282) and The Wheel Alehouse (page 42) before taking a lease on premises in Westgate-on-Sea. Their tenure there was cut short because the landlady was murdered by her husband, so they had to start again, opening here in August 2015. They are pleased to be here because Thanet may now be saturated with micropubs.

They wanted their place to be homely. Indoors is cockney slang for being at home. Gary is – or was – a cockney who spent 25 years doing building maintenance, so the name Inn Doors brings together several relevant themes. A couple of life-size doors hang above the front.

Sandgate is quite a pleasant seaside town sandwiched between Folkestone and Hythe. The beach is across the road and people often visit Inn Doors while walking their dogs along the sea between the two towns. Gary and Jane have pitched their environment between the very busy interior of a micropub such as Fez in Margate and the very plain interior of The Firkin Alehouse in Folkestone, page 126. It's restful, something like a 1930s or 1940s living room, with grey-green the dominant colour in rectangular sections bordered by white. At night it's softly lit by candles.

Jane and Gary stick broadly to micropub rules, but there's a TV out the back where the room narrows, mainly for

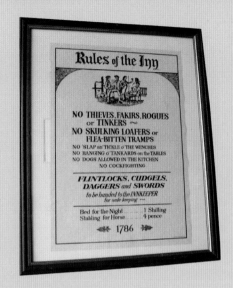

Rules of the Inn

NO THIEVES, FAKIRS, ROGUES or TINKERS ~
NO SKULKING LOAFERS or FLEA-BITTEN TRAMPS
NO 'SLAP an'TICKLE o' THE WENCHES
NO BANGING o' TANKARDS on the TABLES
NO DOGS ALLOWED IN THE KITCHEN
NO COCKFIGHTING

FLINTLOCKS, CUDGELS, DAGGERS and SWORDS
to be handed to the INNKEEPER
for safe keeping ~

Bed for the Night........1 Shilling
Stabling for Horse........4 pence

1786

WHAT THE REGULARS SAY

'Staff are fun and smiling all the time. Great drinks and fabulous platters of meat and cheese to nibble on. If you are a gin fan then you must try out all the different flavours they have.'

'Great landlord and lady. Really good beer Four Candles being my favourite.'

'Super-friendly, great atmosphere, and a lovely little dog too.'

important football games. The three to four real ales change regularly and they offer a couple of bottled craft lagers but the biggest deviation from core micropub values is their extraordinary choice of 43 gins, including rhubarb and pink grapefruit flavoured - both of which have been crazes with customers. Jane says that the gins attract couples and single women.

On our visit we drank The Mighty Oak Brewing Company's Oscar Wilde, a mellow 3.7% dark mild tasting, one customer reckoned, of burnt oak.

Disabled access ✓ not to WC
Child friendly ✓
Dog friendly ✓

STUMBLE INN

Scarborough, North Yorkshire

ESSENTIAL INFORMATION
59 Westborough, Scarborough, YO11 1TS
Telephone: 07837 716774
Email: stumbleinnmicropub@outlook.com
Website: www.stumbleinnmicropub.weebly.
  com
Facebook: www.facebook.
  com/Stumble-Innpub-of-the-
  year-x-1001256913221706
Twitter: @07837_716774

Opening hours:
Monday-Saturday 1200-2300
Sunday 1200-2230

Other reasons to go: Scarborough Castle
www.english-heritage.org.uk;
Scarborough Fair
www.scarboroughfaircollection.com;
Peasholm Park
www.discoveryorkshirecoast.com

No strippers, sword swallowers, bungee jumping or paternity testing – says this micropub's website home page - and no beer twice. Scarborough's first and only micropub as we went to press, out on a limb in a once-thriving North Sea resort, knows how to market itself as the real deal. It's a short walk from the station.

They run up to eight always-changing guest ales on handpump, which is an ambitious number, plus up to 22 ciders and perries. There's no key keg, spirits or lager – it's 100 per cent authentic – a view endorsed by Martyn and Jane Hillier of the Micropub Association when they visited soon after Stumble Inn opened in 2014.

Owner Brian Jacklin worked as a mechanic and MOT tester in Newark until he and his partner got the opportunity "to do something different. We had been part of the real ale scene for years, and knew someone who ran a micropub. We loved Scarborough and after visiting many times decided this was the place for us."

Before Brian converted the premises it was a dressmakers. It's well presented on a pleasant corner site opposite a bookmakers. An outdoor sitting area has three or four tables. Inside the decoration is pleasant but staid: tongue and groove panelling painted green to a waist height dado rail, above that cream painted walls with pump clips, breweriana and framed CAMRA awards. Seating is low level with round and rectangular tables and chairs mixed.

The customers are wide ranging – students, local doctors from A & E, elderly people who love the banter and being involved in group discussions and the communal daily crossword.

Brian offers free samples and one-third

pints of anything in his large range. On our visit we tried something completely different: an award-winning coconut flavoured milk stout 4.3% called Tonkoko from Brew York.

Regulars become friends with each other and with Brian in this very traditional place. As we went to press Stumble Inn was coming up to two years old and Brian had one regret: he should have opened sooner.

Disabled access ⊗ **Child friendly** ⊗
Dog friendly ✓

WHAT THE REGULARS SAY

'Stumbled upon this pub after a long day walking, very warm and friendly welcome from landlady and customers! Love it! Will definitely be back.'

'Wow, what an establishment! Fantastic selection of incredibly well kept ales and ciders.'

'Only a small place, but great atmosphere and excellent beers and ciders.'

CIDER HOUSE

Shoreham-by-Sea, West Sussex

ESSENTIAL INFORMATION
Church Street, Shoreham-by-Sea,
BN43 5DQ
Telephone: 07720 892767
Website: oldstarmicropubsussex.co.uk
Email: oldstar@hotmail.co.uk
Facebook: www.facebook.com/
pages/Old-Star-Ale-and-Cider-
House/271964999611750
Twitter: @oldstar1918

Opening hours:
Monday Closed
Tuesday-Sunday 1200-2100

Other reasons to go: Shoreham Fort
www.shorehamfort.co.uk;
Shoreham Lifeboat Station
www.shorehamlifeboat.co.uk;
Shoreham Farmer's Market
www.adur-worthing.gov.uk

This is a building with a long history – people say there's been an inn here (on and off) since 1300. The current Old Star Ale and Cider House occupies part of the former Star Inn on the former Star Lane (see photo below). The place has also been an ironmongers, a greengrocers, and a pet shop.

Marc Kent and Hugh Robinson opened in August 2014, but this micropub has already changed hands. The new owner is Richard Hasler, whose passion for real ale is shared by the local community. Richard used to be a building surveyor, and his keen eye, knowledge of the local area, and love of real ale set him up for the challenge of running a micropub. He seems to be enjoying his new job and his pub's a popular spot.

Don't be put off by the dark, almost severe outside – the inside is far more welcoming. The tone is softer and warmer – the wood panelling and ceiling are exclusively magnolia, with caged bulbs for lights. A few pictures, photographs and pump clips decorate the walls. There are just three tables in addition to the high-backed chairs and stools, but there is plenty of free floor space for standing. Richard's customers don't seem to mind – as long as the beer and the conversation keep flowing.

The high bar counter wraps around the stillage facility – an auto-tilt array (which helps to tilt the casks to reduce waste) holding around six casks with water-cooled jackets. A further three can be lifted on to the rack when needed. Three or four beers are typically available. During my visit I sampled Black Cat Breweries Nine Tails – a 4.9% ABV dark, full-bodied winter warmer and Brighton Bier's Thirty Three – a 3.3%

ABV dry, crisp and refreshing Pale Ale. Six or more boxed ciders and perrys are served as well as wine (red, white, prosecco, rosé), plus a selection of bottled beers and soft drinks. Pub snacks include crisps, nuts, pork scratchings and Mini Cheddars.

Disabled access ✓ not to WC
Child friendly ⊗
Dog friendly ✓

WHAT THE REGULARS SAY
'It's a welcoming place, I was intrigued when I heard about it opening.'

'It's an old-school, straight-out-of-the-barrel real ale pub'.

'I used to work in a real ale pub which is why I drink in this micropub.'

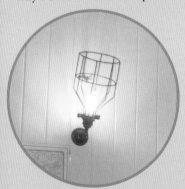

Sittingbourne, Kent

ESSENTIAL INFORMATION
2 Charlotte Street, Sittingbourne, Kent,
ME10 2JN
Telephone: 07927 073584
Email info@thepapermillmicropub.co.uk
Website www.thepapermillmicropub.co.uk
Facebook: www.facebook.com/
   thepapermillmicropub
Twitter: @TPM_Micropub

Opening hours:
Monday-Thursday 1700-2100
Friday 1200-1400 then 1700-2100
Saturday 1200-2100
Sunday 1200-1800

Other reasons to go:
Elmley National Nature Reserve
www.elmleynaturereserve.co.uk;
Sittingbourne Grehounds
www.sittingbournegreyhounds.co.uk;
Saxon Shore Way footpath

A gem tucked away in a quiet, more or less residential area of Sittingbourne, that opened as long ago as 2013 – which in micropub terms makes it positively ancient. Owner Harvey Melia (opposite, far right), formerly a musical engineer, is friendly, relaxed and really cares about real ale. "We're all about the beer", he says. "We had to get the beer storage room right before doing anything else with the interior."

He seeks out guest beers, which he believes are the best of their kind, from all over the country. He also has a strong link with Goachers, the Maidstone microbrewer. Harvey's business partner Marianne (who also happens to be his Mum) is like him, an ale enthusiast and has visited micropubs all over the country (around 140 to date) to get ideas for their venture.

The Paper Mill is on a corner site a few minutes' walk from the town centre and railway station and is named after the town's paper mills which finally went out of business in 2008 after 300 years. There's no bar – ales are brought to you straight from the temperature controlled stillage room. The main drinking area is a squarish space with high bench seating around the edges and high tables: sitting or standing, drinkers are at eye level. Sometimes you're hugger-

mugger with fellow drinkers and this, together with the absence of a bar, makes it a 'pure' micropub, echoing the atmosphere of the old ale houses in peoples' front rooms. It does get pretty packed, but luckily you can spill out into the corridor.

The decoration is bits and pieces from local pubs and breweries, many of them old tin signs or bar towels advertising different beers, "it's all about the beer". Among the breweriana there are some soft toys – don't miss the reindeer (top, middle right).

They make a point of being family friendly – on our visit a young boy playing among the long-haired, tattooed drinkers. 'Commander John', an especially regular regular, helps oil the wheels of conversation by engaging anyone who looks in need of company.

Many of their beers celebrate or commemorate events – for St Patrick's Day and Remembrance day they had special beers for the occasion. And in the mild month of May they promoted the popular type of beer – the Mild.

We drank Oakham Ales' Citra 4.2%, a very tasty citrus flavoured ale; and Tonbridge Brewery Coppernob 3.8%, a dry and medium bitter ale. The excellent Goachers Real Mild 3.4% is always on sale – and for more information about Goachers' ales, see the panel.

Disabled access ✓ **Child friendly** ✓
Dog friendly ✓

WHAT THE REGULARS SAY
'Always friendly and always great fun.'

'Just the perfect pub. Great conversation and excellent beer'

'A great evening which included a guitar.'

WHO BREWS THE BEER?

GOACHER'S BREWERY
telephone: 01622 682112
website: www.goachers.com

Kent's oldest microbrewery, based in the county town, brewing traditional real ales using traditional methods since 1983. Although the brewery moved to a new site in Tovil in the early 90s, the same wooden clad Mash Tun and steam fired Copper are still being used today. The range of beers are brewed exclusively using locally sourced Kentish hops, 100% Maris Otter barley and their own unique strain of yeast.

Skipton, North Yorkshire

ESSENTIAL INFORMATION
1 Albert Street, Skipton, BD23 1JD
Telephone: 07834 456134
Email: info@thebeerengine.co
Website: www.thebeerengine.co
Facebook: www.facebook.com/
   thebeerengineco

Opening hours:
Monday-Tuesday Closed
Wednesday-Thursday 1200-2200
Friday-Saturday 1200-2300
Sunday 1200-2230

Other reasons to go:
Skipton Walking
www.welcometoskipton.com;
Skipton Boat Trips www.canaltrips.co.uk;
Skipton Market
www.welcometoskipton.com

This is an honest Yorkshire micropub where there's never any doubt that it's all about the beer and the conversation. Steve, a retired solicitor and Janet, a retired teacher, both real ale lovers from Trawden, Lancashire, decided to open it as a retirement project in May 2014. They chose their spot well – it's up a pleasant pedestrian alleyway off Coach Street in the centre of Skipton, near the canal. There must be plenty of passing trade from visitors who come for the town's attractions (it styles itself as 'The Gateway to the Dales'), but when we dropped by at 2 pm several regulars were installed and it felt local. The atmosphere was pleasant, relaxed and quiet, the customers mostly 50 plus. The owners' colleague Steve, who shares bar duty, is knowledgeable and enthusiastic.

Inside and out, the place is unassuming but pleasing. The walls are tongue-and-groove timber in two shades of grey; decoration in the form of pictures and posters is far from cluttered, mostly beer related and mildly humorous – 'Free Beer, Tomorrow'. The interior is small and the seating conventional. As if to emphasize the owners' intention to run a beer-focussed micropub, the name Beer Engine refers to the working mechanism of a handpump. Each of the five handpumps on the L-shaped bar always delivers the same style of cask-conditioned ale, so regulars know that, the middle one always has bitter. All five pumps deliver constantly changing ales – and one is always devoted to a strong, quirky ale, 5% or stronger, often sourced via Great Heck, the York brewer.

If you don't want to chat, browse the neat little alcove of shelves for an interesting reference book.

'Great little drinking place. It gets crammed in the evening!'

'This tiny little bar is a gem serving a range of excellent real ales and providing some truly friendly bar staff and patrons who were very quick to start chatting to us.'

'Good selection of traditional beers, great atmosphere and no loud music so you can actually talk. Quite small so soon gets busy, really worth a visit.'

We enjoyed Wishbone Brewery's Epic, a 4.5% hoppy pale ale; and for a change, we tried an unusual bottled ale, Amish Mash: light, fruity and cloudy, like a German Weizen. In addition to the handpumps they offer an interesting selection of bottled beers including four speciality lagers, cider, wine, fruit beers and soft drinks. Food is limited to simple bar snacks. Steve and Janet opened, in 2016, a second micropub in nearby Cross Hills.

If you parked in the long stay car park just across the bridge, before or after your session in The Beer Engine, consider dropping into The Coffee Shop, which faces the parking: a charming, one-off, offering an unusual range of tea and coffee, cakes and light food.

Disabled access ✓ **Child friendly** ✓
Dog friendly ✓

MAWSON'S MICROPUB

Southend-on-Sea, Essex

ESSENTIAL INFORMATION
781 Southchurch Road, Southend-on-Sea,
Essex, SS1 2PP
Telephone: 01702 601781
Facebook: www.facebook.com/
   MawsonsMicroPub

Opening hours:
Monday-Wednesday 1400-2300
Thursday-Saturday 1200-2300
Sunday 1200-2200

Other reasons to go: Southend Pier,
www.southend.gov.uk
Southend Museums,
www.southendmuseums.co.uk
Sea Life Adventure,
www.sealifeadventure.co.uk
Adventure Island, adventureisland.co.uk

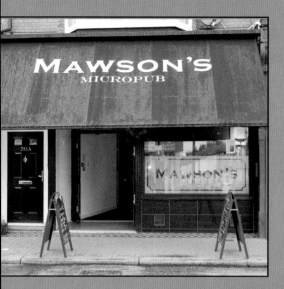

Mawson's Micropub is the brainchild of Mark Mawson - founder of George's Brewery - and the first micropub in Southend. It has a smart black exterior and the awning bears its name in stylish white lettering, giving it a friendly appearance.

Inside, perhaps it's slightly bigger than most micropubs: it used to be an accountants' office, but the only maths that is now done around here concerns how many beers have already been drunk and how many still to go. There is a mix of high and low seating with red leather chairs and benches on both sides of the room, at the end of which is the bar, hand built with wood from a boat. There are some quirky touches, such as a telephone box light, and some homely ones, such as pictures of the Mawson family on the walls, but the decoration is mostly traditional pub style. On the rainy afternoon when we visited, it felt warm and welcoming thanks to the red-washed walls and a pleasant buzz.

Mawson's – as the name suggests – is a family affair: it was opened by Mark, but behind the bar you might also find his daughters, or spot his wife (opposite, bottom) sipping wine at the closest table to the bar. After working as a toymaker and a bricklayer for 26 years, Mark was offered a brewery plant by a friend working at Ramsgate Brewery, who was selling it to make space for a bigger one. After overcoming some location and planning problems, George's Brewery finally opened in Great Wakering in May 2010. Mawson's Micropub was conceived as an outlet for the brewery and is where locals can try something other than lager.

Aside from George's Brewery ales, they offer as many as 50 Belgian beers. They

organise wine tastings where customers give their opinions about which wines they would like offered. We even heard talk of developing an app which would indicate stock levels before a visit. On offer are also fruit-flavoured beers, real ales, ciders, soft drinks, tea and coffee.

They play unobtrusive light music and Mark doesn't mind customers bringing in take-away food. Mawson's is slightly different from conventional micropubs, but the atmosphere and service are authentic.

Disabled access ⊗ **Child friendly** ✓
Dog friendly ✓

WHAT THE REGULARS SAY

'Only place in Southend to get a great selection of premium beer. Friendly staff, and they allow dogs which is rare these days.'

'Shocked and delighted at how good this micropub is.'

'Looking for a pub in Southchurch, look no further than Mawsons... but shh, it's a secret find so only tell those who appreciate good beer and a great atmosphere.'

Spalding, Lincolnshire

ESSENTIAL INFORMATION
1 Sheep Market, Spalding, PE11 1BH
Telephone: 07831 848203
Facebook: ww.facebook.com/
    Priorsovenspalding
Twitter: @PriorsOven

Opening hours:
Monday Closed
Tuesday-Thursday 1200-2000
Friday-Saturday 1200-2330
Sunday 1200-2030

Other reasons to go:
Baytree Owl and Wildlife Centre
www.baytreeowlcentre.co.uk;
Chain Bridge Forge Blacksmith Museum
www.southhollandlife.com;
Gordon Boswell Romany Museum
www.boswell-romany-museum.com;
Moulton Windmill
www.moultonwindmill.co.uk

With around 800 years of history, The Prior's Oven in Spalding is a lovely place in which to enjoy good company and great beer in a relaxed atmosphere. This Lincolnshire micropub opened in December 2013 and is run by the team from Austendyke Ales Brewery in Weston Hills.

Business partners Charlie Rawlings and Nathan Marshall have chosen an interesting spot in which to run their micropub. Grade II* listed, it was built around 1230 AD and was once part of the Priory of Spalding serving as a Monastic Prison for several centuries. After the building of the vaulted chamber, a tower was added by the Lord Prior Clement Hatfield around 1292 to 1318 and a bell once located in this tower would herald the death of felons who had been executed at the prison. The micropub cellar might even have led to a dungeon and legends state an underground passage exists which leads to Monks House, an historic building located a mile away.

Over the years The Prior's Oven (always known as such due to its shape) was used as a blacksmith's shop, a bakery, a tea room and now most recently as the micropub. It may well be small but The Prior's Oven has a lot of charm and character.

The ground floor is dominated by the lovely vaulted ceiling and wrap around bar. As you step inside you could well be drinking in a medieval alehouse. The stags head, tapestries, alcoved shelving and whitewash plaster remind you instantly of the building's heritage. Although perhaps a little cramped, there is ample seating downstairs in the form of barstools and high chairs and most people tend to congregate around the circular counter which encourages group conversations.

A narrow stone spiral staircase leads first to the small toilet and then up to a comfortable seating area, with two sofas and several padded chairs, and also a games room. Up here it's far more spacious, accommodating about sixteen people. You can see some of the original timbers and the simple chandelier now hangs in the space where the original priory bell once pealed.

Serving around six regularly changing beers (including some of their own Austendyke Ales), they stick with local microbreweries such as Tydd Steam, Nobby's Brewery, The Grainstore Brewery and others and also feature local ciders from Spalding based Churchill Ciders. The ale casks which are gravity fed and arranged on auto-tilt stillage are covered by water-cooled jackets and are directly under the serving counter. The cooler unit is in the tiny cellar directly under the bar area. I enjoyed a pint of The Grainstore Brewery's Rutland Osprey, a 4% ABV a refreshing Pale/Blonde Ale with pleasing floral notes and a smooth bitterness.

A small selection of wines, spirits and soft drinks are served. Snacks include Tyrells crisps and there is a regular selection of pork pies, scotch eggs and quiches and there is a monthly meat raffle with proceeds supporting chosen charities.

Disabled access ⊗ **Child friendly** ⊗
Dog friendly ✓

WHAT THE REGULARS SAY
'Amazing building that is worth a visit in itself! And then there's the ales. And then the friendly atmosphere.'

'Great ales, friendly people and excellent service. Best place in Spalding.'

'Great atmosphere, excellent beers of varying tastes, and exceptional company. Loved the circular bar.'

St Ives, Cornwall

ESSENTIAL INFORMATION
Wharf Road, St Ives, Cornwall, TR26 1LF
Telephone: 01736 791665
Facebook: www.facebook.
  com/The-Pilchard-Press-
  Alehouse-250406588683252

Opening hours:
Monday-Wednesday Closed
Thursday-Saturday 1600-2300
Sunday 1200 till ale runs out

Other reasons to go:
Barbara Hepworth Museum
www.tate.org.uk;
Minack Theatre www.minack.com;
National Maritime Museum Cornwall
www.nmmc.co.uk

This is hard to find: it's hidden in a cellar up an alley, off the harbour front, next to a Cornish Pasty Shop, 100 m from the pier, and doesn't advertise itself. Make the effort and you will be rewarded.

Most Cornish pubs serve the summer tourist invasion and are very mainstream, offering food, music and large TV screens. Landlord Nick Simpson says that besides his ales, being unique in Cornwall is his selling point, and it's a fair one: if you want to get away from the tourist crowd, this is the place to go. It was the first micropub to open in Cornwall and as we went to press, the only one.

Nick used to be a solicitor in St Ives until his retirement in 2014, and is now the sole owner of The Pilchard Press, which he opened in 2016.

It has a cavernous feel as most of the walls are white-painted rough stone and the ceiling is low. It's on two mini levels and while not the smallest micropub in the guide, definitely close, fitting only around 25 people. There are only two sets of tables and chairs, a long L-shaped bar with bar stools. Behind the bar are six casks, each with their own blackboard above displaying a description. It's a true micropub, focussing on real ales but also selling real ciders, wine and soft drinks.

When Nick opens on a Thursday there are usually six ales of offer. The casks are not replaced as they run dry, so he may close early on a Sunday if they've run out. He tries to buy from local breweries such as St Ives Brewery, Dynamite Valley Brewing Company and Black Flag Brewery. On our visit we enjoyed The Rebel Brewing Company's Rebel Gold, a 3.8% golden ale with a zesty aroma and clean finish. This was once a pilchard pressing cellar

at a time when St Ives was the pilchard centre of England. The fish were salted and packed ungutted, heads intact, into wooden boxes. The preserved fish, which tasted pretty strong after curing in the salt, were exported worldwide but were especially popular in Catholic countries such as Italy where fish, not meat, was eaten in Lent. A few flakes of salted pilchard did wonders for a bowl of polenta. Freezing techniques finally killed off the salted pilchard trade.

Disabled access ⊗ **Child friendly** ⊗
Dog friendly ✓

WHAT THE REGULARS SAY

'Hidden off the beaten track this little treasure fits the bill for most true pub regulars. Different beers every week with enough choice for everyone.'

'This is the best place ever, keep it a secret though, we don't want many people finding out!'

'Amazing little place. Brilliantly friendly staff and fantastic ale. Gravity fed heaven.'

GROVE ALEHOUSE

Stockport, Greater Manchester

ESSENTIAL INFORMATION
145 London Rd, Hazel Grove, Stockport
SK7 4HH
Telephone: 0161 292 9449
Email: contact@grove-alehouse.com
Facebook: www.facebook.com/
  grovealehouse

Opening hours:
Monday-Tuesday 1600-2230
Wednesday-Thursday 1600-2300
Friday 1400-0000
Saturday 1200-0000
Sunday 1400-2230

Other reasons to go: Staircase House
www.stockport.gov.uk;
Anson Engine Museum
www.enginemuseum.org;
Adlington Hall www.adlingtonhall.com

A long a busy high street, surrounded by a row of shops, lies this modern and chic looking micropub in the Hazel Grove district of Stockport. Owners Kevin and Tina Clarke were already well established beer servers before opening The Grove, as proprietors of the Bird in Hand. Inspired by their nephew to begin this venture, and after eight months of planning, they opened in 2015. Formerly Titterton's Butchers, then a computer shop, their premises are a perfect size, if an odd shape.

The decoration is sparse, with pictures of Hazel Grove in days gone by on the walls. One wall holds notice boards, chalk boards and local art; a laden book shelf of beer in the corner, soon to be replaced with more shelves and more beer; furniture mostly of recycled timber. Many of the fittings were made by the Clarkes themselves with the help of their son. They've created an ingenious cellar in the cupboard under the stairs. A low, fixed bench runs along one wall, and wooden tables and chairs fill the rest of the space, with a few stools at the bar. There's a wooden smoking shelter at the back. There is also free wifi.

The L-shaped bar, providing plenty of leaning space, is in one corner and has five handpumps and a beer mat stating: 'A friend is someone who lets you have total freedom to be yourself'. As at many micropubs, you can buy, for the price of one pint, three one-third pints, so all the beers can be tasted. There are also two to four bag-in-box ciders that rotate regularly. A fridge behind the bar is stocked with bottles from nearby breweries and if you like what you taste there are four-pint containers for take-aways. Shelving next to this offers artisan gin, rum, vodka and

whisky. They also offer Prosecco and wine and a large variety of nuts, Titterton pork pies and pickled eggs. There are also several board games, from Jenga and Connect Four to Chess and Trivial Pursuit, why not challenge a stranger and make a new acquaintance. There's a 10 per cent discount for CAMRA members, Monday-Thursday.

We drank Seven Brother's Brewery's Session craft beer, a 3.8% ale with citrus and tropical fruit flavours; Clark's Traditional 3.8% copper-coloured smooth beer with a hoppy and fruity aftertaste; and H. B. Clark's Atlantic Hop, a 4.0% pale amber ale with a bitter-sweet aftertaste.

Disabled access ⊗
Child friendly ✓ until 1800
Dog friendly ⊗

WHAT THE REGULARS SAY
'Excellent choice of ale, something for everyone.'

'Brilliant, smiling and friendly staff.'

'Proper old school, lovely relaxed atmosphere and lovely ales.'

'Fantastic place. Good ale, friendly owners and good banter.'

GROVE ALEHOUSE
Hazel Grove's First Real Ale   **Micropub**

Kevin and Tina Clarke owners of Grove Alehouse are purveyors of fine local cask ales & craft beers.

We also provide Traditional ciders & Pilsner lager from Outstanding Brewery. UK & Imported bottled beers, ciders & lagers. Wines, spirits & soft and hot drinks.

We also sell Titterton's Pork pies eat in or out.

145 London Road
Hazel Grove,
Stockport
SK7 4HH

Tel: 0161 292 9449

Beer Garden &
Smoking Shelter
TO REAR

OPENING TIMES

Mon-Tues: 4pm-10:3pm
Wed-Thurs: 4pm-11pm
Fri: 2pm-midnight
Sat :   12 noon-midnight
Sun: 2pm-10:30pm

10% C.A.M.R.A discount
Mon -Thurs

Twitter: @grovealehouse
Facebook: grovealehouse
Email: contact@grove-alehouse.com

THE CHIVERTON TAP

Stockport, Greater Manchester

ESSENTIAL INFORMATION
8, Mellor Road, Cheadle Hulme, Stockport,
SK8 5AU
Telephone: 0161 485 4149
Website: www.thechivertontap.co.uk
Email: info@thechivertontap.co.uk
Facebook: www.facebook.com/
    thechivertontap
Twitter: @thechivertontap

Opening hours:
Monday-Thursday 1600-2230
Friday-Saturday 1200-2300
Sunday 1200-2230

Other reasons to go:
Adlington Hall www.adlingtonhall.com;
Hare Hill www.nationaltrust.org.uk;
Bramall Hall www.stockport.gov.uk;
Hat Works Museum www.stockport.gov.uk

The Chiverton Tap was opened in spring 2015 by Andrew O'Shea and Bob and Mary Ellis, who met at the local amateur dramatics society. Andrew teaches hospitality and catering in Greater Manchester and Bob and Mary are lawyers.

Their site is a former draper's shop and the old proprietor's name, Arthur Chiverton, can still be seen in a mosaic at the entrance. Old sewing machines and bobbins are used in the decoration along with a giant tape measure, and drapery memorabilia is incorporated into the front of the bar.

An eclectic mix of tables and chairs gives the place a homely feel, while the double-fronted glass windows make it light and airy. A floor-to-ceiling blackboard attached to the lavatory door lists the ales currently on offer. There is room for about 50 people, and it's recommended to arrive earlier rather than later but, as a dog and child friendly micropub, this is a great place for all the family.

There are six handpumps and six taps for kegs plus a house beer from Bollington Brewery. Three of the kegs always serve beer from The Outstanding Brewing Company. Besides beer and cider they also offer spirits, wine and soft drinks. There's a wide variety of snacks, from pork pies and pork scratchings to lamb and sweet potato patties, nuts and crisps and every Friday from 12pm till 4pm you can get a pie and a pint for £5.

Among the regularly changing beers there are: Sunshine 5.7% from Brass Castle Brewery, a three hop IPA beer; Golden Age 4.2% from Celt Experience Brewery, a golden ale with a dry and bitter

finish; and Sonic Boom 6.8% from Tiny Rebel Brewery, a bold red IPA with American hops.

The Chiverton Tap also plays host to a book club, a knitting club and a home brew club: for more information, see their website.

Disabled access ✓ **Child friendly** ✓
Dog friendly ✓

WHAT THE REGULARS SAY
'Quality beer with a friendly atmosphere.'

'Great atmosphere, rustic but modern.'

'Love the sewing theme.'

THE GOLDEN SMOG

Stockton-on-Tees, County Durham

ESSENTIAL INFORMATION
1 Hambletonian Yard, Stockton-on-Tees,
TS18 1DS
Telephone: 01642 385022
Email: thegoldensmog@hotmail.co.uk
Facebook: www.facebook.com/
   TheGoldenSmog

Opening hours:
Monday-Sunday 1400-2200

Other reasons to go: Preston Park
www.prestonparkmuseum.co.uk;
Wild Animal Adventures
wildanimaladventures.co.uk;
Billingham Forum www.teesactive.co.uk;
Dorman Museum
www.dormanmuseum.co.uk

Smoggies is the name given to people from Teesside. It refers to the pollution produced by local industry and is proudly used by locals - 'Golden Smog' is a nicely positive spin on Teesside's heritage. The micropub was opened in 2014 by John Christie, formerly an army mechanic and now owner of a transport company as well as The Golden Smog. Inspired by the success of micropubs elsewhere he felt that Stockton needed one, and took the plunge. He's a natural landlord: it's hard to believe that this is his first venture into the hospitality trade.

The Golden Smog takes part in many charity events including 'we shall overcome' – a dragonboat race and The pALEgrimage, where people walk or cycle back to the micropub carrying casks of beer from over 20 breweries.

It's located down a narrow alleyway called Hambletonian Yard, right in the centre of Stockton. The outside is surprising: there are no large windows or awning, but a sign leaves you in no doubt as to what this little place serves. It's traditionally furnished, with low wooden tables and stools and the decoration was done by family and friends. One wall is papered with a map of the world, while framed photos of Teesside's heritage decorate the others. There's a framed £5 Stockton-on-Tees bank note, and a work by graffiti artist Karl Striker, also known as 'South Banksy'. The decoration demonstrates clearly which part of the country you are in.

The bar offers four real ales and two ciders and there is a large selection of bottled beers in the fridge, served in appropriate glasses. On our visit there was

only one ale under 5%, but luckily they offer four one thirds of a pint. A regular has made the quirky taster-trays, in the shape of a pub bench. We tasted the lot: Brass Castle's Northern Blonde 3.9%, a malty blonde ale made using hops from the UK's most northern hop farm; Milton Brewery's Cyclops 5.3%, a light copper coloured ale with a fruit and hoppy finish; Brass Castle's Sunshine 5.7%, a three-hop ale; and Wylam Flannel Hammer, a 7.5% porter with a toffee, tobacco and chocolate flavour.

There are also soft and hot drinks, wine, pickled eggs, nuts, crisps and pork pies.

Disabled access ⊗
Child friendly ✓ until 1800
Dog friendly ✓

WHAT THE REGULARS SAY
'What a fantastic place to relax and have a drink.'

'Got to be the best pub in Stockton-on-Tees by a country mile.'

'Lovely pub where people actually chat.'

Stratford-upon-Avon, Warwickshire

ESSENTIAL INFORMATION
12 Greenhill Street, Stratford-upon-Avon,
CV37 6LF
Telephone: 07746 807966
Website: www.thestratfordalehouse.com
Facebook: www.facebook.com/The-
   Stratford-Alehouse-187138211490381
Twitter: @stratfordale

Opening hours:
Monday-Saturday 1300-2300
Sunday 1300-1900

Other reasons to go: Shakespeare's
Birthplace www.shakespeare.org.uk;
Royal Shakespeare Theatre www.rsc.org.uk;
The MAD Museum themadmuseum.co.uk

Stratford may be the birthplace of William Shakespeare, but it's a beer desert – or was. Greene King owns the main pubs, offering dull beer served by ever-changing, disinterested staff. The rest are pub company properties run by revolving-door landlords.

Then Bill, a former postman, decided the town needed somewhere for fellow discerning drinkers who value personal service. With son-in-law Phil he opened on Christmas Eve 2013, choosing the name because he wanted to make clear that his was the first micropub in town. A down to earth place that does exactly what it says on the tin makes a pleasant change among Stratford's twee tea rooms and shops selling tourist tat.

Bill and Phil had no experience of the pub trade, so they had to buy a book on running a cellar and rely on common sense, plus a long- standing passion for real ale. The ale is gravity poured from jacket-cooled casks that sit behind the small bar.

The premises they inherited were pretty basic - a health food shop - but they've worked hard to give the interior plenty of character. Bill and his wife, like many owners, visited Kent micropubs for ideas and have brought in Kent-style bar-height tables. Bill and Phil split bar duty so customers always see the same friendly faces who know many of them by name.

There's no music except on Wednesdays when the local Folk Club perform – they've made The Stratford Alehouse their new home; and the occasional Sunday when people bring their old vinyl records.

Bill and Phil buy from breweries all over the country but their two main suppliers are local - North Cotswold Brewery and

Stratford-upon-Avon Brewery.

On our visit we enjoyed XT Brewing Company's XT1 – a 4.2% characterful, citrus pale ale based on English barley and malt from Bohemia, southern Germany.

Somewhat unusually, their drinking license doesn't allow children. Bill says that their customers understand – and we agree that a micropub can still be personal and friendly even if not family oriented.

Disabled access ✓ **Child friendly** ⊗
Dog friendly ✓

Strood, Rochester, Kent

ESSENTIAL INFORMATION
37 North Street, Strood, Rochester,
ME2 4SJ
Telephone: 07941 449137
Website: www.1050fromvictoria.co.uk
Facebook: www.facebook.
   com/1050fromVictoriaPub

Opening hours:
Monday-Thursday 1600-2100
Friday-Saturday 1200-2215
Sunday Closed

Other reasons to go: Rochester Castle
www.english-heritage.org.uk;
Rochester Cathedral
www.rochestercathedral.org;
Upnor Castle www.english-heritage.org.uk

If you catch any train from Victoria to Rochester and count the arches over the track, on the edge of Rochester at Strood you will find yourself passing under arch number 1,050, which also happens to be the location of this micropub. That's why it was named - nothing to do with raising two fingers at commuter trains - though the three mature gentlemen who started it do describe themselves on their website as grumpy old men.

Bob (70 as we went to press), Gary (68) and Werner (just 59) were a joiner, a plasterer and a master chef in their former lives, and each has a pension, so they don't have the gnawing day-to-day anxiety of what to do next if their venture fails. In any case, the odds on this happening struck us as remote. 10:50 not only has a terrific location under the railway arches but three additional, highly commercial assets: a large, sunny outdoor garden with plenty of seating; a big car park opposite; and no traffic roaring past the front door. It's obviously popular and on our visit was full to the brim with a lively crowd – and no sign of grumpiness from the guvnors.

They did most of the conversion work to the site (owned by Bob) over six months, at the same time as 'researching' ales from various breweries. They made sure they always had a firkin on the spot for themselves and friends who dropped in to see how the work was going. When they finally opened, the pump clips were counted and it was found that they'd really done quite a lot of research.

The inside is littered with mainly railway-themed memorabilia – "a load of old junk" as Bob calls it. Don't miss the vintage cash register.

One of the high spots here is their annual Irish day with bands and Irish dancers in the garden, plus many pump clips to count.

This is a genuine micropub – no music, no food, no TV; conversation flows, often between strangers. They serve real ales, cider and wine and on our visit we enjoyed – what else – the excellent 1050 from Grainstore Brewery – 5% and a great copper colour.

Disabled access ✓ **Child friendly** ⊗
Dog friendly ✓

WHAT THE REGULARS SAY
'Who would have thought there was such a lovely little oasis in the middle of Strood!'

'Great ale, great atmosphere, great location.'

'The best pub for miles, great work guys'

'Wow what a place this is! Any micropub or real ale fan must visit. So much character, the building is just fantastic, in a disused railway arch.'

THE LITTLE GEORGE

Stroud, Gloucestershire

ESSENTIAL INFORMATION
21 George Street, Stroud, GL5 3DP
Telephone: 01453 750300/
0771 293 7883
Email: info@stroudmicropub.co.uk
Website: www.stroudmicropub.co.uk
Facebook: www.facebook.com/pg/
    StroudMicropub
Twitter: @StroudMicropub

Opening hours:
Monday Closed
Tuesday-Thursday 1600-2100
Friday 1600-2300
Saturday 1200-2300
Sunday Closed

Other reasons to go: Woodchester Mansion
www.woodchestermansion.org.uk;
Gloucester Cathedral
www.gloucestercathedral.org.uk;
Great Witcombe Roman Villa
www.english-heritage.org.uk

Landlord John Morgan thought that Stroud needed a quiet and relaxing place in which to drink and have a chat – simple as that. The locals thought so too – on the opening weekend in early 2016 the place was packed to bursting and John has never looked back.

He worked in hospitality for a year, part of which was in The Glengower in Aberystwyth whose bar specialises in real ales. As he learned how to keep the ale in condition his passion for it grew. Before The Glengower he studied Biochemistry at Aberystwyth University.

In keeping with the simplicity of the micropub concept, John kept the name simple too. It's located on George Street and just round the corner from the George Holloway statue which honours one of the largest employers in Stroud's history. George Holloway was a clothing manufacturer who, with his brother Henry, set up a clothing wholesale and manufacturing business in the town, and can claim to have introduced sewing-machines and ready-to-wear clothes to Britain.

Casks sit on view behind the bar and the ale is served by gravity. Four ales are on offer during the week and five at weekends along with three ciders. For events, and during the Stroud Fringe which takes place in August, they increase the choice to six. There's also a wide range of Belgian beers – more than anywhere else in Stroud - and John offers nine different gins including the world's first non-alcoholic gin, Seedlip 108 made with distillates of hay and spearmint.

The furniture is low tables and chairs and there's artwork from local artists on the walls alongside blackboards. John offers

sharing platters of charcuterie and cheese or you can order from Fat Toni's Pizzeria to have food delivered to your table. There are soft drinks for children and free dog treats for furry friends.

There was a bespoke ale - A Little Georgeous 3.6%, brewed by Hal's Ales, an up-and-coming one man band whose operator is slowly tuning a hobby into a business. They serve an ale from here once a month. We also enjoyed Rusty Lane 4.4% from The Kennet and Avon Brewery, a red ale with toffee malt flavours.

Disabled access ⊗ **Child friendly** ✓
Dog friendly ✓

WHAT THE REGULARS SAY
'Great little pub, very friendly atmosphere and gorgeous pies.'

'Good range of lesser seen real ale direct from the barrel.'

'A dog friendly pub, with good beer and dog treats.'

Swansea

ESSENTIAL INFORMATION
2 Dunns Lane, Swansea SA3 4AA
Telephone: 07971194838
Email: jesarmor@icloud.com
Facebook: www.facebook.com/
   mumblesalehouse

Opening hours:
Monday-Tuesday Closed
Wednesday-Thursday 1600-2300
Friday-Saturday 1200-2300
Sunday 1200-2230

Other reasons to go: Oystermouth Castle
swansea.gov.uk;
Dylan Thomas Centre
www.dylanthomas.com;
Clyne Gardens www.swansea.gov.uk

This was the first micropub in Wales. Owners Rod and Karen (bottom left), who have now sold the place, followed the micropub movement from its start, and seeing its success, decided to start their own in 2014. Both are members of the Swansea CAMRA, which gave them the opportunity to launch Mumbles at the annual Swansea beer festival attended by thousands of real ale fans. They now have customers from all around the UK and are packed every night.

A stone's throw from the seafront in Mumbles, on a quiet road just off the high street, it's well located for a beach walk and a beer. You can't quite see the sea from the outside seating area, but walk on to the lane and there it is.

At first, Rod and Karen served ales from casks held in a stillage behind the bar, then quickly upgraded to three handpumps. The casks are now stored in an air-conditioned shed at the back of the premises and besides these regularly changing ales, Mumbles offers one beer: the popular Butty Bach from Wye Valley Brewery. There are also wines and bottled beers, and if you're hungry some great pork pies. Rod collected the beer from the distributors himself as they didn't want to deliver to this relatively remote location. As a result, Rod had a personal relationship with the local breweries.

This micropub seems small from the outside, just a doorway dwarfed by the Slate art gallery next door and above. But inside it stretches back further than you might expect, with the bar on the left plus attractive wooden bar stools and high chairs. A huge blackboard tells you what's on offer and a few pictures decorate the walls. Pale green and white paint gives the interior a clean modern finish.

Mumbles is faithful to the core micropub concept: there is no technology, no lager (a hard decision they haven't regretted) and no music except for a live music afternoon on Sundays - a crowded time to visit - beware.

On our visit we drank Bishops Farewell, a 4.6% light golden beer with a dry finish; and Grumpy Guvnor, a 4.5% black cherry ale with a biscuit malt base and a touch of spice. The line-up changes every week and in the first 18 months alone Mumbles stocked more than 700 different ales. They try to find ales with lower ABVs, such as Tiny Rebel's Cereal Killer ABV 3%, an especially strong seller.

Disabled access ⊗ **Child friendly** ✓
Dog friendly ✓

WHAT THE REGULARS SAY
'What a gem. Pubs like this are so hard to find.'

'Best ale house in Swansea.'

'Excellent beer and a convivial atmosphere. No gastro food or music. What's not to like?'

Tamworth, Staffordshire

ESSENTIAL INFORMATION
51 Lower Gungate, Tamworth, B79 7AS
Telephone: 07989 805828
Email: ontact@kingsditch.co.uk
Website: www.kingsditch.co.uk
Facebook: www.facebook.com/
   The-Kwww.kingsditch.co.ukings-
   Ditch-1508415806063834

Opening hours:
Monday Closed
Tuesday-Wednesday 1700-2100
Thursday 1700-2230
Friday 1600-2230
Saturday-Sunday 1200-2230

Other reasons to go: Tamworth Castle
www.tamworthcastle.co.uk;
Church of St Editha www.stedithas.org.uk;
Erasmus Darwin House
www.erasmusdarwin.org;
Drayton Manor Theme Park
www.draytonmanor.co.uk

Until the 19thC a Saxon fortification, in the form of a ditch, was visible only a few yards away from this micropub. Known as the King's Ditch, it gave this place a name on a plate.

The town also has a long and rich history. The name Tamworth literally means an enclosure by the River Tam, and Tamworth Castle is just a few minutes walk away from here.

Set up by Dave, Ade and Ged in an old bicycle shop this place has plenty of character with bare, brick walls and a mock-Tudor ceiling. After visiting several micropubs in Kent the trio caught the bug and combined to launch their own venture, opening in 2014. Among their aims is to offer a fresh choice of beers compared with other pubs in the area and they do this by searching out new beer from fresh microbreweries.

In common with many micropubs, this place doesn't have a bar, making it open and accessible with no barriers or separate areas within the room. Instead, there is a small counter in the corner where you place your order. You feel as if you are stepping back in time to the days of simply chatting over a pint, no frills attached.

There is a TV, but it doesn't show the latest match. The screen displays the 'cellar', so you can watch your beer being poured on CCTV. We asked Jed and Adrian what had inspired this: they said it was cheaper than knocking a hole between the two rooms.

A long, cushioned bench runs around the walls and wooden tables, plus stools fill, the rest of the space. There's a small upstairs room, so in total the place seats around 40. The walls are decorated with beer clips and a Staffordshire pub crawl poster. There are

take-away food menus, but if you want to buy food, you must also buy a drink - no hardship. There's also take-away beer or cider in two-pint cartons.

When we visited there were four cask ales and no fewer than 15 real ciders on sale. It's no surprise that this place has been awarded the Cider Pub of the Year 2015. They come in a variety of strengths and, maybe not for purists, they offer flavoured ciders such as blackberry and ginger.

We drank: Nene Valley's Starless Stout, a 4.2% oat stout with a hop bite to finish; Exit 33's Mosaic, a 4.1% pale ale with a tropical, fruity flavour; and Wantsum's Golgotha, a 5.5% rich stout with a blackcurrant and liquorice flavour.

Every Wednesday there's a cheese night and pork pies and sausage rolls are always on offer.

Disabled access ✓ not to WC
Child friendly ✓ until 1900

WHAT THE REGULARS SAY
'Amazing service, everyone is so friendly'

'Such a relaxing place to come and enjoy great beer.'

'Bringing back the art of good conversation.'

THE OLD POST OFFICE

Warwick, Warwickshire

ESSENTIAL INFORMATION
12 West Street, Warwick, Warwickshire,
CV34 6AN
Telephone: 07765 896155
E-mail: oldpostofficewarwick@gmail.com
Facebook: www.facebook.com/
   oldpostofficewarwick

Opening hours:
Monday Closed
Tuesday-Saturday 1200-2100
Sunday 1200-1700

Other reasons to go: Warwick Castle
www.warwick-castle.com;
Charlecote Park www.nationaltrust.org.uk;
The Royal Regiment of Fusiliers Museum
www.warwickfusiliers.co.uk;
Stoneleigh Abbey www.stoneleighabbey.org

A four-minute walk from Warwick Castle on a street of Tudor-style and Edwardian houses, this place looks large from the outside. Look closer, and you'll realise that half of it's a barber shop. With matching black paint and red lettering the two businesses have collaborated to make it look as if the building is still as it once was.

Tom had managed and run brewery-owned pubs for 38 years, when he decided to put his experience to good use by opening a micropub. The concept appealed especially because it gave him the freedom to put his own stamp on a pub, and because it enabled him to buy ale from any brewery rather than be tied to specific breweries at specific prices. This hugely important advantage of micropubs is explained more fully in the introduction, page xx, and is why micropubs are booming and traditional pubs are struggling.

The Old Post Office is on split-levels. To get to the bar, you must first negotiate a small, square wood-panelled room packed with memorabilia, trinkets, bookshelves and hunting trophies. Up a few steps is the bar area and beyond this there is another small drinking area.

The decoration is eclectic, collected over several years, and some of the items have been on display in Tom's previous pubs.

Customers can choose to have their beer handpulled, or poured by gravity from the cask. The beers come from local breweries, but the staple option is Saddleback Bitter, brewed by Slaughterhouse Brewery, only a mile and a half away.

There's no food but customers are welcome to bring their own or order a take-away from nearby.

Beers Tom has offered include: Gun Dog

WHAT THE REGULARS SAY

'Looks like it has been open for centuries despite it being only a couple of years old.'

'We loved this quirky place in Warwick, with its fun decoration and handpumped ales.'

Ales' Chilly Dog, a 4% ruby ale with a malty, sweet, faintly chocolate taste; Church End's Just Like Honey, a 4.2% deep gold, autumnal beer, combining spicy hoppiness with a sweet honey flavour; and Wells and Youngs' Young's Special, a 4.5% bronze ale with a rich, malty, orange and hop aroma. The taste is tangy and smokey with a hint of marmalade.

Disabled access ✓ not to WC
Child friendly ⊗
Dog friendly ✓

Welling, Kent

ESSENTIAL INFORMATION

11 Welling High Street, Kent, DA16 1TR

Telephone: 07956 845509

Website: www.thedoorhinge.co.uk

Facebook: www.facebook.com/
thedoorhinge

Twitter: @TheDoor_Hinge

Opening hours:

Monday Closed

Tuesday-Thursday 1500-2100

Friday 1500-2200

Saturday 1200-2200

Sunday 1200-1500

Other reasons to go: Danson Park
www.bexley.gov.uk;
Red House www.nationaltrust.org.uk;
Woodlands Farm Trust
www.thewoodlandsfarmtrust.org

As one door closed another opened; and so began the story of London's first permanent micropub. Opening The Door Hinge in Welling in March 2013 proved to be a right turn for former London cabbie Raymond Hurley. Tired of being a black cab driver, Ray took the plunge. He ditched the keys to his hackney carriage and set up his own ale house, breathing new life into an abandoned shop unit. Like many micropubs, its name was formed from a delightful play on words; in this case celebrating Ray's late mum, Doreen "Dor" Indge.

Stepping into the Door Hinge you're entering Ray's world – in fact, it feels more like you've been welcomed into his home. The Lilliputian pub has a genuine cosiness, and within minutes we were greeted by several affable regulars.

For those who seek a more reflective setting, out back there is an even more intimate 'quiet room' with a real fire and comfortable seats. It's remarkably reminiscent of one's own living room sans the obligatory television. When we visited on a sunny bank holiday weekend the room was not in use, but it's not difficult to imagine how snug it would be on a cold, winter evening.

Drinks and snacks are served from a small bar counter. Beyond it you can see the cooled tap room through a large glass window – patrons can watch their drink of choice being poured directly from a satisfying range of regularly-rotated cask ales kept on stillage.

It was a great shame that Ray wasn't there during our all-too-short visit, and, as a consequence, we were unable to meet the man who is already a celebrated personality in Welling. However, we could still feel his playfulness thanks to the witty prints and

whimsical rhymes amongst the customary assortment of breweriana, pump clips and hop bines.

A couple of the regulars told us how fastidiously Ray keeps and serves his ales to ensure they are in tiptop condition. No wonder then that The Door Hinge was awarded both CAMRA Bexley Branch Pub of the Year 2014 and CAMRA Greater London Regional Pub of the Year 2014 — both just one year after opening. It goes to show that this chap really does have 'The Knowledge.'

A visit to The Door Hinge is wholeheartedly recommended. Just don't be surprised if you find Ray serving drinks and gabbing to you with his back turned — some habits are hard to break!

Disabled access ✓ not to WC
Child friendly ✓ **Dog friendly** ✓

WHAT THE REGULARS SAY
'It's blind to people's backgrounds, promotes conversation and there are no distractions.'

'Ray knows the types of beers I like and those I don't'.

'Many of the customers have become like family to me, and the surroundings feel safe. There are not many pubs I'd feel happy to sit alone, but the Door Hinge is one.'

WHO BREWS THE BEER?

KENT BREWERY

KENT BREWERY serves the Door Hinge
telephone: 01634 780 037
website: www.kentbrewery.com

HIGHLIGHT BEERS:

Pale 4.0%
A favourite with supporters of the local Welling Football Club. A full-flavoured, aromatic, golden Pale Ale.

Prohibition 4.8%
A highly hopped American Pale Ale which has become a firm favourite of Ray the landlord.

Green Giant 6%
A Green Hop IPA made with fresh hops straight from the harvest. Only available in the early Autumn, but the locals talk about it for the other 11 months!

THE LITTLE ALEHOUSE

Wellingborough, Northamptonshire

ESSENTIAL INFORMATION
14A High Street, Wellingborough, NN8 4JU
Telephone: 07787 446460
Email: micropub@outlook.com
Facebook: www.facebook.
com/The-Little-Ale-House-
Wellingborough-734405356668421

Opening hours:
Monday-Tuesday Closed
Wednesday-Thursday 1200-2100
Friday 1200-2330
Saturday 1200-2100
Sunday 1200-1600

Other reasons to go: Jungle Parc
www.jungleparc.co.uk;
The Castle Theatre
www.thecastle.org.uk;
Wellingborough Museum
www.wellingboroughmuseum.co.uk

Wellingborough's first micropub (and the second one opened in the county) is a small and smart little alehouse that ticks all the boxes. Owner Martin Clarke was the landlord of Harrold's Oakley Arms for three years, so he is no stranger to serving real ales. As with so many others frustrated with the mainstream pub scene, he looked to the micropub model as a means to achieve his goals and ideals. He wanted to give something back to the area – a business venture that he could share with the local community.

The dark pub exterior matches the other shop-fronts on the high street – perhaps a little dreary and understated – but the sign stands out with its attractive wood-panel border. The inside is appealing, and the cobalt-blue walls work well with the stained floor and furnishings, and I even liked the faux-brickwork wallpaper. The decoration is simple and uncluttered, with a variety of old, black-and-white photographs on the walls. The shelving, drink and snack boards are made from reclaimed window frames, and the serving counter and stillage rack are solid wood and hand built.

There are four tables, including two made from reused beer casks, and an attractive sheesham wood table by the main window. With a low bench, some bar stools and a few chairs, seating is limited. While the place claims to fit 30, most people would have to stand. It's cosy, with a small electric fire for cold days.

Three rotating ales are served directly from casks, and there is also one handpump. There is one national beer each week, which the customers get to choose: when you buy a drink you are given a 'pea' to place in one of three pots to indicate

your choice. Spend your pennies on beer, 'pea' in a pot, help select a new beer, and the whole cycle starts again. During my visit I enjoyed Phipps N.B.C Beckett's Ale – a 4.5% ABV, rich, dark, honeyed speciality beer, and Nene Valley Brewery's Release The Chimps – a 4.4% ABV Pale Ale with a floral hop flavour. Four ciders are available, and a selection of wines (red, white, rosé, Prosecco) and soft drinks.

Disabled access ✓ **Child friendly** ✓
Dog friendly ✓

WHAT THE REGULARS SAY
'It's very friendly, even when quiet.'

'No telly, no trouble. You can converse with people. It's the way forward'.

Wells, Somerset

ESSENTIAL INFORMATION
38 Market Street, Wells, Somerset,
BA5 2DS
Telephone: 01749 678480
Email: andy@justales.com
Website: www.justales.com
Facebook: www.facebook.com/Just-
   Ales-203076986722145

Opening hours:
Monday-Thursday 1200-2100
Friday-Saturday 1200-2300
Sunday 1200-2100

Other reasons to go: Wells Cathedral
www.wellscathedral.org.uk;
The Bishop's Palace
www.bishopspalace.org.uk;
Mendip Hills www.mendiphillsaonb.org.uk
Cheddar Gorge www.cheddargorge.co.uk

Wells is the smallest city in England, famous for its cathedral and moated Bishop's Palace. It's surrounded by beautiful countryside and the heart of the city dates back to the Middle Ages. It's now home to Somerset's first micropub, Just Ales.

Landlord Andy Le Grange (below left) had been thinking about opening a micropub in the south west for more than a year, believing in the concept because of its adaptability to local needs. Friend and business partner Peter Carr helped him search for the site, and as soon as they saw it they knew it was right because it was in keeping with the city's character: down a small street with stone walls and filled with small independent shops, it was away from most of the traffic but had free parking outside.

Andy and Peter worked in the pub trade for more than 20 years so understood the advantage of being independent and small. They mainly buy from local breweries, but also welcome guest ales from all over the country. Instead of a bar there's a small counter at the entrance with a blackboard behind covering the space under the stairs. The drinking area is on two levels - a couple of steps take you down to the back where casks are lined up along one wall in cold jackets, dispensing the ale by gravity. A selection of local maps and pictures of the area decorate the walls, surrounded by pump clips. There's a games corner and a cider corner in the back plus a shelf displaying the bottled beers on offer. A magazine rack provides reading material and in one corner there's a dog bed.

Besides ale, they offer a big selection of local farm ciders. Snacks include pork pies from the local farm shop, a vintage

cheddar cheese bowl (stored for a month for extra taste), nuts, crisps and scratchings. A loyalty card gives you your 11th pint free. On our visit we enjoyed Black Tor Brewery's Raven, a 4.2% chestnut brown ale with a caramel flavour and summer fruit aromas; and Navigation Brewery's Golden Anchor, a 4.3% golden draught with a biscuit flavour and aromas of fruit and malt.

Disabled access ✓ **Child friendly** ✓
Dog friendly ✓

WHAT THE REGULARS SAY
'Great beer, lovely cider, drinks served the way they should be.'

'Proper pub with fab beers to try all from small producers.'

'Well kept and good variety of real ales. Very friendly owner who also serves probably the best pork pies.'

BAKE AND ALEHOUSE

Westgate-on-Sea, Kent

ESSENTIAL INFORMATION
21 St. Mildreds Road, Westgate-on-Sea,
CT8 8RE
Telephone: 07913 368787
Email: johnmorphy17@gmail.com
Website: www.bakeandalehouse.com
Facebook: www.facebook.com/Bake-
    Alehouse-103188709767943

Opening hours:
Monday Closed
Tuesday-Saturday 1200-1400
then 1730-2100
Sunday 1200-1430

Other reasons to go: Powell-Cotton
Museum www.quexpark.co.uk;
St Mildred's Bay, CT8 8AU;
Ramsgate Maritime Museum
www.ramsgatemaritimemuseum.org

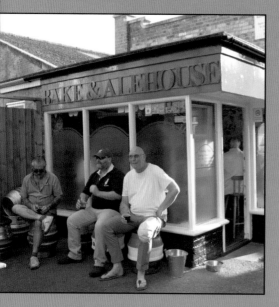

The story of John Morphy, who'd been the new owner of the Bake & Alehouse for about 12 weeks when we visited in August 2016, says much about the micropub movement, about the people who get involved, and perhaps about the independent streak which runs deep in so many Brits.

John had worked here under the previous landlord on several occasions. One evening in October 2015, Peter Williams, then owner (now one of John's better customers), invited him for a casual drink, which he thought a bit odd. "He said he was going to sell it… and that he wanted me to have it. Did I want it? I went home to my wife and said, Yup, he's offered me the ale house. She said, Well, what do you think? and I said Well, I'm interested. I was getting quite stressed at work, I was kind of wanting to kill people, and my wife was telling me I would be dead in two years if I carried on like that. So she said, Just do it.

There was a quick rally round while we thought about the finances, the mortgage and so on. After looking at the trading figures, I went for it. So after 34 years of working as a buyer in the aviation industry I went from a regular monthly pay cheque to this – sleepless nights. But it's absolutely fantastic, I could not love it more. I've now doubled my hours – I'm doing 70, but it doesn't feel like that, it doesn't really feel like work."

He gets a little help from a nephew, but only at busy times "because I don't like people waiting too long – they've always got a thirst, so when they want a beer, they get a beer."

Outside, the premises (many years ago a bakery) has been re-painted a pleasing

Harrods green, but inside John had made few changes by the time we went to press, except planning a new stainless steel kitchen. It doesn't have the traditional raised seating typical of Kent micropubs, intended to encourage conversation, but John still finds that strangers get chatting. "I call this a community centre, I don't call it a pub."

On our visit we tried one of John's most popular beers, Dark Star Brewery's Partridge, a 4% best bitter brewed in traditional Sussex style and relying on a heavy-handed addition of aromatic hops late in the boil.

Besides seven regular beers (he plans to have ten) John sells one or two ciders, crisps, nuts, pork pies from a deli down the road and a local cheese.

Under John's tenure this will always be a genuine ale house (not a cider house), but, he says, "It's as much about the people that come through the door as the beer. The beer should be a given, but I do get told the beer is good."

Disabled access ⊗ **Child friendly** ✓
Dog friendly ✓

WHAT THE REGULARS SAY

'The Bake and Alehouse is a pearl in the oyster that is Westgate. Excellent beers and snacks supported by an excellent host and friendly and amusing clientele.'

'It's got everything: conversation, like minded people, proper beer at proper prices.'

'Best ale house in Thanet by a mile.'

Whitstable, Kent

ESSENTIAL INFORMATION
66 High Street, Whitstable, CT5 1BB
Email: mike@mikemcwilliam.com
Facebook: www.facebook.com/
   The-Black-Dog-Whitstables-Micro-
   Pub-419868708067222

Opening hours:
Monday-Wednesday 1200-2300
Thursday-Sunday 1200-0000

Other reasons to go: Whitstable Castle
www.whitstablecastle.co.uk;
Whitstable Play House
www.playhousewhitstable.co.uk;
The Horsebridge Centre
www.horsebridge-centre.org.uk

All micropubs should be one-offs, but this one does it with knobs on. It's a strange cocktail, possibly even more off the wall than The Firkin Shed in Bournemouth (page 46). The style could be described as dark Gothic or perhaps twisted Victorian. Moreover, the name is rich in possible meanings. 'Black Dog' is a term used famously by Winston Churchill for depression; it's the name of a well known Led Zeppelin song; and in English folklore, black dogs are night-time apparitions associated with hell and the devil. 'Moody' or 'something of the night' are perhaps apt descriptions of the effect – and it may not be for everyone.

Owner Mike McWilliam (opposite, bottom), a photographer, is one of many owners inspired by Martyn Hillier of The Butcher's Arms (page 140), to go it alone. He responded to Martyn's key messages: that micropubs are cheap to start up and simpler to run profitably than mainstream pubs. He puts his customers first and is always watching the quality of his beers and ciders. With the exception of the house ale, Kent Brewery's Session Pale 3.7%, the rest change every week and come from the best microbrewers around the country – "A 365-day-a-year beer festival", Mike says. He also serves wine, soft drinks and snacks.

The outside has an appearance of a medieval apothecary. Inside, it's narrow and deep, with a black floor and crystal chandeliers hanging from the ceiling. The walls are dark green and decorated with ornate gilded picture frames filled with extraordinary art work and artefacts. Tables are chunky and high, in true micropub-style; benches line one side of the room. There's a traditional wooden

WHO BREWS THE BEER?

KENT BREWERY

KENT BREWERY
telephone: 01634 780 037
website: www.kentbrewery.com

HIGHLIGHT BEERS:

Session Pale 4%
Always available here, this light and
hoppy Pale Ale is a favourite with many
local Micropubs.

bar across the back of the room with five
handpumps. It has no purpose, except to
gently tweak the tails of customers who
think they should order drinks there,
and to raise two fingers to mainstream
pubs. The handpumps are fake: beer is
served by gravity from an unseen, 24-hour
temperature controlled beer room.

There is a 'Bizarre Quiz Night' every
month – good fun – as are the loos – be
sure to check them out.

On our visit we drank and enjoyed
Hanlon's Port Stout, a 4.8% dark chestnut-
coloured beer tasting of bitter chocolate
and the port which is added while brewing.

Disabled access ⊗ **Child friendly** ⊗
Dog friendly ✓

WHAT THE REGULARS SAY
'Love the decoration.'

'So great. Don't miss it.'

'Cracking place, everyone is very
chatty.'

THE HANDSOME SAM

Whitstable, Kent

ESSENTIAL INFORMATION
3 Canterbury Road, Whitstable CT5 4HJ
Telephone: 07931 662081
Email: chr15w@yahoo.co.uk
Facebook: www.facebook.com/
   thehandsomesam

Opening hours:
Monday-Thursday 1200-1400
then 1800-2100
Friday-Saturday 1200-1400
then 1800-2300
Sunday 1200-1500 then 1800-2100

Other reasons to go: Whitstable Museum
and Gallery canterburymuseums.co.uk;
Whitstable and Seasalter Golf Course
www.whitstable-golfclub.co.uk;
Whitstable Castle
www.whitstablecastle.co.uk/the-castle

An oversize print of a black and white cat hangs above the door inside Chris Williamson's (opposite, top left) micropub, watching over the drinkers with a look of benign authority – as well he might. For this is Chris's beloved cat, Sam, who died some years ago but is now remembered in this micropub's name.

The Handsome Sam, was opened in 2014 by Chris, a former NHS radiologist. It's a few hundred yards up the road inland from another of Whitstable's micropubs – The Black Dog, page 284, the third, The Tankerton Arms, page 288, is a five minute drive away.

This place has a pretty, seaside style frontage on a somewhat busy main road, with clapboarding on the second storey and an entirely glass front with a red and white striped awning. On the pavement there's a bike rack, which Chris claims could have been the first provided by a micropub.

Inside, it's one of the most spacious micropubs we've seen, partly because of the wide frontage but especially because of the high ceiling - from which a snowman is suspended. Wooden timber frames, exposed in the walls, give it a vaguely historic, mock Tudor ambience. It was an antiques shop before Chris turned it into a micropub, building many of the fittings himself, including the high micropub-style tables. The seating is a mixture of tall stools and cosier benches with cushions in the window bays. Decorations include a collection of guitars, a saxophone and some of Chris's own paintings.

There's no bar and beer is served directly from the large temperature-controlled stillage room, true to micropub form. They drift with one feature though,

there is a 50-inch high-definition TV screen. It's quite unobtrusive, and only used for major sporting events – rugby in particular - Chris reckons that he runs Whitstable's 'rugby pub'. Above all, though, he sees his place as "a customer-oriented local's micropub for those who don't want to walk into town and who like good beer and good conversation."

He sometimes encourages customers to help him pick a beer to stock, provided they help drink it. Regular ales include Gales HSB 4.8% and Gadds' No 5 4.4%. A new brewery called Rother Valley is featured regularly. On our visit we enjoyed Sharp's Special 5%– strongly malty and bitter, with a taste of dried fruits. He also sells Belgian bottled beers, cider, Italian reds, whites and rosés and what Chris believes is Whitstable's cheapest champagne at £20 a bottle.

This place only accepts cash.

Disabled access ✓ **Child friendly** ✓
Dog friendly ✓

WHAT THE REGULARS SAY

'A great place to come and meet new friends.'

'Very simple – a great place for a chat and a drink.'

'A great collection of beers and Chris is so knowledgeable about all of them.'

THE TANKERTON ARMS

Whitstable, Kent

ESSENTIAL INFORMATION
139B Tankerton Road, Whitstable, CT5 2AW
Telephone: 07532 025626
Email: thetankertonarms@hotmail.co.uk
Website: www.thetankertonarms.co.uk
Facebook: www.facebook.com/
 The-Tankerton-Arms-Tankertons-
 Micropub-504417142942355
Twitter: @TankertonArms

Opening hours:
Monday Closed
Tuesday-Thursday 1200-1400 then 1700-
2130, Friday 1200-1400 then 1700-2300
Saturday 1200-2300
Sunday 1200-1500 then 1700-2130

Other reasons to go: Whitstable Castle and
Gardens, www.whitstablecastle.co.uk/the-
castle; Whitstable Museum and Gallery,
canterburymuseums.co.uk; Playhouse
Theatre, www.playhousewhitstable.co.uk

Can anywhere in Britain claim to have more micropubs per head than Whitstable? As we went to press there were three serving a population of about 30,000. The other two, The Black Dog and The Handsome Sam, are on pages 284 and 286.

Perhaps more interesting: each of them is a one-off, as is essential for any genuine micropub. Here at The Tankerton Arms the feature that marks it out is not so much the interior style – which is fairly standard Kent micropub – but the owners, Nigel and Patsy Ranger (opposite, bottom left). The happy atmosphere is all about their personalities – they are naturals – and, perhaps not unrelated – the place is ultra-dog friendly.

On a bright backstreet in Tankerton, a suburb of Whitstable, Nigel and Patsy's place is named after a much-loved mainstream pub, The Tankerton Arms, which stood nearby on the sea front until about 15 years ago when it was sold and turned into flats. The Rangers are among the dozens who have learned the micropub trade from Martyn Hillier at The Butcher's Arms, page 140, where they were regulars, so naturally they run an authentic operation. "We're all about serving great beer," says Nigel - he has a temperature controlled stillage room.

Those seated on benches (with firkins as footstools) and those standing at the chunky, high tables are at eye level. Outside on the tree-lined pavement is a pleasant shady spot with table and bench seating.

Everything about the place – not just the name – is properly local. Locals have donated the decorations – mainly pictures and photos – which line the walls; local day trips can be arranged on Greta, a sailing barge run by a regular, to visit the forts

in Herne Bay; there's a quiz night once a month and occasionally there's 'Cheese Sunday' when you can try Italian cheeses.

Patsy and Nigel's son Alastair helped them start their venture (but has since moved on) and to underline the family ambience children actively welcome.

On our visit we drank Al Murray's Beautiful British Beer – a light bitter; and Westerham's 1965, a full-tasting best bitter.

This may well deserve the award for the most dog-friendly micropub in Britain. Dogs who are genuine regulars get their image reproduced on customised beer mats. The mats are reprinted every six months in order to give as many as possible the chance to be top dog. And don't miss a visit to the loo, which is stuffed with framed photos of local canine celebrities. This place also won the Canterbury & District CAMRA Pub of the Year 2016.

Our reporters commented: 'We can't find any negatives – it's a perfect micropub in every way.'

Disabled access ⊗ **Child friendly** ✓
Dog friendly ✓

WHAT THE REGULARS SAY

'Had an awesome session there yesterday with my wife. Our absolute favourite pub.'

'My dog took me there, what a find. A very welcoming and friendly place to drink. Hopefully my dog will take me back there soon.'

WHO BREWS THE BEER?

KENT BREWERY

KENT BREWERY
telephone: 01634 780 037
website: www.kentbrewery.com

HIGHLIGHT BEERS:

Cobnut 4.1%
This dark and nutty ale goes down well here. There is even a rumour that it was enjoyed on a visit by Pope Francis!

THE RADIUS ARMS

Whyteleafe, Surrey

ESSENTIAL INFORMATION
205 Godstone Road, Whyteleafe, CR3 0EL
Telephone: 07514916172
Email: beer@theradiusarms.co.uk
Facebook: www.facebook.com/
    pages/The-Radius-Arms-
    Micropub/329531410483678
Twitter: @RadiusArmsMicro

Opening hours:
Monday Closed
Tuesday-Thursday 1600-2130
Friday-Saturday 1200-2230
Sunday 1200-1700

Other reasons to go: Chartwell
www.nationaltrust.org.uk;
Titsey Place and Gardens
www.titsey.org;
Croydon Museum
www.museumofcroydon.com

The Radius Arms delivers a smooth ride of an altogether different sort.

Land Rover devotee and former bus driver Vincent Glen (opposite, right, second down) opened up his premises in May 2015, and is already reaping the rewards. At last, the only traffic he encounters is the bustle of happy patrons in his brand new ale house.

Vincent's obsession with all things automotive is obvious. The pub sign is a quirky coat of arms: a pair of crossed radius rods against a forest-green oval background – paying homage to the Land Rover badge. Inside, the pub has a tractor seat (found in Vincent's mother's garden), as well as a Greenham Railway Roadworks lantern that hangs above the toilet entrance, lighting up when it's engaged. There are several car posters on the walls, most donated by satisfied customers.

The decoration is understated — no frills — this is a functional, no nonsense sort of place. The benches were reclaimed from the Olympic Park and the high-legged tables (made from Brazilian Sapele wood) are recycled display cabinets. Both the bar and toilet area are panelled with attractively-stained plywood.

The minimalist decoration means all focus is on conversation. The banner above the front door reads 'It's a never ending beer festival with added conversation' — and it holds true.

Within minutes of my visit I found myself chatting happily to Vincent and some of the punters who had popped in for a pint or two. The atmosphere was instantly accommodating and friendly.

The cask ale stock is regularly rotated. About five ales are available at any one

time, along with about ten ciders and a selection of perry and wines. I sampled Fynes Avalanche – a 4.5% straw-coloured, bittersweet ale, and Kent Breweries Brewer's Reserve 5% slightly malty Strong Pale Ale.

Disabled access ✓ **Child friendly** ⊗
Dog friendly ✓

WHAT THE REGULARS SAY

'This absolutely excellent little gem is an oasis.'

'No lager, no kids, no music, just great like minded people. '

THE HOOPER

Wibsey, Bradford, West Yorkshire

ESSENTIAL INFORMATION
209 High Steet, Bradford, BD6 1JU
Email: info@thehoopermicropub.co.uk
Website: www.thehoopermicropub.co.uk
Facebook: www.facebook.com/pg/
    thehoopermicropub
Twitter: @TheHooperMP

Opening hours:
Monday Closed
Tuesday-Thursday 1630-2200
Friday 1600-late
Saturday 1400-late
Sunday 1400-2100

Other reasons to go: Bradford Industrial
Museum www.bradfordmuseums.org;
National Media Museum
www.nationalmediamuseum.org.uk;
Bronte Parsonage Museum
www.bronte.org.uk

The three owners of this micropub are fans of U.S. chemist and peace activist Linus Pauling, one of whose sayings was: "The way to get good ideas is to get lots of ideas, and throw the bad ones away." So Allison Powell, Graham Lowery and Ryan Bradley found it easy to throw away loud music, large TV screens and the focus on food typical of mainstream pubs, leaving great ale and good conversation. They opened on Christmas Eve 2015.

Locals, and planners, supported the project. The premises, which used to be an estate agent had been empty for some time and The Hooper was seen as likely to bring some life back to this part of High Street.

The inside looks like a mainstream pub, with low tables and benches accommodating around 40 people. The decoration is sparse, with just a few photos of old Bradford and the ambience a bit 1950s. Perhaps it lacks character, but the bar can't be faulted. There are five constantly changing ales mainly from local microbreweries, dispensed by handpump. Unusually for a micropub there is a cellar where the casks are kept cool.

There are eight mainstream pubs within a stone's throw of The Hooper, but none focusses on real ale.

On our visit we enjoyed Slightly Foxed Brewing Company's Fox Glove, a 4.3% golden, full-bodied bitter with a fruity flavour and a hint of caramalt; Bad Co Brewery's Dazed and Confused, a 5.5% milk stout flavoured with chocolate, toffee and crystal malts; and Bradford Brewery's Solero, a 4.2% cloudy, traditional unfined beer with orange and mango flavours. The name? Hooper is the old word for a Cooper – someone who made barrels. Or it could mean a cooper's assistant, who put the metal hoops on barrels.

Disabled access ✓ not to bar or WC
Child friendly ✓ until 1900
Dog friendly ✓

WHAT THE REGULARS SAY

'Good beer, good staff, dog friendly, cracking little individual pub.'

'Great little pub. Love the fact I can try new ales on a regular basis. My wife loves the Belgian wheat beers.'

'Lovely, well kept beer at the right temperature and a good atmosphere.'

OSSETT BREWING COMPANY
telephone: 01924 261333
website: www.ossett-brewery.co.uk

Since 1997 our reputation has been built on producing consistently high quality beers. Whilst we brew a wide range of differing styles we are renowned for our extra pale coloured, heavily hopped ales. Seasonal and one off beers are regularly available.

HIGHLIGHT BEERS:

Yorkshire Blonde 3.9% ABV
Fruity Pale Ale
Our biggest selling beer is a mellow, lager coloured ale. Full-bodied and low in bitterness, the fruity hop aroma results from a generous late addition of Mount Hood hops.

Big Red 4.0% ABV
Ruby Red Ale
A rich, full bodied ruby red ale, bursting with complex flavours. Bitterness and aroma come from the addition of generous quantities of Slovenian grown Atlas hops.

Silver King 4.3% ABV
Citrussy Pale Ale
A simple pale ale, brewed from British and American Cascade hops result in a crisp, dry, refreshing bitter in which the aromas of citrus fruit are pleasingly well balanced. Winner of many prestigious awards.

Excelsior 5.2% ABV
Strong Pale Ale
A classic pale ale, brewed from British pale malt and American Cascade hops this is the perfect drinking experience! Smooth, fruity and full-bodied, but with a deceptive bitterness to complement the high alcohol content this is a deliciously easy-drinking beer.

ALBION ALE HOUSE

Wigan, Greater Manchester

ESSENTIAL INFORMATION
12 High Street, Standish, Wigan, WN6 0HL
Telephone: 01257 367897/ 07411
  081342
Email: albionalehouse@outlook.com
Website: www.albionalehouse.co.uk
Facebook: www.facebook.com/Albion-Ale-
  House-Micropub-350970305077413
Twitter: @AlbionAle

Opening hours:
Monday Closed
Tuesday-Thursday 1500-2200
Friday-Saturday 1400-2300
Sunday 1400-2200

Other reasons to go:
Fairy Glen, Appley Bridge, WN6 9EQ
Museum of Wigan Life www.wigan.gov.uk;
Wigan Golf Club www.wigangolfclub.co.uk

You might think you're in an original Kentish micropub. The tables and chairs are high, and it's tiny. There's a bar, but it only serves to display how many beers they offer – eight handpumps. It's L-shape is perfect for leaning on and for perching drinks.

Becky and Kevin (opposite, top) opened Standish's first micropub in 2014 in a former pound shop. It's bang in the middle of the small town on the main street, so hard to miss and definitely provides a much-needed new drinking place in the local area.

It follows micropub criteria faithfully – there's no TV, no music and no lager and although it has free wifi, mobiles aren't allowed in the bar area. Classic pub games are provided.

It has a bright, modern feel, with a tiled floor and the seats and tables arranged neatly on each side. A feeling of space is created despite the small area. At the back there's a small garden with benches and tables made from casks, likewise a clean, modern space. Upstairs there's a 'cellar'.

Seven of the ales rotate and one – a house ale named Th'Albion made specially for the micropub by Bank Top Brewery – is constant. There are also two ciders, a gluten-free beer, an alcohol-free beer, wine and Prosecco and a selection of malt whiskies. They also have a great selection of snacks such as cheese boards, pork pies, crisps, pickled eggs and gherkins.

The Albion holds micro beer and sausage festivals which are hugely popular, featuring 20 ales that the micropub has never served before along with specially-made sausages including a very hot chilli sausage, which Kevin says, greatly increases beer sales.

On our visit we enjoyed Titanic Brewery's White Star, a 4.8% amber ale with a malty honey flavour; and Redwillow's Directionless pale ale 4.2% with an orange flavour.

Disabled access ✓ **Child friendly** ✓
Dog friendly ✓

WHAT THE REGULARS SAY

'Fantastic place - warm, welcoming and funny with great ales and a great cheese board. Absolutely amazing staff, always feels like a mini holiday when I've been in to visit.'

'Wonderful ale taster selection and excellent wine. The Lancashire cheese selection to complement the beers was perfect and the mini toad in the holes were fantastic!'

'Great wee pub, always a great selection of ales and a cheery face to welcome you.'

Willingham, Cambridge

ESSENTIAL INFORMATION
9 High Street, Willingham,
Cambridge, CB24 5ES
Telephone: 07956 845509
Email: chris@thebankmicropub.co.uk
Website: www.thebankmicropub.co.uk
Facebook: www.facebook.com/
    TheBankMicropub?fref=ts
Twitter: @thebankmicropub

Opening hours:
Monday Closed
Tuesday 1800-2200
Wednesday 1730-2200
Thursday-Saturday 1730-2200
Sunday Closed

Other reasons to go: Danson Park
www.bexley.gov.uk;
Red House www.nationaltrust.org.uk;
Woodlands Farm Trust
www.thewoodlandsfarmtrust.org

The Bank in Willingham was the first ever micropub to open in Cambridgeshire and is still only one of two. It was opened in 2012 by Chris and Linda at a time when most of the pubs in the area had closed down, but this one room classic pub has been an instant success. As a former bank – the name says it all – the building is attractive and full of character – it looks like it has been a pub forever. Located on the high street of Willingham, with a pale green door and window frames it has a chic and modern look to it while maintaining a traditional appearance of a village pub.

Landlord Chris is also the village postmaster, hence the somewhat reserved opening times. However, he is planning to quit his job and the locals are hoping this will mean increase in opening hours.

The effort that has gone into the inside has given it a cosy and classic pub like feel but with plenty of room to stand around for a chat and a drink. There are six small tables and an L-shaped bar in the corner. The walls are decorated with pictures of local interest and the furniture has all been rescued from closed down pubs. With a mixture of exposed brick, wood and plaster the walls give this micropub a traditional feel with sympathetic lighting to top it off.

There are usually five choices of cask ale on offer and bottles and cans are also an option. This is a true micropub - there is no food, no music and no TV, just good beer and conversation, harkening back to the idea of a traditional village pub. However, they do have a tapas night every now and again, which is hugely popular.

When our guest contributor Richard Reeve visited, the landlord, Chris, was having a well earned weekend off after six

months continuous work, however, his stand in Neil was doing a great job and the atmosphere was welcoming and friendly. There were four cask ales on offer served directly from jacket-cooled casks. I tried a pint of Trawlerboys which was excellent and The Kernal, a 5.3% pale ale.

Disabled access ✓ not to WC
Child friendly ✓ **Dog friendly** ✓

WHAT THE REGULARS SAY
'They always have great beers on – more than most other pubs ten times their size.'

'Great night drinking in the Bank micropub, very tasty session.'

Worcester, Worcestershire

ESSENTIAL INFORMATION
22 St Johns, Worcester, WR2 5AH
Telephone: 01905421579/07415526267
Email: chris@bullbaiters.com
Website: www.bullbaiters.com

Opening hours:
Monday 1730-2130
Tuesday-Thursday 1200-1400
then 1730-2130
Friday-Saturday 1200-2130
Sunday1200-1400

Other reasons to go: Worcestershire County
Cricket Club WCCC.co.uk;
The Commandery
www.worcestershire.gov.uk;
St. John-in-Bedwardine Parish Church
www.stjohninbedwardine.co.uk;
Worcester Warriors
www.warriors.co.uk

Landlord Chris Hankins (opposite, right top) has been in the pub trade since 2004 and is currently the longest serving licensee in St Johns. Real ale, to Chris, has always been the most challenging and interesting part of his trade and the micropub allows him to put these skills into practice. Before opening the Bull Baiters Chris had been aware of the micropub concept and was a member of The Micropub Association, so when a shop in St John's came up for rent he leapt at the perfect opportunity.

Right in the centre of Worcester's medieval bull baiting area, just yards from the road that still bears the name Bull Ring, this micropub opened in May 2016 after two months hard work by Chris and a few close friends. The full story and pictures of the conversion are on the Facebook page and documentation for the planning, licensing and change of use are on the website as a useful resource for others thinking of opening a micropub. The Bull Baiters adheres to the original micropub values as faithfully as possible. Chris sells local beers and cider – they are sourced from all over the UK but with a preference for local ones. His is the only micropub in the local area.

The premises used to be a patisserie, then a Polish food shop. The large shop front window displays beer memorabilia and an actual bull ring. Seating is minimal, with benches round the edge of the room and a few low bar stools. There's plenty of standing

room. The furniture and the bar were built by hand and the seating is upholstered in hop pockets. The bar has seven handpumps of small brewery crafted cask ales and the back bar houses a selection of eight ciders. Bar snacks include locally made baguettes, pork pies and scotch eggs.

Conversation is promoted and there is no TV, gaming machines or recorded music.

On our visit we enjoyed: The Wobbly Brewing Company's The Wobbly Welder, a 4.8% full bodied, golden ale with a long smooth finish; and Sadler's Pulling Power, a 3.8% session beer.

Disabled access ✓ **Child friendly** ✓
Dog friendly ✓

WHAT THE REGULARS SAY
'Best place in St Johns by a country mile! Doing an amazing job and I hope you are around for a long time.'

'My husband's favourite place ..loves the banter with Chris .. small and cosy.. just a super little place.. excellent beers all on draught.'

'It's a small 'no frills' pub selling beer to people who like beer and conversation. What's not to like?'

Worthing, West Sussex

ESSENTIAL INFORMATION

27 West Buildings, Worthing, BN11 3BS

Telephone: 01903 529100

Email: anchoredinworthing@gmail.com

Website: www.anchoredinworthing.co.uk

Facebook: www.facebook.com/anchored.
  in.worthing

Twitter: @MicroWorthing

Opening hours:

Monday Closed

Tuesday-Saturday 1200-2130

Sunday 1200-1730

(+30 mins drinking up time)

Other reasons to go:

Worthing Pier www.adur-worthing.gov.uk;

Worthing Museum
www.worthingmuseum.co.uk;

Connaught Theatre
www.worthingtheatres.co.uk

I journeyed to Worthing aboard the Coastliner 700 service from Hove, and came ashore at the fascinating alehouse known as Anchored. It's the pride and joy of former mariner and barman Nigel Watson, who opened his own micropub after visiting Martyn Hillier and The Butcher's Arms in Herne (page 140).

There are no unruly, drunken sailors here – Captain Nigel runs a tidy ship and keeps the micropub ethic right at the heart of what he does. It's a simple, back to basics, real-ale pub with a friendly, respectful atmosphere and a clientele to match. Since opening in August 2013 Nigel has slowly but surely rethought and refitted his premises to become the snug, little refuge it is today.

Easy to locate as you leave Marine Parade and head down West Buildings Road, Anchored stands out a mile with its spacious shop front and large, colourful sign. Big, bold and bright is the idea here, shouting out to the world what's on offer. In contrast, inside is a low-key affair, but it certainly packs a lot into the space available. The small (and it is tiny) interior has raised tables running down each side of the room, with high benches and stool seating. This leaves a narrow central walkway where there is little room to stand. The pub can realistically only fit around 18 people seated, with the odd one or two people standing, before it becomes uncomfortably crowded.

But the intimacy encourages you to meet, and chat openly with, the rest of the customers. The paintwork is sober but the walls are adorned with maps, assorted artwork and pump clips. At the end of the pub is a bookshelf stocked with an eclectic mix of books, beer bottles and paraphernalia – perhaps reflecting the owner's wide-ranging tastes. Out back there is room for an auto-tilt stillage facility which services six firkins. There are three beers on and three to go at any one time. Anchored also has a decent selection of bottled beers which changes seasonally to accommodate different tastes. Six ciders are on offer, one perry and also red and white wine. I personally enjoyed Black Cat Brewery's Hop Smack, a 4% ABV golden citrus beer, and Langham Brewery's Triple XXX, a 4.4% dark winter ale which was smooth, sweet and chocolatey. Sandwiches are available from the café next door, as well as cheese from a local Deli. Nigel doesn't mind if you bring in fish and chips.

Sadly I was not able to meet Nigel in person as he was out at the Lord Mayor's show in London on the day of my visit. Instead, I was entertained and attended to by Stuart, who was a genial host for the afternoon. He succeeded in giving me an idea of Nigel's colourful character.

Disabled access ⊗ **Child friendly** ⊗
Dog friendly ✓

WHAT THE REGULARS SAY
'It's a mini freehouse. It's small scale but friendly.'

'It's friendly — you come in and don't know people initially... but then you talk!'

'I like the continuously changing variations in real ale.'

BROOKSTEED ALEHOUSE

Worthing, West Sussex

ESSENTIAL INFORMATION
38 South Farm Road, Worthing, West
Sussex, BN14 7AE
Website: www.brooksteedalehouse.co.uk
Facebook: www.facebook.com/
    SussexMicropub
Twitter: @sussexmicropub

Opening hours:
Monday Closed
Tuesday 1700-2130
Wednesday-Thursday 1200-1400 then
1700-2130
Friday-Saturday 1200-2130
Sunday 1200-1430ish

Other reasons to go: Cissbury Ring
 www.nationaltrust.org.uk;
Highdown Gardens
www.highdowngardens.co.uk;
High Salvington Windmill
www.highsalvingtonwindmill.co.uk

Just round the corner from Worthing train station, this attractive, modern and trendy looking micropub is the work of husband and wife team Nick and Paula Little, and is housed in a former hairdressing salon. South Farm Road itself was originally known as Brooksteed Road which gave them the name for their new ale house. Both Nick and Paula come from very different employment backgrounds: Nick used to work in IT and Paula in Research and Development. But it was Nick's love of real ale that prompted the change, and their efforts have paid off. They officially opened here on September 5th 2014.

The pub's name is written in bold yellow lettering against a grey background, with a simple logo featuring three pint glasses full of different ales. Inside, Brooksteed Alehouse is spacious, clean lined and brightly decorated, with plenty of room to sit and stand. In fact, the interior is so large that it stretches the traditional definition of a micropub. At the bar front there is space to seat three people. Down the left side are high tables with a long wall bench, along with a low table, sofa and chairs at the back. By the stillage room there is space for an extra few high stools. The place seats 45 people comfortably.

The colour scheme is a tasteful and contemporary blue-grey, orange and yellow, with modern-looking lighting. Hints of the previous occupancy can be seen in one or two of the wall pictures and the reclaimed hairdryer cases which light the table at the far end. Pump clips edge the walls and various pictures hang around the room, but the decoration is far from fussy. The serving area is small. You can place your order here whilst ales are poured direct from

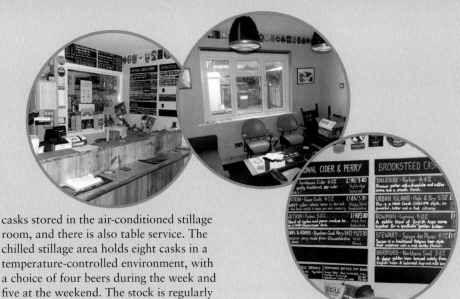

casks stored in the air-conditioned stillage room, and there is also table service. The chilled stillage area holds eight casks in a temperature-controlled environment, with a choice of four beers during the week and five at the weekend. The stock is regularly rotated to maximise variety. During my visit I tried Daleside Porter, a 4.4% ABV rich velvety and smokey chocolate Yorkshire Porter; Urban Island High and Dry, a 5.5% ABV West Coast style IPA with a refreshing bitter finish; and Mr Grundy's Pip, Squeak and Wilfrid, a 4.4% ABV nicely hopped, citrussy Golden Pale Ale.

There is also real cider and perry; red, white and rosé wine; and a decent range of local and foreign bottled beers. Non-alcoholic drinks include teas, coffees, cordials and a variety of bottled soft drinks. The usual bar snacks and basic food are available, and the menu changes depending on the season – antipasto and cheeseboard selections in the summer months, and pork pies and scotch eggs in winter.

Disabled access ✓ **Child friendly** ✓ Under 18s allowed at lunchtime, not in the evening **Dog friendly** ✓

WHAT THE REGULARS SAY

'I like the atmosphere and the distinct lack of gaming machines.'

'It's more about beer and local people — these places obviously engage the owners' passions.'

BARBERS ARMS

Wye, Kent

ESSENTIAL INFORMATION
171 Bridge Street, Wye, Ashford, TN25 5DP
Telephone: 07885 252001
Email: thebarber@barbersarms.co.uk
Website: www.barbersarms.co.uk
Facebook: www.facebook.com/
   barbersarms.co.uk

Opening hours:
Monday Closed
Tuesday 1800-2300
Wednesday-Saturday 1200-1400
then 1800-2300
Sunday 1200-1500

Other reasons to go:
Wye National Nature Reserve;
Godinton House www.godintonhouse.co.uk;
Ashford Designer Outlet
www.godintonhouse.co.uk

When our reporter Richard Reeve arrived by bike one Friday evening he found the place packed with a younger-than-usual crowd for a micropub and a friendly, buzzy atmosphere. There were plenty of bikes outside, also a little unusual, and there was music playing. If everything else stacks up, music needn't prevent a micropub from being genuine, in fact owner Graham Austen (opposite, top right) says the right sort of music at the right volume actually contributes to a genuine micropub atmosphere, which should be relaxing. Background music helps mask conversations: some people don't want to be overheard, and knowing they might be makes them tense.

In all other ways this is a true micropub, serving cask-conditioned ales from a cold room plus basic bar snacks (and free peanuts). The decoration is simple but not perfunctory: tobacco stain effect paint on the walls; hops hanging from the ceiling; an ingenious bench incorporating barrel parts and outside a red-and-white stripped awning typical of old barber's shops. The bar at the back is the focus, an arrangement Graham likes because it gives people freedom to talk to him or not. Behind the bar is a beer room in which jacket-cooled firkins are racked on scaffolding poles.

Graham sells usually three real ales plus real ciders both of which he buys from far and wide in order to provide something new most of the time. On our visit we drank Skinner's 3.8% Ginger Tosser, a reliable everyday golden ale tasting of honey and ginger.

The micropub occasionally hosts live music but Graham's main event, fast becoming a local institution, is his end-of-June beer festival in a marquee on the

village green.

For many years Graham was a roofer
and cabinet maker until a knee injury made
it unwise for him to continue climbing
ladders – opening Barbers was his response.
So he's an enterprising type and it was no
surprise to learn as we went to press that
he had plans to open another micropub at
nearby Charing in early 2017.

Wye is a large village on hilly ground
between Ashford and Canterbury.

Disabled access ⊗ **Child friendly** ✓
Dog friendly ✓

Other Micropubs

The micropubs in this section, as explained under our Selection Criteria on page 11 are not second best, but for various reasons -see below- we don't think they are as mainstream as the micropubs on pages 24-305. Many of them are terrific - don't overlook them. More will open: please let us know about them.

- Often have more than one room.
- Serve roughly as much key keg and lager as real ale.
- Often music and sports TV play a part.
- Food – not just snacks – is an important feature.

Belper, Derbyshire

ESSENTIAL INFORMATION
6 Campbell Street, Belper, Derbyshire,
DE56 1AP
Telephone: 01773 823 117
Email: contact@arkwrightsbar.com
Website: www.arkwrightsbar.com
Facebook: www.facebook.com/Arkwrights-
REAL-ALE-BAR-649464885092852

Opening hours:
Monday-Friday 1600-2300
Saturday-Sunday 1200-2300

Other reasons to go:
Kedleston Hall www.nationaltrust.org.uk;
River Gardens www.visitambervalley.co.uk

There is no formal door into this micropub. Instead double wooden gates lead you into the outdoor seating area before revealing the door into the place itself. Arkwright's Real Ale can't be called a pure micropub due to the large TV on the wall (only played by request on silent), the lager at the bar and the home made hot food available. It can however, be said to take great pride in its attention to and knowledge of real ale. It's the only drinking place in the area to do so and it has brought drinkers from miles around because of this.

Paul Carroll worked upstairs in The Strutt Club, a members bar, when he discovered the space wasn't being used for anything. He decided to transform it and has created a place with a family like atmosphere where people can come and enjoy a drink and a natter.

The name comes from two places: The owner of the grocer's shop in *Open All Hours* (TV series, 1976-1985), a photo of the cast is hung on the wall to the right of the door. And Sir Richard Arkwright, who built the second water powered cotton mill in the world, in Belper.

The bar has six handpumps serving ales from all over the UK, the more unusual the better. There are two measures of take out cartons: 4 pints and 18 pint boxes and there is a loyalty card, which gives you a beer free once its full, for the regular regulars. On Sunday night there is live music and there are occasional beer raffles.

Disabled access ✓ **Child friendly** ✓
Dog friendly ✓

Bristol

ESSENTIAL INFORMATION
22 Chandos Road, Bristol, BS6 6PF
Telephone: 0117 973 1498
Email: Chums.Mark@mail.com
Website: www.chumsmicropub.co.uk
Facebook: www.facebook.com/
    CHUMS-903685713040516

Opening hours:
Monday-Thursday 1600-2230
Friday-Saturday 1200-2300
Sunday 1200-2200

Other reasons to go:
Bristol Zoo www.bristolzoo.org.uk;
SS Great Britain www.ssgreatbritain.org;
Bristol Museum and Art Gallery
www.bristolmuseums.org.uk

Disabled access ✓ Child friendly ⊗
Dog friendly ✓

The name of this place says much about micropubs: they're meant to be places where you arrive among strangers and leave among friends, which is why landlord Mark Farrell named his micropub after his group of walking mates. He used to work in The Three Tuns, a ten-minute drive away from here, so he hasn't moved far and he knows the area and his customers well. The decision to go for a micropub was driven by the high rents paid by mainstream pubs - he wanted to sell real ale at a fair price.

Chums is the second micropub in Bristol following The Draper's Arms, page 56, also a ten-minute drive.

These premises were a convenience store and Mark had his work cut out to get the place into shape. After a radical refit it has half-height wooden panelling on the walls; the furniture is benches and low tables; and it's decorated with landscape drawings. It opened in early 2016 and remains faithful to the basic micropub criteria of no music, no TV, no wifi and no gaming machines. Most of Bristol's mainstream pubs have a serious emphasis on food, leaving few where people can simply sit and chat. However, as much as we like this place – and the welcome really is friendly, with Mark knowing the names of many of his regulars, it's in the back section because he sells almost as much lager and key keg as cask-conditioned real ale.

Between four and six ales rotate regularly and come from three main sources: Wye Valley Brewery, XT Brewery and Butcombe Brewery.

Chums is a great addition to the Bristol drinking scene and Mark has created a hub of real ale enthusiasm.

Broadstairs, Kent

As we went to press there were three micropubs in Broadstairs – this one, The Four Candles (page 58) and Yard of Ale (page 60). There's nothing wrong with this place, but the other two are so authentic that we thought we'd note the difference by putting The Thirty-Nine in the back section.

At present this is a genuine micropub: chunky tables and high seating round the edge of the room; cold room; four cask-conditioned gravity-fed real ales always on offer, outnumbering the single key keg that dispenses a quality Belgian ale. However, owner Sean Harding, a former police sergeant, doesn't buy exclusively from small brewers. He will stock any beer of interest from a wide range of brewers large and small, not just in the UK, and he says that his emphasis might not always be mainly cask-conditioned real ales.

The Thirty-Nine Steps is in a good location in a pleasant, quiet road off the bottom of the High Street, where it moved from two doors along in late 2016. It's a couple of minutes walk from the cliff top front at Viking Bay. Pleasant shops, some with traditional frontage, are all around.

It's neat, newly furbished and well kept. The wall decorations (with three obligatory Thirty-Nine Steps film posters) are uncluttered and nicely framed, otherwise unremarkable. However, the ceiling, covered with a mind- boggling collection 1,500 pump clips, is an eye catcher.

On our visit we enjoyed Worthington White Shield 5.6% (cask version) an original India Pale Ale made to an old recipe: copper coloured, hoppy with a malty backbone, and proving that there are excellent offerings from big brewers if you know where to look.

THE BOREHOLE

Bromsgrove, Worcestershire

ESSENTIAL INFORMATION
5 Charlotte Street, Broadstairs, CT10 1LR
Email: info@thethirty-ninesteps.co.uk
Facebook: www.facebook.
   com/The-Thirty-Nine-Steps-
   Alehouse-482311068465594

Opening hours:
Monday-Thursday 1200-2200
Friday-Saturday 1200-2300
Sunday 1200-2200

Other reasons to go:
The Potteries Museum and Art Gallery
www.stokemuseums.org.uk;
Trentham Estate www.trentham.co.uk;
Alton Towers www.altontowers.com;
Water World www.waterworld.co.uk

Disabled access ✓
Child friendly ✓ until 2000
Dog friendly ✓

This is a terrific family-run small pub selling mainly real ales hand drawn from firkins kept in a cool room, but it's not quite a genuine micropub. With a capacity of 70 people, it's relatively large, but this matters less than the two taps dispensing pressurized lagers, which mean that strictly it ought to be in this back section, not the main section.

The Borehole is one of two sales outlets for Lymestone Brewery, a family-run microbrewer located a stone's throw from the pub which sells locally in the West Midlands area and further afield. The freestanding brick building occupied by the pub was originally the gatehouse for a brewery, built 1889, that covered the whole of the industrial estate on which the pub stands. 'Borehole' refers to the boreholes on this site which supplied water for the old brewery. The premises were a music school before a major refurbishment gave it this new lease of life. It opened March 2015.

The Borehole always serves five or six Lymestone Brewery real ales, plus guest ales from small brewers in the area and further afield. On our visit we tried one of Lymestone's own ales, Foundation Stone 4.5% golden IPA. This is made with 100% English ingredients and has a very mellow, rounded flavour. The finish (aftertaste) is distinctly spicy, thanks to the unusual hedgerow hop, Boadicea. This was originally discovered growing wild in a hedgerow but then cultivated commercially.

Brad and his wife Viv run the brewery and the pub's hands-on, with some help from staff and from their daughter. Take a look at their website to get a feel for their close knit team and find out about their brewery tours.

THE LITTLE ALE HOUSE

Bromsgrove, Worcestershire

ESSENTIAL INFORMATION
21 Worcester Road, Bromsgrove B61 7DL
Telephone: 07773 247179
Email: baconterrance@yahoo.co.uk
Facebook: www.facebook.com/
   littlealehouse
Twitter: @TezzaAles

Opening hours:
Monday Closed
Tuesday-Wednesday1500-2215
Thursday-Sunday 1200-2215

Other reasons to go:
Avoncroft Museum www.avoncroft.org.uk;
Liz Monk Studio Pottery and Gallery
www.lizziesfarm.co.uk;
Hagley Hall www.hagleyhall.com

Disabled access ✓ not to WC
Child friendly ⊗ Dog friendly ✓

Owner Terry Bacon has put in some hard graft since opening in October 2013 to make this the local place to come for great beer – it holds an entry in the 2016 Good Beer Guide.

Terry hosted Bromsgrove's first Winter Ales Festival in 2016, an idea that originated from his regulars. The plan was to hold the event in the micropub until it became clear that a much bigger space would be needed. The venue changed to Lickey End Social Club, where Terry is now hoping to hold the event annually.

The Little Ale House's premises were formerly a hair salon, with an all-glass front. There's no particular theme: one side of the pub has traditional wooden tables and chairs with some leather sofas and coffee tables, while the other side has micropub-style high tables and padded benches – you have to mount a step to reach them and there are beer barrels on which to rest your feet. There is also seating outside the front. It's not particularly cosy as micro-pubs go – instead the attention has been paid mainly to the beer and its quality – and you couldn't complain about that. There is little decoration, apart from a few advertising posters and framed awards on the mainly bare walls.

Four to five cask beers are on offer at a time, served by gravity from a metal stillage behind the bar and if you are a card-carrying CAMRA member there is 20p off a pint of real ale. There is also a selection of ciders, perries and wine available along with tea and coffee. You are welcome to bring your own food from one of the many takeaways.

The Little Ale House

BURSLEY ALE HOUSE

Burslem, Stoke-on-Trent, Staffordshire

ESSENTIAL INFORMATION
Wedgwood Place, Burslem, Stoke-on-Trent,
ST6 4ED
Telephone: 01782 911393
Email: bursleyalehouse@gmail.com
Facebook: www.facebook.com/
    bursleyalehouse
Twitter: @BursleyAleHouse

Opening hours:
Monday-Thursday 1200-2300
Friday-Saturday 1200-2330
Sunday 1200-2230

Other reasons to go: The Trentham Estate
www.trentham.co.uk;
Apedale Heritage Centre
www.apedale.co.uk;
Gladstone Pottery Museum
www.stokemuseums.org.uk

Burslem is mentioned in The Domesday Book, where it's described as a small farming hamlet until after the Black Death when it's described as a medieval town. By the 1800s, when the Trent and Mersey Canal was completed, the town flourished on the back of the local pottery trade and became known as The Mother Town. Today it has Britain's last working industrial district – an area where people both live and work.

The centre of Burslem is red-brick Victorian buildings, many with ornate façades. It's not a thriving area: many of the buildings are derelict and there's a distinct lack of places in which to hang out, but Bursley Ale House has begun to fill this gap. Darren Bailey, Alan Collinson, Chris Myatt and John Slack opened it in what was Chambers Wine Bar, wanting to create a unique drinking place not only for locals but for people from further afield.

The building looks like a mainstream pub and has a large garden at the front. Inside there are two levels (the top one available for hire) and it's warmed by a real coal fire. The bar has five handpumps delivering rotating ales plus two rotating ciders. Next to the bar is a cooling cupboard with two levels and a glass front, where eight casks are kept. The furniture is low tables and chairs and the walls are decorated with pictures of old Burslem.

As much as we like this place it doesn't conform to micropub criteria: there's a TV, they offer lager and they serve more substantial food than simple bar snacks.

Disabled access ⊗ **Child friendly** ✓
Dog friendly ⊗

Canterbury, Kent

ESSENTIAL INFORMATION
48 Northgate, Canterbury, Kent, CT1 1BE
Telephone: 01227 464952
Facebook: www.facebook.com/
    Thethomastallis
Twitter: @thomastallisale

Opening hours:
Monday 1700-2130
Tuesday-Saturday 1200-2300
Sunday 1200-2200

Other reasons to go: Canterbury Cathedral
www.canterbury-cathedral.org;
The Canterbury Tales
www.canterburytales.org.uk

Mark Robson, owner of The Just Reproach, an authentic micropub in Deal, page 98, opened this place in 2016 as his second venture.

The Thomas Tallis is a charming, unusual mini-pub, not a true micropub: it's run by a manager, not the owner; it has three rooms, not one; and it serves more key keg ales than real ales.

It's far from being a clone of The Just Reproach though. This is thanks, to its unique setting in a medieval building, part of the historic Hospital of St John. One of the walls could date from 1084 but most of what you see now is from the 14th to the 16th centuries.

Of the three rooms, the front two, have seating typical of genuine micropubs; one has a log burning stove. The third room has conventional, low tables and chairs where you can chill over a game of Scrabble and a view of the gardens of St John's Hospital. It was a pub – The House of the White Swan - from the 1830s to 1913. Manager Dave is right to call it "Canterbury's oldest newest pub".

A menu card describes the current beers and you'll be given some dice - 'the dice of destiny' - to help you decide which beer you want to drink.

They sell real ales and cider from Kent plus craft ales in casks or key keg from around the world. Dave keeps going back to The Four Candles in St Peter's, Broadstairs. The owner of this pub has a tiny brewery in his basement and the Thomas Tallis is one of the very few serving its delicious beer.

Disabled access ⊗ **Child friendly** ✓
Dog friendly ✓

Carterton, Oxfordshire

ESSENTIAL INFORMATION
5 Carters Walk, Alvescot Road, Carterton,
Oxfordshire, OX18 3DH
Telephone: 01993 845663
Email: soalehouse@gmail.com
Website: www.siegeoforleans.co.uk
Facebook: www.facebook.com/
   SoOAlehouse

Opening hours:
Monday-Thursday 1500-2300
Friday-Sunday 1200-2300

Other reasons to go:
Cotswold Wildlife Park and Garden
www.cotswoldwildlifepark.co.uk;
Crocodiles of the World
www.crocodilesoftheworld.co.uk;
Wren Gallery www.wrenfineart.com

Landlord Chris Jones says his place isn't a true micropub, more a microalehouse. Chris was inspired by the idea of taking an empty shop and turning it into a hub for the community, focussing on real ale and making sure the customer came first. However, he wanted to put his stamp on the place so he doesn't follow all the micropub rules. In particular, he plays music and he offers a range of cocktails. Carterton only had two pubs before Chris arrived, both of which were very mainstream and boring. Chris' answer was adapting the micropub model to create a new, fun place for Carterton.

Chris has co-owned the Cotswold Arms in Burford for ten years and Simon his manager used to work in theatre in London's West End. They have pooled their experiences to create a well-run bar with plenty of artistic touches.

There are four constantly changing ales as well as craft wines, spirits, ciders, and the bespoke cocktails mentioned above. They often have live music, the occasional DJ and put on some unusual events.

And the name? Carterton has a link with the Siege of Orleans, a battle in the Hundred Years' War between England and France. Land on the town's north side was owned by a family all of whose males died in the siege – the last killed allegedly by Joan of Arc. The siege ended on 8th May 1492 and this pub opened 586 years later to the day.

Disabled access ✓ Child friendly ✓
Dog friendly ✓

Chesterfield, Derbyshire

ESSENTIAL INFORMATION
405 Sheffield Road, Whittington Moor,
Chesterfield, S41 8LS
Telephone: 01246 260876
Email: info@the-beer-parlour.co.uk
Website: www.the-beer-parlour.co.uk
Facebook: www.facebook.com/pages/The-
    Beer-Parlour/119336671452701
Twitter: @beerparlourches

Opening hours:
Monday-Thursday 1600-2100
Friday 1600-2200
Saturday 1200-2200
Sunday 1300-1730

Other reasons to go:
Hardwick Hall www.nationaltrust.org.uk
Bolsover Castle
www.english-heritage.org.uk

Don't be put off by the appearance of this little place: the outside needs renovating and there are plans to do so. Inside, it's another story. High tables and stools, acquired from the local gym are everywhere, and a grandfather clock stands in the corner. Stephen and Dawn are extremely friendly and welcoming and go to great lengths to find good ale from around the world for their customers. The more unusual the better, and they search out beers that people haven't had before.

They opened The Beer Parlour because they felt that other pubs in the area sold too many spirits and didn't have a focus on good beer. Their bottled collection is large with Belgian, Dutch and Bavarian beers on offer, plus numerous handpumps on the bar. You can taste the beers before buying and there are several take away options from four pints to 72-pint firkin.

The decoration is mainly made up of amusing signs such as 'Beauty is in the eye of the beer holder' and 'Beer is the answer but I can't remember the question'. There are of course the obligatory pump clips covering the walls, recording the many beers sold here in the past.

This place opened round the corner in very small premises, and was so popular that it had to move here. It's a fabulous little place, but, the bar is large, and they serve several lagers, so unfortunately it has to be in the back section.

Disabled access ✓ not to WC
Child friendly ✓ **Dog friendly** ✓

THE SAXON BEAR ALE HOUSE

Christchurch, Dorset

ESSENTIAL INFORMATION
5 The Saxon Centre, Fountain Way,
Christchurch, BH23 1QN
Telephone: 01202 488931
Website: www.thebearbeerfamily.co.uk
Facebook: www.facebook.com/
thesaxonbear

Opening hours:
Monday-Wednesday 1600-2200
Thursday-Saturday 1200-2300
Sunday 1200-2230

Other reasons to go:
Christchurch Market www.visit-dorset.com;
Christchurch Quay;
Christchurch Priory
www.christchurchpriory.org

Disabled access ⊗ Child friendly ⊗
Dog friendly ✓

This is the sister micropub of The Wight Bear in Southbourne, Bournemouth, (page 50). It's likewise the work of Nicola and David Holland and looks and feels almost identical to The Wight Bear – the main difference is the shape of the room – long and narrow. It's called The Saxon Bear because Christchurch was a Saxon settlement and this is reflected in the micropub's Saxonised bear logo. It's located between Waitrose and Bargates, near Saxon Square. Don't miss the 'Carlsbog'- the toilet (below) where you can vent your distaste for gassy, tasteless lager.

It's definitely a good place with a pleasant atmosphere and a big national and international range of bottled beers. At present it's a true micropub. One wall is bright red and covered in musically themed decoration. A string of lights adorn the ceiling, the tables and benches (the timber reclaimed from Bournemouth Pier) are appropriately high and there is plenty of standing room. For more information, read The Wight Bear entry. If, however, the Hollands expand their Bear brand into a mini chain, then it runs the risk of becoming less and less owner managed - ie not such a genuine micropub.

Cowes, Isle of Wight

ESSENTIAL INFORMATION
5a Shooters Hill, Cowes, Isle of Wight,
PO31 7BE
Telephone: 01983 294027/ 07791514668
Email: mark@cowesalehouse.co.uk
Website: www.cowesalehouse.co.uk
Facebook: www.facebook.com/COWES-
ALE-HOUSE-452641661472068

Opening hours:
Monday-Thursday 1200-2300
Friday-Saturday 1200-0000
Sunday 1200-2230

Other reasons to go:
The Sir Max Aitken Museum
www.sirmaxaitkenmuseum.org;
Cowes Golf Course
www.cowesgolfclub.co.uk;
Carisbrooke Castle
www.english-heritage.org.uk

A small pub, rather than a true micropub which opened in 2013. They serve five regularly changing real ales straight from the barrel, but there's lager too. Food is limited to traditional pub snacks including cheese platters and. It will appeal to those who like their pubs to be 'real', rather than pub-restaurants. Decoration is fairly simple. One wall is painted with a seascape mural while others are painted cream with framed photos. Barrels serve as tables with a few arm chairs and bar stools. At the back there's a small terrace. The atmosphere and welcome are friendly and there is live music on Friday evening and Sunday afternoon. The owner managers also run a sister establishment at Newport, page 329 (the smallest pub on the Isle of Wight).

Disabled access ✓ **Child friendly** ⊗
Dog friendly ✓

BEER DOCK

Crewe, Cheshire

ESSENTIAL INFORMATION
159 Nantwich Road, Crewe, CW2 6DF
Telephone: 01270 747170
Email: sam@beerdock.co.uk
Website: www.beerdock.co.uk
Facebook: www.facebook.com
/Beerdock.co.uk
Twitter: @BeerDockcouk

Opening hours:
Monday-Wednesday 1000-2000
Thursday-Saturday 1000-2300
Sunday 1200-1700

Other reasons to go:
Nantwich Museum
www.nantwichmuseum.org.uk;
Crewe Golf Course
www.crewegolfclub.co.uk;
Little Moreton Hall
www.nationaltrust.org.uk

Disabled access ⊗ Child friendly ⊗
Dog friendly ✓

On the face of it not really a micropub at all – it's a shop with a huge stock of worldwide beers which you may take away or drink on the spot. There are six key kegs and only one cask-conditioned ale. It has two rooms: downstairs is essentially the shop and upstairs is for drinking only, for private parties or for events such as Meet the Brewer.

The name of the game here, in contrast to the purist micropub, is stocking every kind of beer – bottles, cans, cask and key keg, but all of them available to drink in or take out. The aim is to support a wide range of small breweries producing interesting beer. Owner Samuel McGarrigle opened in 2013 with 150 different types of beer in bottles only but soon expanded: now there are 600 beers in stock at any time – it was the first such place in Britain.

The interior is 'modern industrial' -scaffolding supports extra-solid wooden shelves on which the bottles and cans are displayed. The taps are at the back of the ground floor on a white tiled wall. Seating is German beer tables in a line downstairs and individually upstairs, where the decorative style is exposed brickwork and original floorboards.

You'll be drinking mainly with 25-55-year-old blokes but all ages and both sexes get the point of the place. The atmosphere is friendly and of course there's a bunch of local regulars.

Beer dock is the colloquial name used on the US East Coast for an off licence that sells beer. Samuel's Dad went to the States in 1977 and his Uncle Sherman always referred to the beer shop as the beer dock. The name stuck in his head until Sam needed a name for his new venture.

Devizes, Wiltshire

ESSENTIAL INFORMATION
28a St. John's Street, Devizes, SN10 1BN
Telephone: 01380 721443
Website: thevaultsdevizes.com
Facebook: www.facebook.com/
    thevaultsdevizes
Twitter: @VaultsDevizes

Opening hours:
Monday-Sunday 1200-2100

Other reasons to go:
Wiltshire Museum
www.wiltshiremuseum.org.uk;
Marden Henge
www.english-heritage.org.uk;
Wadworth Brewery Visitor Centre
www.wadworthvisitorcentre.co.uk

Disabled access ✓   Child friendly ⊗
Dog friendly ✓

This is a great place, but not as pure a micropub as those in the main section. On weekdays, there are three cosy ground-floor drinking areas as well as the bar, but at weekends they open up a large basement room which makes the place bigger than a classic micropub.

There are six firkins (five for real ale, one for cider) and four key kegs, two of which sometimes offer interesting but on occasions relatively mainstream pilsners or lagers. Don't let that stop you coming, but if you are a real ale nut don't expect the overwhelming emphasis to be on cask-conditioned ales from microbrewers.

What they do brilliantly here is their selection of craft bottled beers from all over the world, with expert barmen to help you explore them. Ricky plus two other helpers run the place, liaising with co-owners Malcolm Shipp of The Kennet & Avon Brewery and Chaz Hobden of West Brewery. Malcolm has been in the beer trade for some years and is one of the early brewers of gluten-free ale. You can buy bottles at the bar, of course, or to take away from the bottle shop in the basement. Buy six and there's a 70p discount per bottle.

It's in a pleasant street near the centre of Devizes opposite Giddings the wine merchant. Inside, the decoration is unremarkable – painted brick walls and a few framed pictures. Besides cider and soft drinks they do tasty pies with six different fillings.

On our visit we tried Kennet & Avon Pillbox, a light and fruity session pale ale.

Playing cards are available at the bar. Water bowls and treats provided for dogs.

Folkestone, Kent

ESSENTIAL INFORMATION
The Old High Street, Folkestone CT20
Telephone: 01303 246766
Email: kippsalehouse@gmail.com
Website: kippsalehouse.blogspot.co.uk
Facebook:www.facebook.com/
　Kippsalehouse
Twitter: @Kippsalehouse

Opening hours:
Monday-Thursday 1200-2200
Friday-Saturday 1100-2300
Sunday 1200-2200

Other reasons to go:
Westenhanger Castle
www.westenhangercastle.co.uk;
Brockhill Country Park www.kent.gov.uk;
Kent Battle of Britain Museum
www.kbobm.org

With seven taps dispensing kegline beer and ten real ales, this is half way between a mainstream pub and genuine micropub. There is background music and they serve plates of food, including vegetarian dishes.

It's a relatively big space, holding 50-70 when full, formerly occupied by restaurants, a shoe and a flower shop. The owner, Andrew Pook, an environmental consultant, comes in three or four times a week. He used to own The Thirty-Nine Steps Alehouse in Broadstairs, which is a similar place, much more customer and market led than a true micropub.

Folkestone drinkers are not all into real ales, he says, so besides the keg beers (which include ones from Belgium and North America) he stocks plenty of bottled beers.

On our visit we enjoyed Madcap Brewery's Syndale Ale 4.2% made with green hops, tasting fresh and grapefruity – a 'breakfast beer'.

No mistake, this is a good place with a community focus where most get a friendly greeting as they enter. Customers take over some nights to organize quiz, game and even poetry nights. The name comes from the title of the H.G. Wells's novel Kipps: the Story of a Simple Soul – the author once lived round the corner.

Disabled access ✓　**Child friendly** ✓
Dog friendly ✓

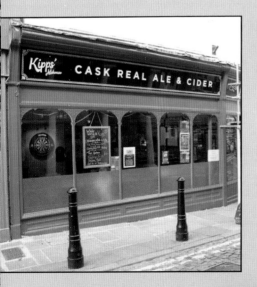

Grantham, Lincolnshire

ESSENTIAL INFORMATION
27 Watergate, Grantham, NG31 6NS
Telephone: 01476 330 274
Email: grantham@beerheadz.biz
Website: www.beerheadz.biz/beerheadz-
    grantham
Facebook: www.facebook.com/
    BHZgrantham
Twitter: @BHZgrantham

Opening hours:
Monday-Thursday 1300-2300
Friday-Saturday 1200-0000
Sunday 1200-2200

Other reasons to go:
Belton House www.nationaltrust.org.uk;
Grimsthorpe Castle www.hha.org.uk;
Woolsthorpe Manor
www.nationaltrust.org.uk

This is the sister pub of BeerHeadZ, Retford, page 234. Outside it's painted black, somewhat gothic, but the inside is quite a contrast – bright orange and blue.

The furniture consists of low tables and chairs. Owner Phil tries to find new and exciting beers for example Abstract Jungle's Easy 4.4%, an American brown ale, flavoursome and easy drinking; Lincoln Green's Gin and Beer It, a 5% fragrant pale ale, infused with gin. The gin is flavoured with juniper berries, plus orange and lemon peel; and Milestone Raspberry's Wheat Beer, a 5.6% strong, dry tasting craft beer with a raspberry flavour finish. As well as draught beers he sells bottled beers from all over the world.

The upstairs area is available for parties and groups at no cost.

Although a wonderful, eye-catching place, this is part of an expanding chain, which is why it's in the back section – a shame because it currently feels, like its Retford counterpart, like a one off.

Disabled access ⊗ **Child friendly** ⊗
Dog friendly ✓

THE REDEMPTION ALE HOUSE

Heanor, Derbyshire

ESSENTIAL INFORMATION
3 Ray Street, Heanor, DE75 7GE
Telephone: 07887 568576
Email: theredemptionalehouse@gmail.com
Facebook: www.facebook.com/pg/
   TheRedemptionAleHouse
Twitter: @redemptionmicro

Opening hours:
Monday-Wednesday Closed
Thursday 1200-2200
Friday-Saturday 1200-2230
Sunday 1200-2200

Other reasons to go: Kedleston Hall
www.nationaltrust.org.uk;
Denby Pottery www.denby.co.uk;
Pewit Golf Course www.erewash.gov.uk

Y ou get a log burner and a yard – good for year-round drinking. Bernadette Lawley and her son James opened it to encourage community get-togethers and that is exactly what they have achieved in this cosy place.

Bernadette spent 25 years working in social housing, but for several years before opening here was involved in beer festivals and other micropubs. James does two jobs - one in finance and one behind the bar.

The room is designed to encourage clusters of drinkers, with a mixture of high and low tables and chairs and a bar at the back with the cool room visible beyond. The yard is full of colourful chairs and pot plants. The top half of a stable door leading to the interior is kept open, so from the yard you can see the blackboard featuring drinks choices. Inside, there's a bold statement wall of blue and gold wall paper, while the rest of the room is painted blue.

The premises has had a varied history. Before the micropub it was a temporary library and before that a butcher's, a motorcycle shop and a camping supplier.

On our visit we enjoyed Whim Ales' Flower Power, a 5.3% hoppy pale ale with a grapefruit and herb flavour.

This is a brilliant place, but it serves four keg beers which is why it's in the back of the guide.

Disabled access ✓ not to WC
Child friendly ⊗
Dog friendly ✓

Hedon, Hull

ESSENTIAL INFORMATION
Watmough's Arcade, St Augustine Gate,
Hedon, Hull, HU12 8EZ
Telephone: 01964 601100
Facebook: www.facebook.com/The-Hedon-
Inn-907342609337388

Opening hours:
Monday-Thursday 1200-2300
Friday-Saturday 1200-0000
Sunday 1200-2300

Other reasons to go:
Wilberforce House www.hullcc.gov.uk;
Hull Maritime Museum
www.hullcc.gov.uk

Plenty of space here – there's room for 40 chairs, all picked up at local auction houses. Hedon is about 30 miles east of Howden along the Humber Estuary, beyond Hull, and the Inn is located in a car park near the town centre.

Co-owners Shirley Bamforth and Paul Smith took over the office of a former carpet shop in 2015 to create their characterful space: you're not literally head on with your fellow drinkers, but you might be in spirit.

One keg lager is sold to make customers from their previous pub feel at home.

Regular beers include Timothy Taylor Bootmaker and Titanic Plum Porter. Or, from the cider fridge you could try Mad Jack or Hazy Daisy. They do simple snacks such as black pudding and peanuts, and no cooked food. It's a simple, genuine place which Shirley and Paul want to be "all about real ale drinkers and people socializing." They see their venture as a "traditional but trendy little pub where people can chat and have a laugh. No music, no fruit machines, no shots."

Disabled access ⊗ **Child friendly** ✓
Dog friendly ⊗

ALE HOUSE

Henlow Camp, Bedforshire

ESSENTIAL INFORMATION
300 Hitchin Road, Henlow Camp,
   Bedfordshire, SG16 6DP
Telephone: 01462 817410
Facebook: www.facebook.com/
   The-Old-Transporter-Ale-
   House-798956783478628

Opening hours:
Monday Closed
Tuesday-Thursday 1500-2230
Friday-Saturday 1200-2300
Sunday 1200-2100

Other reasons to go: Henlow Greyhound
Stadium www.henlowdogs.co.uk;
Barton Hills National Nature Reserve
www.gov.uk/government/publications/
bedfordshires-national-nature-reserves/
bedfordshires-national-nature-reserves

When renting DVDs went the same way as VHS, many video shops were left vacant. Like The Firkin Shed (page 46), this place is in a former Blockbuster shop that's been transformed into a cosy drinking space. The location, on a busy road and roundabout is not ideal, and they have a TV which means that according to our criteria, it's not a true micropub. However, it's still a good place, worth knowing about.

Opened in 2014, Steve and Jay furnished it with a mixture of café-style tables and comfy sofas – so you really can relax. The decoration is inspired by all things transport related: a miniature penny farthing, a series of old American number plates, helicopters, cars and motorcycles all have a place. Customers regularly make their own contributions which gives the place an authentically personal feel.

A small bar serves four to six real ales directly from the cask and there is a selection of ciders in polypins, plus spirits, wine, shots, soft drinks and tea and coffee. Rolls, pickled eggs and pork scratchings are on offer, or you can order a take-away and bring it in.

There's a darts board, a meat raffle is held regularly and there are occasional live music nights.

We drank Smokin' Angel, a 4.5% porter from Leighton Buzzard Brewing Company; and Buntingford Brewery's Highwayman, a 3.6% light brown ale with hints of toffee and a fruity bitter-sweet aftertaste.

Disabled access ⊗ Child friendly ✓
Dog friendly ✓

Howden, East Yorkshire

ESSENTIAL INFORMATION
3 Market Place, Howden, DN14 7BJ
Telephone: 07817713232
Facebook: www.facebook.com/The-Tailors-
 Chalk-Howden-1094363927257792
Twitter: @howden_chalk

Opening hours:
Monday-Friday 1600-2300
Saturday-Sunday 1200-2300

Other reasons to go:
Howden Minster
www.english-heritage.org.uk;
Blackbird Gallery
www.blackbirdgallery.co.uk;
The Ashes Park

One small room, formerly a tailor's shop, is crammed with six small tables and hugger mugger seating for around 15. It feels lived in, with homely touches and humorous decorations.

Owner Tony Bonser couldn't be there when we visited, but we met his wife and son. They were serving just four other customers, soon after 5 pm on a Friday evening, so it was difficult to guess what the atmosphere would be like in a full house. An old turntable record player and a cardboard box of 12-inch vinyl LPs occupy a prominent spot and we wondered whether conversation and music might compete. Customers sometimes bring their own records.

Alongside the lager pumps are constantly switched beers which might include Northern Light from The Orkney Brewery or Crystal Jade from a small brewer in nearby Brough.

The micropub is in quite an attractive street in the town centre, with Howden Minster 75 yards away and, a few doors down, a mainstream pub, The White Horse. Interesting to see the traditional and the alternative so close together in a smallish town.

Disabled access ⊗ **Child friendly** ⊗
Dog friendly ⊗

GALLAGHER'S ALE HOUSE

Keighley, Bradford, West Yorkshire

ESSENTIAL INFORMATION
1-3 East Keltus, Keighley, BD20 8TD
Telephone: 07834 456134
Facebook: www.facebook.com/Gallaghers-
 Ale-House-1134149759936215
Twitter: @GallaghersMPub

Opening hours:
Monday-Tuesday Closed
Wednesday-Thursday 1500-2200
Friday 1300-2300
Saturday 1200-2300
Sunday 1200-2200

Other reasons to go:
Bronte Parsonage Museum
www.bronte.org.uk;
Skipton Castle www.skiptoncastle.co.uk;
Bolton Abbey boltonabbey.com

This is the sister micropub, opened December 2015, of The Beer Engine at Skipton, page 250. Both are owned and run, with help, by Steve Banks and Janet Langton. They have set up their second place in the former premises of Gallagher's betting shop.

It's a genuine micropub, no question, but because we are reserving the main entries in the guide for genuine micropubs that are one offs, rather than repeats, we are putting this in the back section. It seems to be very similar to The Beer Engine: as in The Beer Engine they offer five always-changing ales and in particular Steve and Janet have repeated here their handpump set-up: a different style of beer for each pump which never changes position.

The walls are mainly plain, and the key decorative feature seems to be the blackboards that announce the current ales, but that doesn't mean that the atmosphere is stark or uncongenial – quite the opposite, especially when full.

We sympathize with Janet and Steve over a review that they got on Tripadvisor recently. The reviewer said the beer 'tasted flat'. For an unfair, ignorant remark this takes some beating. Janet's online reply politely, pointed out that real ale is designed not to be fizzy, like lager… well there's always someone… it's bad that this kind of comment can't be deleted.

There's parking round the corner by the Co-op store.

Disabled access ⊗ **Child friendly** ⊗
Dog friendly ✓

Macclesfield, Cheshire

ESSENTIAL INFORMATION
43 Sunderland Street, Macclesfield,
SK11 6JL
Telephone: 01625 615938
Email: info@thetreacletap.co.uk
Website: www.thetreacletap.co.uk
Facebook: www.facebook.com/
   thetreacletap
Twitter: @thetreacletap

Opening hours:
Monday-Wednesday 1200-2300
Thursday-Saturday 1200-0000
Sunday 1200-2300

Other reasons to go:
Jodrell Bank Observatory
www.jodrellbank.net;
Adlington Hall www.adlingtonhall.com;
Nether Alderley Mill
www.nationaltrust.org.uk

Sitting at a bar in Manchester, Bronwyn Riley had a sudden desire to run her own. She had recently seen a tiny shop near the station in Macclesfield, that had been offered for rental for several months. After going through planning permission and licensing they opened 18 months later in December 2010. She's since been able to convince husband Tim to join the business full time.

Bronwyn used to be an equity analyst and Tim a fund manager. They got fed up with sitting behind a desk all day and unsurprisingly find their new working life is a welcome contrast.

Bronwyn's brother came up with the name. Macclesfield's nickname is Treacletown. Apparently a barrel of treacle fell from a cart on Hibel Road and the poor came to scoop it up.

Painted mostly dark red with low wooden tables and chairs, the place has a traditional feel. Beer memorabilia covers the walls. Bronwyn and Tim are well known for their pie and mash – proper food, not entirely in keeping with micropub criteria, which is why it's in the back section.

The Treacle Tap hosts regular book clubs, live music, language conversation groups and 'Meet the Brewer' nights.

Disabled access ✓ not to WC
Child friendly ✓ **Dog friendly** ✓

THE NEWPORT ALE HOUSE

Newport, Isle of Wight

ESSENTIAL INFORMATION
24a Holyrood Street, Newport, Isle of Wight
PO30 5AZ
Telephone: 07791 514668
Website: www.newportalehouse.co.uk
Facebook: www.facebook.com/newportale.
house/?fref=ts
Twitter: @NewportAleHouse

Opening hours:
Monday-Thursday 1200-2300
Friday-Saturday 1200-0000
Sunday 1200-2230

Other reasons to go:
Carisbrooke Castle
www.english-heritage.org.uk;
Classic Boat Museum
www.classicboatmuseum.org;
Newton Old Town Hall
www.nationaltrust.org.uk

The sister of The Cowes Ale House, see page 318, and like its sister, not quite a micropub, more of a small traditional pub specializing in real ales. It can claim to be the Island's smallest pub, with The Cowes Ale House tucked in behind as the second smallest. It's furnished more like a traditional pub than a true micropub, with leather mini armchairs arranged around tables, a prominent bar and typical pub paraphernalia decorations. No food is served, only snacks (including soup) and there's no loud music. There's a choice of well-kept real ales.

Newport, the main town of the Isle of Wight, is at the top of the Medina River, three miles inland from Cowes, with access by bus from Cowes.

Disabled access ✓ not to WC
Child friendly ✓ **Dog friendly** ✓

Preston, Lancashire

ESSENTIAL INFORMATION
56 Lancaster Road, Preston, Lancashire,
PR1 1DD
Telephone: 07932 517444
Facebook: www.facebook.com/Guild-Ale-
   House-862032483883107
Twitter: @GuildAleHouse

Opening hours:
Monday-Thursday 1200-2130
Friday-Saturday 1200-2300
Sunday 1200-2200

Other reasons to go: Harris Museum
www.harrismuseum.org.uk;
Lancashire Infantry Museum
www.lancashireinfantrymuseum.org.uk;
Turbury Woods Owl and Bird of Prey
Sanctuary www.turbarywoods.co.uk

Disabled access ✓ Child friendly ✓
Dog friendly ✓

Gary and his wife Jane rescued this beautiful Georgian building (with pilasters on the upper two floors) from demolition after it had stood empty for three years.

Gary was brought up in the hospitality industry - his grandparents and parents ran pubs and clubs. He worked in a variety of places before becoming a manager at a sports and social club where he began to explore the world of real ale. After reading about micropubs in 2011 he decided they were the way to go.

He fell in love with the premises at first sight and spent a year sorting out leaking roofs, damp, rotten timber and loose plaster. The bar alone has its own story - Gary bought it off eBay but it came with two major problems: the bar was in Yorkshire, and it was still in a pub. He rallied his mates together including Dave Bishop, co-owner of Bishops Crook Brewery, and after eight hour's work and a bucket full of screws the bar was finally theirs. Gary opened in late 2015 and to celebrate their work Dave brewed a unique ale for the place and named it Two Screws.

The interior has been done up in a light, modern style but respecting the character of the old building. There's modern art on the walls juxtaposed with a coffered ceiling and chandelier style lighting. The furniture is a mixture of high and low tables and chairs but it's minimal - mainly the space is for standing. The open staircase lends a feeling of grandeur.

There are seven real ales on handpump and six keg beers. This 7:6 ratio sadly puts this lovely place in the back section, along with the gaming machine next to the bar.

RITA'S PANTRY

Redcar, North Yorkshire

ESSENTIAL INFORMATION
1 Esplanade, Redcar, TS10 3AA
Telephone: 07739 392822
Email: ritaspantrypub@icloud.com
Facebook: www.facebook.com/
    ritaspantrypub
Twitter: @Ritaspantrypub

Opening hours:
Monday-Thursday 1500-2200
Friday 1500-2300
Saturday 1200-2300
Sunday 1200-2200

Other reasons to go:
Kirkleatham Museum
www.redcar-cleveland.gov.uk;
Winkies Castle www.winkiescastle.co.uk;
Redcar Beacon

Disabled access ✓ not to WC
Child friendly ✓ **Dog friendly** ✓

Redcar is a seaside town south of the Tees Estuary. To get a view you need to climb the Redcar Beacon on the sea front. Inland, opposite the Beacon is Rita's Pantry, opened by Neil Dooley in a former amusement arcade in late 2015. It's a five-minute walk from the station.

Rita was Neil's grandmother, who had a pantry full of treats, which is how he sees his micropub.

The interior decoration is unimaginative. There are round tables, wheel-backed chairs and brick-effect wallpaper behind the bar. One feature – a whole wall papered with maps – is unusual and effective, and there's a fireplace. Inside, there's room for around 40 people.

Three cask-conditioned ales are served alongside two key keg lagers and although the real ales are the focus, the 2:3 lager to ale ratio makes this a borderline micropub, which is why it's in the back section.

Still, this is a good place, the smallest pub in Redcar, and the only one in around ten miles of local coastline that has sea views. Neil offers free tasting samples and as the bar is by the door he manages to greet most people as they come in. The atmosphere is friendly and his three helpers are chosen for their knowledge of ales.

On our visit we enjoyed Salamander Brewery's Caligula, a 3.8% pale ale - dry, hoppy and refreshing.

Neil, originally from Redcar, was a primary school teacher for six years before starting Rita's Pantry and before that worked for a county council encouraging people into sport. He says his new life "doesn't feel like work".

Rochester, Kent

ESSENTIAL INFORMATION
318 High Street, Rochester, Kent, ME1 1BT
Telephone: 07889 214000
Email: rochestermicropub@
virginmedia.com
Twitter: @TheFlippin_Frog

Opening hours:
Monday Closed
Tuesday 1500-2100
Wednesday-Thursday 1200-1500
then 1700-2100
Friday-Saturday 1230-2300
Sunday 1200-1900

Other reasons to go:
Rochester Castle,
www.english-heritage.org.uk
Upnor Castle, www.english-heritage.org.uk
Rochester Cathedral,
www.rochestercathedral.org

There are one or two places in this guide where we've hated applying the strict definition of a micropub – and this is one of them. It's a terrific place but not a true micropub because of its emphasis on food, so it has to be in the back section. Very good food too, for example chicken and aubergine with cous-cous, or pork loin with home-made baked beans.

The French couple who run it – charming Melanie and her Hells Angel lookalike partner Cyril have panache, creating a friendly atmosphere heightened by amusing banter between staff and regulars. Never a dull moment – people are flocking here instead of the nothing-special local eateries.

They offer three local, real ales from jacket-cooled casks behind the bar; a choice of ciders, a gin and in summer Pimms.

There are Kent-style high tables and seats at the front window and elsewhere slatted low- level seating. The kitchen, where you can see Mel and her minions slaving, is open to view at one side and at the back is a tiny concrete outdoor area shared with a local who has been known to shuffle off, not too happy, when drinkers arrive.

The name? Mel and Cyril are French, or Frogs. And crêpes, the French version of a pancake, have to be flipped half way through cooking.

Disabled access ⊗
Child friendly ✓ **Dog friendly** ✓

ESSENTIAL INFORMATION
49 High Street, Wath-upon-Dearne,
Rotherham, S63
Telephone: 01709 872150
Email: wathtap@gmail.com
Website: www.wathtap.co.uk
Facebook: www.facebook.com/pg/
  WathTap/about
Twitter: @WathTap

Opening hours:
Monday-Sunday 1200-2300

Other reasons to go:
Clifton Park Museum
www.rotherham.gov.uk;
Roundwood Golf Sports and Social Club
www.roundwoodgolfclub.co.uk;
Magna Science Adventure Centre
www.visitmagna.co.uk

Disabled access √
Child friendly ⊗ Dog friendly √

It's a shame to put this place in the back section, but the almost 50:50 ratio of real ale to fizzy keg drinks means it is not a true micropub. However, it's beautifully done up inside, and has heaps of character. One half is smartly tiled in cream and green with a huge clock making it feel like an indie London café. Also on this side there are two sets of high tables and chairs. The other half is plastered cream with green panelling below. This area has more of a traditional pub feel, with low tables and chairs and a couple of cushioned casks done up in rich reds and golds - traditional and modern sit comfortably side by side. The bar is wooden, L-shaped and panelled with six handpumps delivering rotating ales. Spirits line the back of the bar and include sloe gin, whisky and rum.

This is Rotherham's first micropub and owners Mel and Rory have had customers from as far away as Australia.

Blackboards show what is on tap and below them are pump clips showing what's to come. A word of the day hangs above the bar, on our visit it was xenophobia. Typical bar snacks are available and takeaways are welcome. The exterior is pretty average, part of a mock-Tudor terrace with pebble dashed fronts. The white and blue tiles are the only thing that make it stand out.

On our visit we enjoyed: Elland Brewery's Ebeneezer, a 4.6% golden ale with a marmalade flavour; Saltaire's Winter Ale, a 4.9% traditional strong bitter with a malty base and a touch of sweetness; and Acorn Brewery's Cracker, a 4.1% straw coloured seasonal ale with a lemon and grapefruit flavour.

THE BOOKSHOP ALEHOUSE

Southampton, Hampshire

ESSENTIAL INFORMATION
21 Portswood Road, Southampton,
SO17 2ES
Email: bookshopalehouse@outlook.com
Facebook: www.facebook.com/
    BookshopAlehouse
Twitter: @BookshpAlehouse

Opening hours:
Monday-Sunday 1200-2300

Other reasons to go:
Solent Sky Aviation Museum
www.solentskymuseum.org;
Bargate Medieval Gate House, SO14 2DJ;
Medieval Merchants House
www.english-heritage.org.uk;
Itchen Valley Country Park
www.eastleigh.gov.uk

Owner Jon Harris describes this as a place "for drinkers with a book problem." The second-hand bookshop where it's located has been a feature of Portswood life for more than 30 years.

When its owner died, Jon, a regular customer, decided to take it over because he didn't like the idea of it being run by anyone who didn't appreciate its role at the centre of the community. Though he didn't have any idea about book selling, selling beer was another matter. So he opened a micropub within the bookshop and the two operate harmoniously under the same roof.

Jon had worked for 20 years in bars, pubs, clubs, music venues and festivals alongside his day jobs, most recently in social care.

The front window displays firkins and books and in large lettering declares 'Secondhand and Antiquarian books'. Smaller lettering asks 'Pint?'. The bar offers four handpumps of real ale, four ciders, a selection of bottled beers and a small assortment of spirits and wines.

As per form, there is no hot food, instead Jon encourages customers to use the local restaurants and anyone is welcome to bring their own food into the micropub.

Unusually for a micropub The Bookshop Alehouse doesn't try to stay local with their beer. They come from far and wide, from the Isle of Wight to Italy and New Zealand. Some of them don't even come from microbreweries - "what's important is great beer, basically, we prefer smaller brewers, but great beer is great beer and we're into great beer."

Disabled access ✓ not to WC
Child friendly ⊗ **Dog friendly** ✓

THE BUTCHER'S HOOK

Southampton, Hampshire

ESSENTIAL INFORMATION
7 Manor Farm Road, Southampton,
SO18 1NN
Telephone: 02381 782280
Email: hello@butchershookpub.com/ dan@
   butchershookpub.com
Website: www.butchershookpub.com
Facebook: www.facebook.com/
   TheButchersHook

Opening hours:
Monday-Tuesday Closed
Wednesday-Thursday 1800-2300
Friday 1600-2300
Saturday 1300-2300
Sunday 1400-2200

Other reasons to go:
Solent Sky Aviation Museum
www.solentskymuseum.org;
Bargate Medieval Gate House, SO14 2DJ;
Medieval Merchants House
www.english-heritage.org.uk

We really like this place, even if it isn't a true micropub, especially its buzzy vibe. However as we went to press, six to eight of their ales were from key keg, against three or four from firkins, so reluctantly we have to put it in the back.

Dan Richardson and Anthony Nichols, co-owners, opened in 2013. Dan used to be a product designer and Anthony a graphic designer. Both had worked in mainstream pubs and were serious real ale nuts. Bored with their jobs, and wanting to see a good local pub with a focus on real ale in their part of town, they started looking at empty shops, realizing how they take the heart out of a community, they settled on an old butcher's shop.

Bulbs in jam jars hang from the ceiling, and the decoration is a nice mix of old and new. A local artist named Adam exhibits his screen prints, the obligatory pump clips collection is on the ceiling and the gents lavatory is amusingly decorated with newspaper cut-outs.

The place attracts a really broad range of customers – we saw students rubbing shoulders with elderly drinkers. They don't play music and they aren't as strict as some micropubs about mobiles but customers are considerate, taking their calls outside.

Dan says he can't imagine running a pub without being mad about beer. They also stock about 20 bottled beers, a draft cider, six wines but no spirits. They do the occasional quiz night, a live music night and a pie cooking night when people bring their own pies, a judge delivers his verdict and the winner takes home a case of beer.

Disabled access ✓ **Child friendly** ✓
Dog friendly ✓

Southampton, Hampshire

ESSENTIAL INFORMATION
8A Portsmouth Road, Southampton,
SO19 9AA
Telephone: 07437 935223
Facebook: www.facebook.com/
   OlafsTunCraftAleBar
Twitter: @OlafsTun

Opening hours:
Monday-Tuesday Closed
Wednesday-Thursday 1800-2200
Friday 1600-2300
Saturday 1200-2300
Sunday 1300-2130

Other reasons to go:
Solent Sky, www.solentskymuseum.org
Southampton City Art Gallery, www.
southampton.gov.uk
Netley Abbey, www.english-heritage.org.uk

This suburb of Southampton started life as a Viking settlement on the River Itchen and was ruled by Olaf I of Norway in the 10th Century. Tun means town and so the place was called Olaf's Tun. Recorded in the Domesday Book of 1086 as Olvestune, Olaf's Tun later changed its name to Woolston because of its trade in wool. So this place's name is nicely grounded in local history.

Landlords Neil Horlock and Neil Horsfall decided that after years of being on the customer side of the bar they wanted to do more with their passion for real ale. They both still have full time jobs, Neil Horlock as an aeronautical engineer and Neil Horsfall as an administrator for a railway company, but with the help of their wives Ros and Christina, who also have full time jobs, they opened Olaf's Tun in 2016.

They offer ales served straight from the barrel into the glass along with four keg beers, bottled beers, cider, and wines. However, the ratio of real ale to key keg beers is around 50-50, and so we have to put Olaf's Tun in the back of the guide. Other than that, it can't be faulted. As in a traditional Kent micropub there are high cushioned benches and tables, the casks are kept in cooling jackets and the landlords try to support local businesses by using local breweries as much as possible, but also search for unusual ales from further afield.

Disabled access ✓
Child friendly ⊗
Dog friendly ✓

OVERDRAFT CRAFT ALE BAR

Southampton, Hampshire

ESSENTIAL INFORMATION
383 Shirley Road, Southampton, SO15 3JD
Telephone: 023 8077 5823
Email: mikha@hotmail.co.uk
Facebook: www.facebook.com/
    overdraftcraftale

Opening hours:
Monday-Wednesday
1700-2230
Thursday 1700-2300
Friday 1500-2330
Saturday 1300-2330
Sunday 1400-2230

Other reasons to go:
Southampton City Art Gallery
www.southampton.gov.uk;
Medieval Merchants House
www.english-heritage.org.uk
Solent Sky Museum
www.solentskymuseum.org

The Butcher's Hook, page 335, the first Southampton micropub, was the inspiration for this place. Father and son Amrik and Mikha liked The Butcher's Hook atmosphere so much that they decided to open their own. "When people drink real ale and craft beer in a relaxed environment, the atmosphere is fantastic."

Mikha wouldn't call himself a beer expert – "there are a lot out there" – but he felt he could put his stamp on a micropub and create a unique place.

Amrik used to work in the property industry after a career in music as a journalist and band manager. After leaving university in Bristol, Mikha worked in one of the popular Patty and Bun comfort food restaurants in central London. Both had transferable skills to bring to the venture.

The site is a former Westminster bank, which provided easy ideas for the name. The bank's vault is perfect for keeping ale at a cool temperature.

This place is not a pure micropub – they play music and they have as much keg beer as real ale – which is why it's in the back section. However, the music is entirely played on vinyl and the keg beer is constantly changing along with the cask ale. They buy the beer from all over the country and are always trying to source new ones. You'll find six to ten cask ales and ten keg craft beers.

Regular and irregular events occur, including DJ nights, live music nights, brewery tap takeovers and BBQs.

Disabled access ⊗
Child friendly ✓ until 2130
Dog friendly ✓

ESSENTIAL INFORMATION
10 Newport Street, Tiverton, EX16 6NH

Opening hours:
Monday-Thursday 1200-2300
Friday-Saturday 1200-0000
Sunday 1200-2230

Other reasons to go:
Knightshayes www.nationaltrust.org.uk;
Tiverton Canal Company
www.tivertoncanal.co.uk;
Tiverton Castle www.tivertoncastle.com

As we went to press we believed that this was still the only genuine micropub in Devon – Exeter Beer Cellar, page 341, is not strictly a micropub and nor is The Taphouse and Bottle Shop in Newton Abbot, page 342. However, we're putting it in the back section because the owner was unavailable to provide up to date information, and it's had a somewhat chequered history.

Duncan Binks and his then partner opened in 2010 when there were only between ten and 20 micropubs in the whole country. It was called Goldy's then, but when they separated the name was changed to Courtenay's. Since then Duncan has sold it, the new owner, Marilyn, leaves no contact details in the usual places and its entry hasn't been updated on The Micropub Association website. We're recommending it with caution – readers' reports welcome.

It occupies a pretty curved corner site (once a pet shop) on Castle Street, which used to be called Frog Street because a stream ran down the middle which presumably contained frogs.

As far as we can gather, Courtenay's remains a small version of a mainstream pub. On the right is a fine wood panelled bar; the floor is dark wood and the place is fitted out with traditional pub furniture. Behind the bar is a metal stillage holding four jacket-cooled casks, nicely integrated into the bar surround. Three or four real ales are usually offered, plus at least three real ciders, bottled and canned beers, wines and spirits.

Disabled access ⊗   Child friendly ⊗
Dog friendly ⊗

PRAIRIE SCHOONER TAPHOUSE

Urmston, Greater Manchester

ESSENTIAL INFORMATION
33 Flixton Road, Urmston, Greater
Manchester, M41 5AW
Website: prairie-schooner-taphouse.co.uk
Facebook: www.facebook.com/
    prairieschoonertaphouse
Twitter: @pstM41

Opening hours:
Monday Closed
Tuesday-Thursday 1500-2230
Friday-Saturday 1300-0000
Sunday 1400-2200

Other reasons to go:
Museum of Science and Industry
www.msimanchester.org.uk;
Imperial War Museum North
www.iwm.org.uk;
The Whitworth Art Gallery
www.whitworth.manchester.ac.uk

Despite being larger than most, this place is faithful to core micropub values. The premises were formerly a golfing retailer, then a fireworks shop before Robert MacRae and Christian McKie took over in 2014. Both had been volunteers at local beer festivals, which helped them work out that there wasn't much to dislike about making a living from selling beer. 'Prairie Schooner' is the colloquial name for the wagons used in parts of the U.S.A. – Robert originates from Kansas. The Kansas flag hangs proudly inside.

The micropub is divided into two sections, with the bar in the middle. The back has armchairs and low tables and is the main drinking space. The front part has a couple of bar-high wooden tables and chairs but is mostly taken up with bottle-laden shelves and is a retail area for takeaway customers. You are likely to go home with your pockets clinking. They also do gift boxes, and discounts on cask ale for CAMRA members.

There are four handpumps and three craft kegs, along with an ingenious cellar system which has been set up behind the bar. We drank Howard Town Brewery's Super Fortress 4.4%, a ruby ale with a caramel flavour; and Blackedge Brewing Company's Blonde 4.5%, a citrus flavoured ale. They also stock traditional cider and perry, wine, Prosecco, a few spirits and soft drinks alongside crisps, nuts and sweets.

Disabled access ✓ (ask for ramp)
Child friendly ✓ (until 1800)
Dog friendly ✓ (during quiet times on a lead)

Time ran out in late 2016, leaving us unable to include several micropubs that should be in the Other Micropubs section. As new ones open most months, there will be some that didn't even make this list. Sorry... Let us know if you've been left out and we'll catch up with you in the next edition.

Arcade Alehouse, Barnsley
31 The Arcade, Barnsley, S70 2QP.
Located in a former cake shop, there is one regular ale and five changing ones. The furniture is low mainstream pub stools and benches. The seating is on two levels with the bar downstairs. The toilet is upstairs. Every Thursday there is a poetry workshop.

Mind the Gap, Broadstairs
156 High Street, Broadstairs, CT10 1JB.
Set on two mini levels – a bar and cold room are upstairs and the seating area is downstairs. The place is close to the train station and is railway themed. There's a mixture of sofas and pub stools, a luggage rack holds battered leather suitcases and a national rail sign decorates one wall.

Chesham Brewery Shop, Chesham
8 Market Square, Chesham, Buckinghamshire, HP5 1ES.
A shop with a bar. There are eight draft beers, two draft ciders and over 150 bottled & canned craft beers from around the UK. A bar lines one wall and shelves of bottles another. An awning provides sheltered seating outside. The wall behind the bar is white and black tiled with ten taps coming directly out of it.

The Ale House, Clitheroe
12-14 Market Place, Clitheroe, BB7 2DA.
On a characterful market place, the street is charming and on a hill with great views of the surrounding hills. This place specialises in bottled beers and has six handpumps offered from a bar at the back. There are regular live music nights and some sports.

Barley Hops, Congleton
Swan Bank, Congleton, CW12 1AN.

A beer café with the feel of a traditional pub but with a focus on real ale. An L-shaped bar offers three handpumps and shelves of bottles cover one wall. The seating is high and low tables and stools.

Offbeat Brewery and Bar, Crewe
Thomas Street, Crewe, CW1 2BD; beer@offbeatbrewery.com.
The beer is brewed on site then sold in the bar. Michelle runs the place. There are bottled beers, ciders and a growing selection of gins. There's a focus on events and small, experimental brews.

Freed Man, Deal
329 Dover Road, Deal, Kent, CT14 7NX.
More of a mini pub than a micropub. There are ales, wines, spirits and one rotating lager. Wonderfully decorated with ensigns and sailing memorabilia, the whole place is wood panels - you are never bored.

Station House, Durham
The Station House, North Road, Durham, DH1 4SE.
A three minute walk from the station, tucked under the viaduct. Ale is served from the barrel, seating is high and low stools and chairs and windows at the back allow customers to see into the cold room.

Exeter Beer Cellar, Exeter
2 South Street, Exeter, EX1 1DZ.
Six cask ales, nine keg and more than 50 bottled beers. The food is American and more substantial than just pub snacks, making this place more of a mini pub. The exterior looks like an American diner, the interior is filled with bright red high stools in a long thin room.

Cobblers Arms, Filey
2 Union Street, Filey, YO14 9DZ.
A former Cobblers shop on a charming street of butchers, cafés and a church. There's a bar with handpumps, low bench seating and occasionally live music. Dog and family friendly.

Continued on next page

Little Ale House, Harrogate
7 Cheltenham Crescent, Harrogate, HG1 1DH.
In a row of terraced stone buildings, the outside appearance is smart and attractive. The interior is smaller than suggested by the exterior. A small bar at the back offers four handpumps and four keg beers. There's a small yard at the back.

The Real Ale Classroom, Leicester
22 Allandale Road, Leicester, LE2 2DA.
Run by two former teachers, the furniture is recycled school desks and lab style stools. The decoration is quirky and a juxtopision of modern and classic - a stags head sits alongside industrial style lampshades.
There's live music and a monthly pub quiz. Surrounded by cafés and independent shops this is a great place to come for an after lunch or dinner drink.

Office, Morpeth
The Toll House, Castle Square, Morpeth, NE61 1YL.
This is the outlet for Acton Ales Brewery. There are five handpumps and three keg beers. On the corner of Castle Square, this place is just down the road from medieval chantry houses and Morpeth Castle. It's more modern than it looks on the outside.

The Taphouse and Bottle Shop, Newton Abbot
Tuckers Maltings, Teign Road, Newton Abbot, TQ12 4AA.
This place has been a bottle shop for many years and recently expanded to become a micropub as well. Next door is Tuckers Maltings and on the other side is Teignworthy Brewery. The place is fairly large but in a historic building full of character.

Hamelsworde Brewery and Tap, Pontefract
41B Kirkby Road, Hemsworth, Pontefract, WF9 4BA.
Formerly Londis, there is a brewery at the back and a drinking area at the front. The ales are brewed in small batches and are always different. The clean and modern inside is cosier and more atmospheric than the pebble-

dashed exterior gives away. It's family friendly and there's disabled access.

Drift Micro Bar, Poole
7 The Quay, Poole, BH14 9BY; 01202 667528.
Definitely micro: three tables fashioned from chopped up surfboards and a mini-counter made from driftwood occupy the lobby-entrance area of the Italian restaurant upstairs. Draught real ales, craft keg beers, bottles and ciders; gin lounge upstairs. An alternative to the mainstream pub-dominated Quay.

Smuggler's Run Real Ale House, Poole
184 Ashley Road, Poole, BH14 9BY; 01202 385399;
www.smugglerspubs.co.uk.
One of a mini chain of (currently) two small pubs owned by Bournemouth Brewing Co. A substantial range (up to 12) of draught real ales and craft keg beers from local and national microbreweries. Buy food from the Chinese takeaway next door and eat in the pub. Its sister establishment Smuggler's Cove is on nearby Parr Road.

Green Hops Real Ale Bar, Stockton-on-Tees
55 The Green, Billingham, Stockton-on-Tees, TS23 1EW.
Inspired by Sherlocks (page 192). The place used to be the cellar of the Half Moon Club so there was no need to apply for an alcohol license. There are four Real Ale pumps, lager, real ciders, wine and spirits. There's also a TV that shows sports. It's opposite a small green.

Taphouse, Wimborne Minster
11 West Borough, Wimborne Minster, BH21 1LT.
Beautifully laid out and decorated, high wooden benches and stools line a brick bar. Shelves display knick-knacks and wire brackets encase lightbulbs. Everything has been thought through and executed well. Ales are served straight from the cask behind the bar with eight on offer.

In this index, micropubs are arranged in alpha order by name.

INDEX

GUIDES

Charming Small Hotel Guides

Austria, Switzerland & The Alps

Britain & Ireland

France

Germany

Italy

Spain

On Foot Guides

London Walks

Paris Walks

New York Walks

Venice Walks

Prague Walks

Rome Walks

Boxed walking guides

Great Pub, Great Walk

Weekend Walks

Lake District Walks

London and the South East

Walker's Britain

Cycle Escapes London

Cyclist's Britain